The
Imperial Shah
An Informal Biography

The Imperial Shah

An Informal Biography

Gérard de Villiers
with Bernard Touchias and
Annick de Villiers

Translated from the French by June P. Wilson
and Walter B. Michaels

An Atlantic Monthly Press Book
Little, Brown and Company—Boston—Toronto

First American Edition
T07/76

**LIBRARY OF CONGRESS CATALOGING
IN PUBLICATION DATA**

Villiers, Gérard de, 1935-
  The imperial Shah.

   "An Atlantic monthly book."
   Translation of L'irrésistible ascension de
Mohammad Reza, shah d'Iran.
   Bibliography: p.
   I. Mohammed Reza Pahlavi, Shah of Iran,
1919-   2. Iran — Politics and government —
1945-   I. Touchais, Bernard, joint author.
II. Villiers, Annick de, joint author.   III. Title
DS318.M65V5413 1976   955'.05'0924 [B]
ISBN 0-316-18152-8   76-10985

B
Pahlavi

Atlantic-Little, Brown Books
are published by
Little, Brown and Company
in association with
The Atlantic Monthly Press

Designed by Susan Windheim
Published simultaneously in Canada
by Little, Brown & Company (Canada) Limited
Printed in the United States of America

Illustrations

Preface

IT IS NOT MY INTENTION to judge Mohammed Riza Pahlevi, the Shah of Iran. My only concern is to tell the story of this man of many contradictions with one foot in the past and the other in the future. Once a frail and romantic young man little given to serious pursuits, he is now the undisputed ruler over 33 million Iranians, and one of the world's most powerful heads of state. And even though he has distributed to his people his private domain encompassing one quarter of Iran's arable land, he remains one of the world's richest men. A man with a winter palace and a summer palace who smokes Gauloises and speaks an Oxford English with a French accent. A mystic who has spent his life battling his country's regressive religious hierarchy. A man who has created one of the most fearsome police forces in the modern world but who systematically pardons those who try to assassinate him. And even while his country has one of the highest rates of illiteracy in the world, and he is considered a despicable dictator by many, his social programs are more advanced than Sweden's.

I've known Iran for more than fifteen years. I've met the

Shah on numerous occasions. I've watched with my own eyes the evolution of his country—underestimated by foreigners, overestimated in Iran—and the undeniable progress achieved under his reign.

It has not been easy to write this book; no one in Iran can or dares to speak out. If the answer to a specific question threatens to be embarrassing, the Iranian shrugs it off or changes the subject. Nor does the power of the political police and SAVAK make the task easier. When some of my Iranian friends learned I was writing a book about their Shah, they simply fled. Also, the Iranian archives are inaccessible, and every event has at least two interpretations. On the other hand, the Shah three times agreed to answer all my questions without dodging a single one. It was thanks to these conversations, the testimony of knowledgeable witnesses, and detailed investigations in Iran, Europe and the United States, that my collaborators and I were able to piece together the story of the irresistible ascent of Mohammed Riza Pahlevi, Shah of Iran.

GÉRARD DE VILLIERS

The Imperial Shah

An Informal Biography

Chapter 1

His Imperial Majesty, the Shahinshah Mohammed Riza Pahlevi, was in good humor when he got out of bed at 6:30 AM on February 4, 1949, even though he had been up late the night before with a female companion. Three observations were enough to dispose of any desire to linger in bed.

First, from his windows in the Winter Palace in the center of Tehran's residential district, he could hear the crunch of new snow under the boots of the palace guards as they strode back and forth in their tight-fitting uniforms with the high collars of royal blue that reached right up to their chins.

Second, beyond the iron grill that surrounded the Winter Palace, the city's street cleaners were talking in loud voices as they spread sand and coarse salt in anticipation of the morning traffic.

Last, high above the great plane trees and pines in the palace park, the stars still shone in the predawn sky.

The first two observations indicated that, after ten days of freezing weather, the day would continue cold, and the third, that the sun would shine.

On this particular Friday — all Fridays are holidays to Muslims — as soon as the ceremonies celebrating the fourteenth anniversary of the University of Tehran were over, Mohammed Riza would be free to go to his stables and choose which among his several dozen thoroughbreds he wished to have saddled. Then, finally alone and far from problems of state, he would give free rein to his horse and ride for hours along the stony edges of the desert just outside the city limits.

The University of Tehran had been built in 1934 by Riza the Great, the present Shah's father, on the Shahriza, the wide avenue that crosses the city from west to east and which the Iranians consider their Champs Elysées. It consisted of three splendid buildings forming a U around a mosque and surrounded by carefully manicured gardens. It had always been one of the capital's trouble spots, the cradle of burgeoning ideas, passionate discussions, plots and counterplots.

Early that morning, an impressive array of uniformed men had taken up positions. And in addition to the police and the army, there were the mustachioed athletes of the secret services, distinguished by their steely eyes and jackets bulging with unseen weapons.

One item made the police particularly nervous: a meeting of the Tudeh, Iran's large Moscow-controlled Communist party which had been scheduled to take place two days before in the suburbs of Tehran, had been suddenly postponed to this very day, Friday, February 4, when the Shah was making his first public appearance in a long time.

As a result, the crowd — growing, despite the glacial cold — was kept at a distance by a cordon of police, and anyone wishing to enter the university was being required to show a permit.

Around 10:00 AM, the less important guests began to arrive — minor officials, a few hand-picked students and journalists. At eleven, three men marched up to the sentry. Since they

Village women sifting grain. *Marilyn Silverstone, Magnum*

had no permits, they were refused entry. They protested vehemently, but to no avail. So they left, followed closely by plain-clothes men who had found their behavior peculiar. One of the three, a dark young man of medium height with a thick mustache and a camera hung around his neck, consulted his companions and then headed for the center of the city. The police let him go, but as the other two began to circle the university, taking Bisto Yek Azar Street in a westerly direction, the police followed after. The men soon vanished in the dense crowd, only to reappear suddenly, a hundred yards ahead, climbing the iron railing and jumping over the wall. The police split into two groups. One went in pursuit over the railing, the other returned to the main entrance in the hope of catching them from the opposite direction. Neither group was successful.

Toward 12:30, the third man came back and presented himself to the sentry once again, this time in the company of a very thin, clean-shaven young man. His camera was still hanging around his neck, he held a proper permit in his hand made out to one Nasser Hossein Fakhr Arai, twenty-eight years of age, authorized by the newspaper *Partcham Islam* (The Flag of Islam), and signed by the paper's publisher, Dr. Faghidi Chirazi. No one recognized him. He was allowed to pass and his companion went on his way.

Nasser Hossein Fakhr Arai reached the Law School entrance and joined the group waiting for the procession to pass by. He talked to no one. Nobody seemed to know him, but nobody noticed anything odd about him either, despite the fact that his camera was hardly professional equipment. In fact, it was one of those cheap cameras sold in Tehran for the equivalent of forty U.S. cents. Fakhr Arai's chief worry seemed to be to hold onto his place in the front row of the press section, as close as possible to the red carpet on which the official procession would approach. But this didn't seem unusual either. His colleagues were all fighting for position. After all, it was their job.

But curiously enough, while the other photographers were already snapping away at the first arrivals, he took no pictures. He simply clutched his camera to his chest and kept craning his neck as if he were looking for someone in the crowd.

At 2:00 PM, the officials began to arrive—members of the university, the government, the imperial court. They all drove up in large American and British limousines, looking solemn and dignified, and responded with studied disdain to the sharp salutes of the functionaries assigned to greet them and conduct them to their places. The military were especially impressive in their dress uniforms—a bizarre mixture of British elegance, Prussian rigidity and Soviet ponderousness—all the influences that had successively acted on Iran over the years. There was even, among the older men, that slightly supercilious tilt of the head peculiar to French officers, which they had retained from their days at Saint-Cyr, the favorite military school of Riza the Great. But what they all had in common—and this was typically Iranian—was the number of decorations on their chests. They were literally covered with medals, and when they marched, these set off a cacophony of clattering metal. With an air of modesty, they tried to mute the jangle with one hand, but their gaze remained as fierce as ever. Most of them wore boots, and each carried a large regulation revolver in a black leather holster.

As they gathered in groups, there was a chorus of *salaams* and salutations, while servants in white jackets scurried about serving tea and biscuits from large silver trays. It was not unusual, even for a civilian, to accompany the *salaam* with a noisy clicking of heels. The hierarchies were clearly marked:

while an inferior's bow was accepted with stiff condescension, one bent over double before someone higher up the ladder. In this still feudal country, there were only two classes: the powerful and the poor.

In the dining room at the Winter Palace, the Shah was finishing his lunch. Even though it was a holiday, he had worked the whole morning. After a half hour of gymnastics, a quick breakfast and a cold shower, he was at his desk at 7:45. He first read the papers, both Iranian and foreign, then his mail and dispatches. After that, he signed the letters he had dictated the day before. A little after ten, he received Mohammed Saed, then prime minister, led in by Hormoz Pirnia, the palace master of ceremonies who backed out, bowing.

The two men studied, among other things, the dossier on the university, and Saed placed before his sovereign the speech he would be delivering shortly, which a young member of his staff had written. They went over the text together, then checked off the details of the ceremony.

The Shah made only minor changes. The ceremony bored him; he found it a tiresome ritual. Mohammed Riza was not yet thirty and he much preferred riding to making speeches. As soon as they had finished with the dossier, the prime minister retired so that his sovereign could get ready.

Now the Shah was alone at the lunch table. He drank very little but smoked incessantly. The servants came and went silently, Hormoz Pirnia keeping a watchful eye on them from his station by the sideboard.

At twenty-nine, the Shah was one of the world's most eligible bachelors. He had been free for three months now, since divorcing Fawzia, King Farouk of Egypt's very beautiful sister. He had seen her only once before their marriage. Fawzia bore him a daughter, Princess Shanaz, but no sons. That was the official reason for the divorce, but the truth was that they didn't get along and had early gone their separate ways.

Dark skinned, athletic, five feet ten inches tall, the Shah was appealing to women, with his sad, penetrating eyes and his shy and disarmingly youthful smile. Actually, the shyness was an act. He was a true lady's man, and it was rumored that since his divorce, he had had affairs not only with young women from Tehran's top society but with movie stars. The Shah never denied these rumors, and since one of his chief characteristics is secrecy, no one actually knew the truth. One thing, however, was certain: he preferred tall blond Europeans, especially the Scandinavian type, and they arrived in Tehran in droves. All this, even though (rumor had it) he tended sometimes to treat them rather cavalierly.

By 2:30, there was a constant coming and going of official cars, depositing the privileged few who were to join him in the official procession. It was time to leave for the university. The Shah made his appearance, dressed in a general's uniform with stars on his epaulets and braiding on his cap. He wore no medals, only a few bars sewn on his pocket.

The official Rolls-Royce drove up and the procession got under way. The black limousines made an impressive sight as they headed down Kakhe Avenue in the direction of the Shahriza, followed by some thirty motorcycles, their sirens going full blast.

It was a beautiful day: snow had been falling for weeks (Tehran is stifling in summer and has one of the heaviest snowfalls of any city in the world in winter). It covered sidewalks, terraces, and in the bright sunlight, the glare was intense. To the north, only a mile or two away, the foothills of the Elburz, the great mountain range that drops abruptly

down to the Caspian Sea on the far side, were completely
white and appeared so close and so high that they seemed
about to crush the city.

A little after three, the procession slowly wound its way
into the gardens of the university, and the Shah's Rolls came
to a stop at the end of the red carpet, about seventy-five feet
from the main steps. The chief of the Imperial Guard opened
the door and the Shah stepped out. At the same moment, the
Imperial Guard saluted smartly and struck up the national
anthem. Dr. Mohammed Sadjadi, the minister of national
education and former rector of the university, presented Dr.
Sassi, the current rector, to the Shah, and then the deans of
the various faculties and their professors in their black gowns.
Behind the Shah stood his younger brother, Gholam Riza,
Colonel Daftary, chief of the military police, and the guard
commanders.

The Shah shook hands with everybody, then turned to Colonel Chafaghate, his escort's commander, and signaled to him
to have his men stand at ease. It was time to enter the great
hall of the Law School where the guests were waiting.

The photographers were snapping away from alongside the
carpet as the Shah strode toward the steps. Everybody, that
is, but Fakhr Arai who was standing next to the first step.
The Shah came abreast of him, stopped for a second, mechan-
ically adjusted his tie and started up the steps.

Then everything went very fast. Fakhr Arai opened his
camera as if to take out the film inside, but instead took out
a small revolver. Standing six feet from the king, he held the
revolver behind the camera and quickly loaded it. Three shots
rang out, one after the other: the Shah's cap blew off as if in
a sudden gust of wind. He stopped, staggered, and seemed
about to fall, but then he righted himself and turned, his face
deathly pale, toward the would-be assassin who was moving

closer, exasperated at his own clumsiness. Even though the Shah's face and neck were covered with blood, the three bullets had miraculously only grazed his scalp.

What happened next was almost unbelievable.

The most obvious course of action for any one of the bystanders would have been to grab Fakhr Arai and disarm him. But at first, not a soul moved. Then, in the next second, there was a stampede. Police, guards, faculty, cabinet ministers, officers and generals laden with medals and armed with large service revolvers, all of them scattered. They shoved, elbowed and trampled on each other in a desperate attempt to get out of the fanatic's range. And so it was that the two men now faced each other in a large empty circle, one armed, the other empty-handed, his eyes blurred by the blood streaming down his face.

For the fourth time, Fakhr Arai pulled the trigger and this time the Shah spun around and started to fall, his face in his hands. Fakhr Arai moved in for the kill. The Shah looked done for; blood was spurting from his right cheek and from under his nose. And he had only himself to look to for his survival. Right away, he had identified his attacker's weapon as a 6.35 automatic with an ivory grip (it happened to be a Belgian Herstell) which usually held six cartridges. Fakhr Arai had loaded the weapon, which meant that it had been empty and therefore had only the six bullets in the chamber. With extraordinary self-possession, the Shah had counted the shots. There could only be two bullets left. His eyes riveted on his assailant, he started to dart this way and that, jumping from left to right, up and down the steps, ducking and dodging in a paroxysm of movement. Fakhr Arai shot his fifth bullet and there was a new gush of blood from the Shah's shoulder. With a desperate effort, the king ducked at the very moment that Fakhr Arai, now at point blank range, pulled the trigger for the sixth time. Nothing happened. The gun had jammed. He kept pressing the trigger, but to no avail. Wild with rage, he took the gun by the barrel and rushed at the Shah to strike him with the butt.

At this moment, the crowd realized that Fakhr Arai was no longer dangerous. Their courage restored, they began to move in and he started running. A shot rang out and he fell, hit in the leg. It was General Sarfat who had fired the shot. Fakhr Arai got to his feet, and, limping, retraced his steps, threw his pistol at the Shah's Rolls-Royce in a gesture of insult, and raised his arms.

"I give myself up," he shouted.

He was seized by Assram, the Shah's chauffeur. The police and a few officers drew their revolvers.

"Don't shoot! I want him alive!," the Shah ordered, but no one seemed to hear him.

Struck by two bullets in the thigh and abdomen, Fakhr Arai fell backwards. Colonel Daftary beat him with the butt of his revolver. The lynching went on for almost ten minutes, and Fakhr Arai was not the only victim. A young Czecho-slovakian student who had tried to pull him away also got a beating.

As for the Shah, he was calmly walking back and forth, mopping his face with his handkerchief. None of his wounds was serious. There was no bone damage to his face and his left shoulder functioned normally. The fourth bullet only grazed his upper lip, and the fifth glanced off his collarbone. He was suffering only from loss of blood. And violent emo-tion.

Many years after the event, the Shah told me: "I am no longer afraid of death. I faced it one day on the steps of the University of Tehran; there was no way of avoiding it, and yet I did. Why? Because I didn't panic. I remember calmly taking in the situation, with a clarity that surprises me to this day. For example, while my full attention was on Fakhr Arai, I saw out of the corner of my eye that one of my officers had crawled under a car, his face white with terror. For charity's sake I won't tell you his name, but he was immediately dismissed."

At the same moment, on Bisto Yek Azar, Danesh and Anatole-France, the avenues that encircle the university, small groups of men were trying to force their way against the crowd drawn to the university by the sounds of screaming and gunfire. A few policemen had the presence of mind to follow them, but again without any luck. Most of those taking flight managed to disappear into the crowd; the others were picked up by cars that pulled away with a screech of tires.

A little later, several cars that resembled these—it was never proved that they were the same—arrived at Eman Zadeh Abdellah where the Tudeh Party was holding its meeting. Thousands were present, many of them armed with revolvers. Others carried the large wooden clubs used in the national Iranian game of Zur-Khaneh. People wandered about, talking, while emissaries rushed in every direction. Fifteen minutes later, the meeting was over and everyone returned to Tehran. Weapons and clubs had disappeared. Their faces were drawn and silent.

At the university, the Shah angrily refused a stretcher. He would accept only handkerchiefs to mop the blood on his face and neck. He was determined to get on with the ceremony. It took all the persuasion at his brother's command to convince him that he must have medical attention. So, walking alone and without support, he climbed back into his car.

Youssef-Abad Hospital was only a few hundred yards west on Nosrat Avenue. The royal Rolls, escorted by a few motorcycles, sirens wailing, arrived a little before 3:30, barely fifteen minutes after the first shot had been fired.

The hospital had been alerted by telephone, and five surgeons and doctors, among them General Ayadi, the Shah's personal physician (he still is), were anxiously awaiting the king's arrival. When they saw him walk in smiling, there were sighs of relief, and when they started to examine him and sew up his wounds, they were doubly astonished. His injuries were so superficial that it took little more than an hour to finish with the sutures. By 4:30, the Shah was back at the palace.

At virtually the same moment, Fakhr Arai died of his wounds. The five bullets he fired at his sovereign had very nearly ended an extraordinary adventure begun seventy-one years before, at the end of the last century.

Chapter 2

WHILE IN EUROPE AND AMERICA, the Gay Nineties were metamorphosing into the Belle Epoque, in the southern section of Tehran, an impoverished and illiterate donkey-driver was launching the dynasty of the Pahlevis.

Persia was falling apart. The empire that in ancient times had stretched from Greece and Egypt and the Caucasus to the Indus River, had been reduced to a patch of land that grew smaller every year. The Russians took the Caucasus and Azerbaijan, the British the Persian Gulf. Afghanistan seceded.

In theory, the Qajars were the country's rulers. In practice, they ruled only Tehran and its environs. The rest of the country was in open rebellion. To travel across Persia, a strong escort was essential. Bands of brigands roamed the roads and sowed terror in the villages. Nor were they alone. Turks, Russians, British and Germans exploited the country in successive waves. Persia was dying and the Qajars were doing all they could to hasten its end. Their only interest was pleasure.

Nasr Ed Din Shah spent all his time in Europe. He was a familiar figure at all the watering places, casinos and parties on the Continent. His special passion was expositions: Vienna in 1873, Paris in 1878 and 1889. He spent whole months at these events, squandering his fortune, while back home, the treasury was empty. And so he mortgaged everything. To the British, he gradually turned over the telegraph, railroad construction, mining concessions (with the exception of precious metals), the forests and undeveloped lands, all public works, the proceeds from customs for twenty-five years, the management of banks, and much more. To the Russians, he handed over the tobacco monopoly—in other words, the vast opium trade.

When he was assassinated in 1896, he was bankrupt.

No sooner had his son, Mosaffer Ed Din Shah, mounted the throne than he hastened to follow his father's example. This was made easy for him: the Russians decided to compete with the British by the simple expedient of having their commercial banks ready at all times to lend the Shah money. He would make his withdrawal, leave for Europe, return for more, leave again. From time to time, the Russians added up his bill, presented him with the total debt and agreed to wipe it out on condition he gave them another concession.

But the British returned to the attack. On May 28, 1901, they made a move which changed the course of Persia's history: on that day, William Knox d'Arcy obtained for 200,000 gold francs in cash ($40,000), oil rights for virtually the entire country.

In Turkey, the "Young Turks" were rebelling against the Sultan and demanding a constitution. Inspired by their example, the Persians took action, and in August, 1906, Mosaffer was forced to accept a constitution. He survived his capitulation only a few days.

The reign of his successor, Mohammed Ali Shah—another Qajar—brought little improvement. As the unrest grew—the entire country was now in a state of ferment—the Russians and the British removed their masks. When, in August, 1907, they signed the pact defining their respective zones of influence in Asia and the Near-East, they included Persia. After declaring that they both recognized the country's independence, they immediately set about carving it up. The Russians took the north, the British the south, and a neutral zone was left in the middle.

Meanwhile, the Shah decided to use force to put an end to the spreading anarchy. But it didn't work; nobody obeyed him. Outraged, he organized a coup d'état in June, 1908, dissolved Parliament at the point of a gun, and put the "Young Persians" behind bars. Tehran was silenced, but in Tabriz and Azerbaijan, civil war broke out. The red flag went up everywhere and the regular troops laid down their arms. There were pitched battles in the streets, raids and looting. Terror reigned throughout Persia. The Russians and British had thus far been content to watch from the sidelines, but now they began to worry. They wanted a weak Persia certainly, but not a revolutionary one. Who could tell what kind of strong government might emerge out of the chaos?

The British Navy steamed into the Persian Gulf, the Russian Cossacks occupied Tabriz, the Turks joined in and crossed the border. None of them was able to bring the chaos under control. Bands of insurgents moved into Tehran, unseated Mohammed Ali (who sought refuge in the Russian legation) and placed his son Soltan Ahmed on the throne.

He was twelve years old; he was the last of the Qajars.

At that same moment, in the stony desert to the south of Tehran, the barefoot, illiterate donkey-driver was tending his herd. It was he who would replace the last of the Qajars.

Little is known of his origins; even the year of his birth is uncertain. Depending on the source, it varies from 1870 to

1880. However, the year – 1878 – given in his official biography sounds plausible, although the actual date – March 16 – is open to doubt.

In his *Memoirs*, the present Shah wrote: "My father was born in 1878 in the province of Mazanderan on the Caspian. His origins were entirely Persian. His grandfather was even singled out for his courage in one of the Afghan wars. His father commanded a regiment stationed in Mazanderan. Riza Khan, as my father was called in his youth, was only forty days old when his father died." According to the Shah, his grandmother was forced to flee the region, crossing the Elburz Mountains to reach Tehran. At that time of year, there were no roads through the mountains, only mule paths, and the trip was especially difficult for a woman who usually had to follow the caravan on foot. One day, the group was caught in a blizzard. By evening, when they stopped for the night, the infant Riza was blue with the cold. His mother revived him by undressing him in the stable and rubbing him with straw. Once in Tehran, they lived in the most desperate poverty. And the Shah went on: "When he was fourteen, he enlisted in the Persian Cossack Brigade, formed the year after his birth. He was completely illiterate, education then being exclusively a privilege of the rich and powerful."

Princess Ashraf was less charitable about their grandfather's origins and probably closer to the truth when she said: "Actually, our father was of very humble birth."

To anyone flying over the vast capital today, it is hard to imagine what Tehran was like in 1878. A few palaces, which – except for Golestan, the royal palace – were no more than large villas, a few mosques, the bazaar swarming with merchants, donkeys and camels – like any classic *suk*. The rest was hovels of mud or brick. The only luxurious buildings were the foreign embassies. The total population was barely eighty thousand, periodically decimated by epidemics. The city was surrounded by a wall and a moat that was always dry, with only one gate, which was closed at night to keep out marauders.

While the top society and the embassies feasted, the common people were close to starvation. Some families lived off the harvest of a single nut tree. Those best off were the brick makers (brickworks were virtually Tehran's only industry), but even they were barely able to survive. Many did not have so much as a roof; they slept outdoors summer and winter, next to the *djubs*, the open mains that carried the melting snow down from the Elburz and across the city where the women did their laundry and drew their drinking and bath water. At night, bands of cutthroats took over the town, while the men tried to forget their misery in the opium dens.

Nothing is known of the first years that Riza and his mother spent in Tehran. How did she manage? Did she find work? Did she have family? It's all a mystery. All anyone knows for certain is that by the time he was five, Riza was driving a herd of donkeys, his staff a stick studded with nails. Despite his youth, he was very strong. At five, he already looked eight. The people of Mazanderan, like the Caucasians and those who live on the shores of the Caspian, have always been known for their unusual height and strength. The present Imperial Guard is largely made up of these men. Even so, Riza was a special case. Broad-shouldered, with rough-hewn features, the child's outstanding trait was his ruthlessness. This allowed him to dominate his comrades, his fists doing the rest. By the age of ten, he was the uncontested leader of the children in his neighborhood.

There were barracks nearby, and Riza began to haunt them to watch the soldiers. Theirs was not an easy life: more often than not, they were paid in bricks, and to survive, they had to sell eggs, split wood, and rent their services to the highest bidder. But even so, their lot seemed a comparatively desirable one.

One day, the boy walked boldly into the recruiting office. He had chosen a Cossack regiment. The top officers and instructors were czarists, assigned to Tehran to help form an elite corps in Persia. Riza was twelve. The recruiting officer smiled and asked his age. Riza answered proudly: "Eighteen."

He was staking everything on his physique. He was already five feet eight inches tall, and although still beardless, his voice had begun to deepen.

But the lie was too outrageous, and the sergeant laughed in his face. Crestfallen, Riza admitted his real age, and was told to come back when he was older. He left, holding back the tears, but he had made an impression: his pluck had struck home, and so had his bearing. The army had a good recruit in the making.

Riza's strong point was perseverance. He would hang around the barracks, rendering small services, making himself useful, taking part in the exercises, asking questions, making friends. And two years later, his strategy paid off. The now six feet tall fourteen year old was accepted into the regiment.

But he had to wait a long time before he could fight. After a period of training as tough as that of today's American marine, he was assigned as orderly to the German embassy, then to the Belgian. The German embassy has preserved to this day a *djavaiz* (laissez-passer) signed by the future Shahinshah, his shaky and awkward signature that of an illiterate who has learned to form the letters in his name by heart.

At seventeen, Riza married one of his cousins, Maryam Khanum, whom he found very beautiful and very gentle.

In 1896, he was eighteen, almost six foot six, and he made a striking impression astride his horse, with his thick mustache, and fiery eyes glistening under his fur hat. The country was once again in an uproar, and there were punitive expeditions against the dissident tribes. Riza saw to it that he was in the thick of every battle, and his indifference to danger, his flair, his talent as a leader greatly impressed his officers. In the Persian army then, there was no rank between simple soldier and lieutenant. That gave Riza his chance. At twenty, he was promoted to lieutenant. From then on, his name was Riza Khan, "khan" in Persian meaning "chief."

He was now able to give full rein to his appetite for leadership. For two years, he was in every battle. With varying results. In Mazanderan, he cut up the Bolsheviks; in Recht, he was beaten back with his entire brigade. On this occasion, one of his dominant traits—a terrible temper—showed itself in all its fury. Enraged at the setback, he put the blame on the White Russian officers who were flanking the expeditionary force, and insulted them with such savagery that he just missed being demoted and even court-martialed. But the incident was glossed over, which proved to him what prestige he already commanded.

In early 1904, Riza's wife died giving birth to a daughter, Hamdan-Os-Saltaneh.

From then on, wherever a rebellion needed putting down, Riza Khan was there. Winter and summer, he was in the saddle. He ate half-cooked meat and rice cakes and slept on the ground, rolled up in a rug next to his horse. He was a fearsome disciplinarian: the smallest blunder meant the knout, and Riza never hesitated to use it. But his soldiers continued to admire and even like him and his reputation as a fighter grew.

In 1903, he won the title of Riza Maxim.

He was serving under Prince Firuz, a Qajar. The two men

knew each other well, since between assignments to foreign embassies, Riza had served as the prince's personal bodyguard. Their troop was returning to Kermandjur in the Zagros Mountains near the Iraqi border when it was caught in ambush. The mountain people were three times as numerous and very well armed while the Cossacks had only two machine guns — Maxims. It soon became obvious that their retreat was cut off and that they would be massacred on the spot. Riza Khan shoved aside the men operating one of the two machine guns who, in their terror, had managed to tangle their ammunition belts, took the gun in his arms, lifted it onto a mound of dirt and, shouting at the top of his lungs, emptied the whole magazine into the enemy. Then he pulled the gun down, reloaded it and moved it thirty yards away, shot off another round, and repeated this process in seven or eight different locations. Thoroughly ashamed, the gunners recovered their courage; Riza gave them back their gun and ordered them to follow his example, shooting as fast as possible in order to make the enemy believe there were several guns instead of just the one. It took three men to imitate him. Then he ran to the other gun and repeated his routine. In twenty minutes, his assailants had retreated in panic. Riza Khan had become Riza Maxim.

After this adventure, it might have been expected that Riza would be satisfied to rise rapidly through the ranks, his military career threatened only by the possibility of an enemy bullet hitting its target one day. But in fact something very different happened, something rather rare for men who have felt the thrill of battle in their blood. Riza began to think, to reflect; he formed opinions about men and events.

His comrades-in-arms had only one thing on their minds:

slaughtering as many brigands as possible. Officers weren't supposed to think. Riza made two observations: first, he was an officer, but more than that, a Persian officer. Persian, not Russian. That was significant. The others paid no attention to this fact because they were blind to everything that wasn't sword, horse, rifle or machine gun, but Riza was outraged: their orders came not from Tehran but from Moscow. The pious fiction that the Russian officers were in Persia only to serve as advisers didn't go down. The Russians' game was as clear as day: under the pretext of helping the Persian army, they were insidiously gaining control of it. And whoever has the army holds the power. This conflicted with one of the emotions closest to Riza's heart—love of country.

So, secondly, Riza began to wonder about the people he was being sent to fight. Now, no officers' mess is completely cut off from the world. News reached them; they talked, they discussed. Riza heard references to the "Young Turks" who were threatening the rule of Sultan Abdul Hamid. He learned that a similar movement had taken root in Persia—the "Young Persians." He probably even met a few during his leaves in Tehran. As he listened and learned, he gradually came to understand the whys and wherefores of events. His political education was under way.

Many of the bands devastating the provinces were made up of brigands, but not all of them. One day, he had the chief of the partisans he had just captured brought before him. The man was his age, spoke Persian, and didn't sound like a butcher. Before he died of his wounds, he talked about nationalism, liberty, patriotism, and pleaded with Riza to open his eyes to the motives of the Russians, the British, and all the other foreigners whose only goal was to colonize Persia and cut it up like a pie. Deeply disturbed, Riza had him buried with full military honors.

Mohammed Ali Shah's coup d'état in 1908, the repression of the "Young Persians," the Russian, British and Turkish incursions of the next year, followed by the king's abdication, all these were fuel for Riza's awakening political consciousness. At thirty, Riza Khan, now a captain, was an officer who fought because he was ordered to fight, but who was beginning to be devoured by the suspicion that he was fighting for the wrong side. But there was also no point in becoming one of the desperadoes he had been fighting for so long, and ending up—as most of them did—shot to death in ambush.

So he decided to wait. And at night in his tent, he studied. The six-foot-six giant would humbly seek the instruction of a subordinate who had gone to school. Soon, Riza was ordering books and newspapers. He learned history, political science, economics, and studied the foreign news.

Then lightning struck in the person of Kemal Ataturk.

Though still obscure, the future leader of the Turkish revolution was becoming the theoretician of the "Young Turks." He was three years younger than Riza Khan, but as soon as Riza heard of him and read his speeches and analyzed his actions, he made him his mentor. What Mustafa Efendi, called Kemal ("Perfection" in Turkish), was doing in his country, he, Riza Khan, would do in his own.

Persia was growing sicker by the month. Its finances were in a catastrophic condition, the maladministration and the corruption of its petty officials were a spreading cancer. *Bakshish* was king. The only services that functioned at all were those run by the Europeans, and they held all the key positions. Anarchy was bleeding the country dry. If you wanted to get from Tehran to Meshed in the northeast alive, you had to go through Russia, and to go to Khuzistan in the southwest, you had to travel by way of Turkey and Mesopotamia. The poverty of the people was frightful. Even the army was disintegrating. It had nothing but half a dozen old cannons.

It was now 1914. World War I had broken out, and for the Persians, the worst threat was from Turkey. Backed by the Germans, Enver Pasha, the new Turkish leader, wanted to proclaim a holy war which would result in nothing less than the conquest of Egypt, North Africa, Arabia, Palestine, Syria, Iraq, Afghanistan, and of course, Persia.

The invasion of Persia got under way in 1915. It was completely chaotic. The Turks moved into the north near Tabriz, fighting the Russians who soon won it back. As they retreated, the Turks avenged themselves by ravaging the villages in their path. Persia signed a treaty with Germany, whose officers immediately set about recruiting tribal warriors. Kabul, the capital of Afghanistan, was the Germans' ultimate goal. At the same time, the British landed troops in the Persian Gulf and headed north.

By the end of the year, Tehran and Qom were in Russian hands, the Russians having expelled the Germans. By April, 1916, the Turks had eliminated the British, whom they defeated at Kut-el-Amara in Syria, seized Kermanshah Hamadan and pushed as far north as Qazvin.

At this point, the plague broke out, decimating the Turkish ranks, while the October Revolution in St. Petersburg and Moscow caused the departure of most of the Russians. By the end of 1918, having been beaten on all other fronts, the Turks abandoned Persia. The country was left to the British.

In August, 1919, Sir Percy Cox, chief of the British mission, imposed an accord that officially recognized Persia's independence, reserving for Britain only the status of "protector," and the responsibility to provide financial and military aid. In theory, Persia was free; in fact, she had become a British protectorate.

Bled white by five years of war, the Persians were already numb with despair. But no sooner was the war over than their troubles resumed. When the White Russian army tried to seek refuge in Persia, the Bolsheviks landed in Enzeli on the Caspian Sea (now Bandar-e-Pahlevi) and formed an alliance with a local rebel named Kutchek Khan, creating the Socialist Republic of Guilan. In no time, they had taken over all the Caspian provinces, even though when Lenin came to power, he solemnly promised to forgo the Czarists' designs on Persia. Meanwhile, the Britons' brutality toward their Persian victims provoked a rash of protests from abroad. There was open revolt against the occupying forces in Tehran. The Persian people's hatred of the British was such that they virtually welcomed the Russians with open arms. Short of a miracle, Persia was on the way to disappearing from the map for all time.

This was the climate in which Mohammed Riza was born. On October 26, 1919, Tadj-Ol-Moluk, Riza Khan's second wife and the daughter of a Caucasian sergeant, gave birth to twins—a boy and a girl. Mohammed Riza was born second, after his sister Ashraf. Two years before, Tadj-Ol-Moluk had borne a daughter, Shams. The birth of the future king took place at Ahmadiyeh, at the time Tehran's one and only hospital. The mother and the two infants then returned to their small house in Shahr-E-Now, a neighborhood of small shops and businesses. Even though he was an officer, Riza Khan had little money and lived very modestly.

The father was fighting in the north when the twins were born. But the moment he learned he had a son, he rushed back to Tehran. (There is some confusion about the neighborhood where the Shah was born. According to him, it is now the capital's red-light district, rebaptized Zone Number 10; his ministers maintain that the district was leveled and is now part of the industrial zone.)

Chapter 3

MOHAMMED RIZA HAD A DIFFICULT START in life. His sister Ashraf was a healthy, lively child, but he was small and delicate. For a long time, his parents feared for his life.

Not long after his son's birth, Riza Khan was promoted to colonel and second-in-command of all Persian forces. The family moved to a larger house on Hassan Abad Street. He was earning a thousand rials a month (about $13 at the time) — a small fortune. Stationed ninety miles west of Tehran at Qazvin, he was at the strategic point that controlled the routes to Turkey, the Caspian Sea and the southern oil fields. And Riza had twenty-five hundred cavalrymen under him — a considerable force. It is thanks largely to these men that Mohammed Riza, the frail child of the twenties, is the Shah of Iran today.

That Riza Khan would have an important role to play was obvious to everyone, even at court. His reputation as a strong man was widespread; the officers' circle and the capital's drawing rooms were familiar with his outbursts against the country's decadent ways. Now, Riza had formed a close friendship with one *Sayyid* Ziaeddine Tabatabai, a thirty-year-

old journalist and son of a *mullah* in the Shiite clergy, and
also with a young officer, Lieutenant Mortez Khan, who was
to play a key role in the present Shah's life as well.

The three men shared the same admiration for Mustafa
Kemal, the same hope for their country's salvation, and the
same hatred for the decadence and corruption of the Qajar
dynasty. In his newspaper, the sayyid constantly fulminated against the court and its entourage. To Riza, meeting
Tabatabai was a revelation; he had found the perfect ally. The
sayyid had everything he lacked: great culture, entrée into
influential circles, experience in politics. On his side, Tabatabai
was overwhelmed by the forty-two-year-old giant and his
driving passion to remake Persia into a free, independent and
powerful nation.

But what could three men do alone in a country living
under the heel of two armies of occupation? Only one thing:
make peace with the enemy, seem to play its game, and keep
nibbling away to reclaim their country. But, make peace with
which enemy? The Russians? Out of the question: Russia was
geographically too close, and besides, the Russians were Communists. Neither the sayyid nor Riza wanted a Red republic.
What they wanted was to do exactly what Mustafa Kemal was
doing in Turkey: reestablish complete independence as the
essential first step.

Britain, on the other hand, was far away, weak and under a
cloud. Riza instinctively knew he must choose Britain. Also,
the British shared his fear of a Russian invasion, and therefore needed a strong government in control. The Qajars were
incapable of providing it, hence the British must look elsewhere. And quickly; the Russians were on the move.

In the Foreign Office in London, Riza Khan's dossier,
begun at the start of the century, had grown increasingly
thick. The British studied their files, compared reports,

weighed the pros and cons of the various men who might fill the role. The choice was easy. Riza Khan was their man. All that was needed now was to make contact.

There are two versions of how this occurred. According to one source, the British spoke only to Tabatabai—who was one of their agents. This is possible; anything is possible in Persia. According to the second, the two men were discreetly contacted together. Where the interviews took place and what the terms agreed upon were is a secret Riza took with him to his grave, and which the British still have locked up in their archives. All that is known is the approximate date: August, 1920. Nor is there any doubt that each side tried to deceive the other. The British promised them heaven and earth if Riza were able to exert full power. Riza went out of his way to appear compliant, accepting the entire British proposal on bended knee. Together, they decided that their first move would be to weed out the elite corps of the Persian army, in other words, the Cossack Brigade that constituted the Russian presence. On this point, the two parties were in perfect accord. The British were delighted to see the Russian influence sapped by an intermediary, and Riza had the backing of a British guarantee to "renationalize" his troops.

As a first step, Riza invited the Russian lieutenants to leave the country. Protestations from the Soviet ambassador. In reply, he was reminded that these officers were, after all, only "advisers"; they had given their advice, and their presence was no longer needed. The Russians were themselves in the midst of a civil war. They had more important problems on their minds than the fate of the officers assigned to Persia. They gave in. Riza Khan increased the pressure. First the Soviet captains, then their commanding officers, were thanked in turn. By the end of November, 1920, all the Russians had left, except for their chief. Two months later, he personally submitted his resignation to Riza Khan.

Meanwhile, Riza Khan was supposed to be waiting for British instructions—as stated in their agreement. But instead, after what appeared to be a six-weeks' hibernation in his garrison at Qazvin, he suddenly went into action. Well before dawn, on February 21, 1921, Riza, together with the sayyid and Mortez Khan who had secretly joined him, set off in the arctic cold for Tehran with his 2500 cavalrymen. It was a bald-faced power play. Under the terms of the agreement, Riza should have alerted General William Edmund Ironside, his superior in the British hierarchy. He did nothing of the sort. When at 10:00 AM, Riza reached Karaj, about thirty miles from Tehran, Ironside had just woken up and was having his morning tea. By the time the news was brought to him, it was too late to do anything.

After a fifteen-minute stop in Karaj, Riza set off again and was in the capital's outskirts an hour later. A few shots were fired, but by three in the afternoon, Tehran was completely under his control. Not a drop of blood had been shed.

That same evening, Prime Minister Sepahdar-Azam offered his resignation to the Shah and the sayyid was promptly named in his place. Riza Khan, promoted to general on the following day, took over the War Ministry.

The first lap was won. They had thumbed their noses at the British. And in the face of the fait-accompli, the British could hardly disavow Tabatabai and Riza. So they ratified their promotions.

In his first public proclamation, the new general declared: "The inhabitants of Tehran are invited to obey and keep quiet." Then he had all the former ministers and the capital's leaders put in prison. Nobody stirred. Some nervous types had feared that the great powers might intervene. But within five days after the occupation of Tehran, the Russians signed a treaty of friendship with the new government, promising to respect Persia's independence, and renouncing all concessions and zones of influence. The Turks departed from the areas they still occupied. The British pulled back to the Persian Gulf. It didn't take them long to realize that Riza Khan had the makings of a powerful leader. So why not leave it to him to restore order? What they wanted were the oil wells in the Khuzistan which had produced almost a million and a half tons in 1920. They were content, for the time being, to be allowed to exploit them in peace.

Then, too, the British were delighted at the speed with which the new government was bringing order to the country. In a matter of months, the Socialist Republic of Guilan had been liquidated, and Kutchek Khan arrested and executed. The chiefs of the principal Persian tribes — the Qashqai, Bakhtiari, and Kurds — were on their knees. Everywhere, people were being weeded out, brought to trial and executed. Riza Khan was given the title of Sardar Sepah, or Chief of the Armed Forces, and he used it to gain control of the police and militias, and to set up a corps of *gendarmes* — rural police copied after the French. In addition, he sent his own men to recruit foreign advisers, especially in France, for he was much impressed by Saint-Cyr, France's military academy. By now, all the strings of power were in his own hands. But this signaled the start of the fatal rupture between him and the sayyid. Tabatabai took umbrage at his associate's rapid rise and, in one of those reversals common to politicians, chose the only solution that might turn things in his favor: he betrayed him.

Riza Khan had made no attempt to hide from the *sayyid* the fact that he was only waiting for the right moment to revoke the 1919 Anglo-Persian accord. Tabatabai was on his way to the British embassy on Ferdowzi Avenue when Riza, alerted by his spies, had him stopped and immediately dismissed him. Tabatabai fled to Mesopotamia.

Curiously enough, Riza Khan refused the post of prime minister when the Shah offered it to him. Apparently he didn't think the situation sufficiently stable. He preferred running things from behind the scenes, so that his straw men would have to take the responsibility for decisions displeasing to the British. Meanwhile, he continued to spin his own web, collecting taxes due his ministry, installing his own men in every provincial post, formulating new laws which he brazenly imposed on the prime minister, finally convincing the Shah that he should repudiate the Anglo-Persian accord. Stunned, the British were forced to accept it.

With this behind him, Riza Khan grew even bolder.

He had been building a small modern army (the old one didn't have even a thousand rifles of the same caliber), equipped it in France, raised the soldiers' pay and recruited with a vengeance, all with incredible speed. By October, Riza felt he had enough power to take the next step. He deposed the prime minister, Mochir-Ed-Dowleh Pirnia, put himself in his place, and "advised" the Shah to do what the young king (he was twenty-three) was more than eager to do: go amuse himself in Europe. Ahmad Shah didn't have to be told twice. He named his brother regent and left that very evening. He never saw Persia again.

Was it coincidence? The meeting of two destinies? The very next day, October 29, Mustafa Kemal, Riza Khan's "god," ordered the Turkish National Assembly to depose the caliph of Constantinople, and was unanimously elected President of the Turkish Republic. Riza was struck by the news and immediately considered following suit. He kept repeating: "Better a healthy republic than a weak and corrupt monarchy." But he prudently waited to see how things worked out in Turkey.

In March, 1924, convinced that Mustafa Kemal had succeeded, he went to work. On the day of Nowruz, the Persian New Year which is celebrated on the first day of spring, he convened Parliament and submitted his project. Not a single objection. A study committee was appointed, but unfortunately, the prime minister had overestimated his people's docility. When he summoned the top Shiite clergy to the holy city of Qom, he found himself faced with a regiment of unyielding lawmakers. They argued for three-and-a-half hours, but the priests wouldn't give in. In their eyes, a republic was pure folly; the monarchical system had run Persia for too many centuries. They warned Riza that if he persisted, they would have to oppose him.

Wild with rage, Riza Khan fumed all the way back to Tehran. By the time he reached home, he had come to a decision: he would force a republic down their throats.

At that time, one of Riza's closest collaborators was Charles Banel, a Frenchman not yet twenty-five. Now, Amanolah Mirza Djahakbali, a former czarist cadet officer and a friend of Riza's since the early battles in Azerbaijan, had been, since early in 1923, the head of the Persian military mission in Paris. Riza needed not only rifles, machine guns and artillery, but also planes and pilots. Charles Banel was a young pilot who had gone into aviation after the war and was eager for action. When Djahakbali contacted him, he jumped at the chance and left on the next freighter with three dismantled old planes which he started to put together the moment he docked in Bandar Abbas. From there, they had to be carried by hand to Isfahan, the airport nearest to the coast.

Banel was ready for anything and had taken part in every

expedition against the rebels' strongholds. Those were the heroic days! When Banel took off in his plane, he had bombs under his seat, between his legs, everywhere he could find room. And he released them by hand even as the rebels were shooting at him.

Riza had taken a great liking to the French mercenary with the blue eyes who was almost as tall as he, and like him, totally fearless. As soon as he returned from his setback in Qom, Riza summoned Banel. He needed him to bring off his republican revolution. His plan was child's play. Banel was at Isfahan at the time. He was to fly to the Tehran airport where two tanks would be waiting for him which only he and his mechanic knew how to operate. His role was purely a psychological one: No one had ever seen a tank in Tehran.

Banel was delighted with the plan. On the given day, with Riza's troops in a state of alert, Banel started up his engine on the Isfahan airstrip, picked up speed . . . and flipped over. A wheel had hit a hole in the tarmac. Banel was not hurt, but when the people who had been watching his flying machine from a respectful distance came running up, they asked him why he was flying his plane upside down. The Persians hadn't even realized that his plane had turned over!

What republican inclinations Riza Khan had did not survive the mishap. It is also unlikely, given what is known of his character, that his idea of a republic was in any way related to a democracy. In any event, he never spoke of the project again. Riza explained the weakening of his republican ardor with these words: "It is true that I wanted to establish a republic. But to the Persians, republic means Bolshevism, or at least something close to it. That was enough to make them not want it. In the end, I came around to their views."

With Riza's plot exposed, it was too late to turn back. But he showed some hesitation: Three different times, he asked the Shah to return. On the first occasion, the young king who, like his father and grandfather, was shuttling between Switzerland and the Riviera and watering places in France and Germany, didn't even answer him. Then he reported that he would return, but they must be patient: He wasn't well. By the end of summer, 1925, the last of the Qajars announced he was coming back. He would leave Marseilles on September 25. On the twenty-third, riots broke out in Tehran. The mob demanded bread and the Shah's return. Riza put down the revolt, made a number of arrests, but the bazaar remained restive. Ahmad Shah let it be known that he had thought things over and decided not to return after all.

On October 29, the Constituent Assembly met and a young deputy named Davar proposed that the Qajars be deposed and power turned over to Riza Khan. Two days later, the deed was done; the Shah's brother was sent into exile and Riza Khan was named regent.

Elections were called to set up a new assembly, and on December 12, its 280 members unanimously proffered the throne of the King of Kings to His Highness the Regent, General Riza Khan.

It goes without saying that Riza Khan's precipitous rise had a telling effect on the life of his young son.

To make sure his son had an education worthy of a future ruler, Riza Khan engaged a tutor, and as he also wanted a European influence on his son, he engaged a French governess, Madame Arfa, the wife of a Persian, who taught him to read, write, and speak French like a native.

Although he loved his children dearly, Riza Shah was a very strict father. The present Shah wrote in his *Memoirs*: "We were all terrified by him. One look from those piercing eyes could freeze us to the spot. At the family table, we never dared to express an opinion. Besides, we didn't have the right to open our mouths unless we were asked a direct question. On the other hand, he never punished us — never the smallest spanking."

Riza Shah eventually had nine children. Two-and-a-half years later another son was born to Tadj-Ol-Moluk; then, in quick succession, Riza took two more wives, the first bearing him still another son, the second five children. Tadj-Ol-Moluk was never disturbed by the presence of competing wives, for polygamy was a familiar custom in Persia. And since she was the mother of the firstborn, hence the "principal wife," she played the enviable and intimidating role of "queen mother" in the Persian court.

Whatever his preference among his children might have been, Riza Khan treated Mohammed differently. His oldest son, from whom he expected so much, was allowed to get away with nothing. As Mohammed Riza was to say later, his was an unhappy and browbeaten childhood. In addition, his health continued to be poor; he suffered constantly from colds and bronchitis. But when things looked darkest, he had the affection of his governess to compensate for his terrifying father.

It was on April 25, 1926, that Mohammed Riza made his definite entry into History. On that day, his father was crowned in Golestan Palace, the Qajars' Thousand and One Nights, resplendent with Venetian mirrors, marble, gold and crystal, and priceless fabrics hanging everywhere. When the giant of the steppes reached the palace entrance, he was met by the country's highest dignitaries. Riza climbed the monumental staircase and entered the great throne room where a crowd awaited him. On his heels came the members of his family — only the men, of course, women having as yet no right to take part in official functions – the members of the government, Parliament, and the generals. Speeches followed, to loud applause. The prime minister placed on Riza Khan's shoulders the cloth of gold that symbolized Power and Glory, and put in his hands the scepter and globe encrusted with precious stones. He then handed him the imperial crown and, like Napoleon, Riza Khan placed it on his head himself.

Savad Kuhi, the donkey-driver from Mazanderan and subsequently the intrepid cavalryman Riza Maxim, had at forty-eight, become Riza Shah Pahlevi. He was emperor, as twenty-five hundred years before him, Cyrus and Darius had been king of kings in ancient Persia. And for the first time in a hundred and thirty-eight years, Persia had a Persian ruler. (The Qajars, who had come to the throne in 1787, were Turks.) As for his predecessor, the last of the Qajars, he had just died in Cannes as the result of too stringent a diet.

In the crowd, a uniformed child was taking in the spectacle, spellbound. The crown prince, Mohammed Riza, was six and a half years old. He had been separated from his brothers and sisters, and was attending an elementary military school which his father had created expressly for him, with the sons of Riza Shah's companions-at-arms to keep him company.

Riza Shah's orders were that his son must not only be treated like everybody else, but even more harshly. The school was installed in Saadabad Palace – the "house of happiness" – recently built by Riza Shah on the barren hills north of the city at an altitude of 5600 feet. He hated Golestan Palace: it was too big and too pretentious, with its great stairs and vast mirrored rooms where he shook with the winter cold. Besides, Golestan was a Qajar palace. And Riza, founder of a new dynasty, wanted his son and successor influenced only by himself.

Chapter 4

MOHAMMED RIZA HAD NO SOONER BECOME crown prince than he was put to a severe test, one that was to leave a permanent mark on his character. He was stricken with typhoid, the first of his several brushes with death.

At this time, especially in Persia where doctors were still few and far between, typhoid was a serious disease. In the young prince's case, it took such a disturbing turn that Riza Shah feared for his son's life. Abandoning receptions and meetings to sit helpless and despairing by his son's bed, Riza Shah began to feel pangs of guilt. Had the Spartan education he imposed on the child been too much for him?

At long last, Mohammed Riza recovered. As he looked back on it, it seemed like a true miracle. The night before his fever broke, he had had a dream. He saw Ali, the prophet Mohammed's son-in-law, holding in one hand the double-edged sword often seen in Persian paintings, and in the other, a bowl containing a liquid which he told the sick child to drink. The child obeyed. The next morning when Mohammed Riza woke up, his fever had subsided and he was well in no time.

Ever since that day, Mohammed Riza has been convinced

that he is under God's protection, and so need never fear danger or be afraid of taking risks. This explains a great deal about him: his self-assurance, his amazing courage in the face of repeated attempts on his life, his certainty that he has a mission to fulfill for his country.

Soon after, a second miracle occurred, reinforcing his mysticism, and again preceded by visions. That same summer (1926), he was on an excursion in the mountains above Tehran and had reached the vicinity of a small cemetery — Emamzadeh-Daud. To get to it, one had to climb a steep hill, either on foot or by horse. One of his relatives, an army lieutenant, had placed him on the pommel of his saddle. Halfway up the hill, the horse lost his footing and the child fell head first on a rock. The blow was so hard that he passed out. When he came to, he heard his companions marveling that he didn't have so much as a scratch.

The child told them that as he fell, he had had a vision of Abbas, one of the Islamic saints, and that Abbas had protected his forehead with his hand to prevent him from cracking his skull on the rock.

Not long after, he had a third vision. Taking a walk one day with his tutor near the royal palace, he saw a man approach with a halo around his head. As they passed each other, the child recognized him as the Iman, Mohammed's descendant who, according to Islamic law, had disappeared but was expected to return to save the world.

"Did you see him?" he asked his tutor.

"See who?" the tutor replied. "There's no one here to see."

The Shah's mother was deeply religious and a mystic in her own right, and must have encouraged these tendencies in her son. She was positively fanatical in her observance of all the Muslim rituals. She organized *Taazieh* (Mysteries) in the streets of Tehran and even took part in them, together with her husband and son. Many years later, the Shah remarked that he had been especially fond of the snacks and syrup drinks which were distributed on these occasions.

Soon after his third vision, the prince fell sick once again, this time with diphtheria, followed by malaria. And again, his family feared for his life. Then, once again, he made a sudden and seemingly miraculous recovery. Riza Shah was of course relieved to have his son restored to health, but he was exasperated by the child's tales of miracles and apparitions. He berated him constantly, reminding him that he was a crown prince and that instead of mooning around like a girl, he should grit his teeth and behave like a future king. The endless admonitions often drove the boy to tears, which caused his father to stalk away, angrier than ever.

And yet, Riza Shah adored his son. When his anger had passed, he would take him on long walks and talk to him with deep affection. Back at the palace, they could often be heard singing old Persian songs together. He was also a talented mimic, and when he was in a good mood, his children would pester him to do an imitation of someone they knew — and not always a flattering one.

Riza Shah was so afraid of his son's becoming soft that he went out of his way to eradicate the comforts and luxuries that had marked the Qajars' way of life. Using himself as an example, he continued to wear the plain uniform of a Cossack officer, his socks were homemade, and his boots were often in need of repair. His only luxury was a small silver cigarette case he kept in his pocket next to his handkerchief, a present from Tadj-Ol-Moluk which he had cherished for years. And, a throwback to the days of Riza Maxim, he slept on a mattress on the floor. During the early days of his reign, he continued — even during an audience — to sit on a rug as he had in his army days. Food meant nothing to him. For breakfast, bread,

Riza Shah with children, including present Shah. *Henri Cartier-Bresson, Magnum*

cheese, butter, eggs and tea, and usually rice and chicken at the other two meals. This was the classic Persian food – of the poor, not the rich.

The last Qajar's study was full of precious rugs, gems, miniatures, paintings, valuable European antiques, and bowls and bowls of flowers. Riza Shah's had a plain inlaid table, one chair, a couch for visitors, one rug and a large map of the world. That was all.

To his son's regimen of privation, Riza added work. There again, he made himself the example. Up at five, even on Fridays, he spent the morning reading newspapers and reports and receiving a constant stream of visitors. Lunch with his family at 11:30, then a walk in the garden until 2:30 when the visits began all over again. Ministers, ambassadors, generals, businessmen, but also and quite often, the common people. He usually had dinner at eight and was in bed by ten. His only distractions were hunting and walking in the mountains above Saadabad, or in summer, through the Caspian forests.

If Mohammed Riza is in total control of Iran today, it is because, having won his throne by naked force, his father was equally merciless in establishing a lasting power base. The brutality of the former Cossack was never far from the surface. On one occasion, he actually resorted to defenestration. One of his ministers had committed a blunder, and instead of groveling before his sovereign and accepting a tongue-lashing, he tried to justify his mistake. Riza Shah took him by the arm, dragged him up to a window, opened it and shoved him out. He was also said to have kicked another minister to death.

He was equally cruel to foreigners. One day, the new Greek ambassador came to present his credentials. His name was

Kyriakos. Now, in Persian, "kir" means the male genitals, "kos" the female, and "ia" signifies "or." As the ambassador entered, the chamberlain announced at the top of his voice: "His Excellency, the envoy of the King of the Greeks, Mr. Kyriakos."

Stunned silence and embarrassed smiles. The Shah, like everybody else, heard "Kir ia Kos."

He leaned toward the chamberlain and whispered: "Is his name Kir or Kos?"

The chamberlain blushed and stammered. The Shah, without looking at the ambassador, announced: "If he hasn't made up his mind, throw him out!"

As a result, Greece broke off diplomatic relations with Persia.

On another occasion, the Persian ambassador to Washington — this was during Roosevelt's administration — had done a poor job of parking his car and an overly zealous American policeman gave him a ticket in spite of his diplomatic license plate. When word of it reached Riza Shah, he recalled his ambassador and immediately severed diplomatic relations with the United States. It took endless diplomatic maneuvering to restore relations.

Meanwhile, Mohammed Riza was pursuing his studies at military school. His health was gradually improving. Instead of breaking him, the rigorous training seems to have given him strength. In addition to riding and gymnastics, the ten year old was introduced to boxing. His boxing master wore a pince-nez, and Mohammed's greatest delight was to give him a jab that sent the glasses flying. Classes lasted from eight in the morning until five in the afternoon, with a break from 11:30 to 1:30. Besides the traditional subjects, he had long hours of military instruction, practicing with weapons and going on maneuvers in the countryside even in rain and snow.

His foreign language was French, taught by a Frenchman. There were twenty-one students in his class, all of them the sons of top officials and the military. Their uniform, copied after the cadets at Saint-Cyr, included boots, and a somewhat more supple and wider cap that sported a plume on parade and ceremonial days.

Starting with his eighth birthday, Mohammed not only had breakfast alone with his father every day, but also began attending meetings of the Council, parades and inspections. A photograph from this period shows him in the courtyard of a barracks surrounded by thirty officers — the general staff of the Pahlevi Cavalry Guard, of which he was colonel. His hands in his pockets, and flanked by officers standing rigidly at attention, the boy looks very proud. A far cry from the days of illness and visions.

The future king was also taking his first lessons in the practice of absolute power. First, legislative power. Ostensibly, there was a Parliament of 136 deputies elected by all citizens over twenty-one, except the military and criminals. Citizens between thirty and seventy years of age were eligible. Jews and Zoroastrians each had one deputy, and the Armenians, two. Deputies were elected for two-year periods and could be reelected until they reached the age of seventy. As there were no actual political parties, hence no opposition, Parliament's function was simple: it was presented with laws and it passed them unanimously.

On the executive side, there was a Council of Ministers made up of eight ministers and three under-secretaries of state. The president of the Council had, as usual, no real power. The Shah himself presided over all Council meetings. All he asked of them was to execute his directives. They did.

From his father, Mohammed also learned national pride and how to deal with the world beyond Persia's frontier. To establish peaceful borders, Riza Shah had concluded treaties of friendship with Iraq, Afghanistan and Turkey. Despite their wartime difficulties, he was quick to patch things up with Turkey. He admired Kemal Ataturk too much to let bad memories fester.

Agreement on Persia's fifteen-hundred-mile frontier with Russia had been reached earlier. On the British side, matters improved after his revocation of Sir Percy Cox's ill-disguised "protectorate." Then the king turned to a "minor problem" that was especially dear to his heart: He did away with the preferential treaties which the various foreign powers had imposed on the Qajars.

In the area of foreign relations, all that remained was the oil problem. And that was so complex that it remains a problem to this day. But more of that later.

Inside Persia, Riza Shah launched a far-reaching revolution in customs and manners. He was inspired in this by Kemal Ataturk who, during the three years following his seizure of power, ordered all men to cut their beards and dress in European style, and forbade women to wear veils. The Persian national dress was wide pants and a long tight-fitting jacket, with an *aba*, or loose cloak, over that and a turban, or cap, on their heads. The women wore the *chalvar*, or wide pants, and over these, a *pirane*, or tunic, that hugged the body. On their heads, they draped a *chador*, a black veil wound in such a manner that only the eyes showed.

Riza Shah shared Kemal Ataturk's belief that, to modernize a country, one had to start by abolishing the native dress. It was the only way to shake the people out of their ancestors' ways and prepare them for the twentieth century. He had some difficulty putting the men in European clothes, especially in replacing the turban, or *kolah*, with a hat. The opponents of the hat, with the clergy in the lead, protested loudly, especially in Meshed, the center of the Islamic Shiites. To comply with the Shah's orders, the governor of Meshed had to resort to extreme measures: he summoned the rebels under the pretext that he wished to listen to their views . . . then ordered them at gunpoint to undress. Six months later, all Persians, from caravan leaders to shopkeepers, were dressed in European style.

To solve the problem of the *chador*, Riza Shah arrived one day at an official inauguration with his wife and daughter unveiled and wearing skirts, jackets and hats. He had them photographed and ordered "all Persians to follow their example."

A little later, he learned that an *imam* in his mosque had launched on a diatribe against the queen because he had seen her arm unveiled. Wild with rage, the Shah leapt into his car — not even waiting for his armed escort — drove straight to Qom and beat the *imam* with such force that he bent his cane.

From that day on, no veiled woman was allowed on a Tehran bus. Two weeks later, they were forbidden taxis. Then it was movie houses and stores. Finally, the police were given orders to tear the veils off the last holdouts, the women instinctively picking up their skirts to hide their faces. In two months, the *chador*, which dated back many hundreds of years, had disappeared. Angriest of all were the husbands. The *chador* had served as a cover-all; from now on they would have to buy their wives dresses.

The Shah today is one of the world's richest men — and one of its sharpest businessmen. This is no accident: His father used the same vigorous tactics on his own account as he did for his country.

In a few years, the erstwhile donkey-driver had become immensely rich. Although he turned Golestan Palace over to the public — he never liked it anyway — he followed a very different course with the Qajars' other residences and those of Persia's first families. He appropriated Niavaran, today his son's Winter Palace, and Saadabad, the Summer Palace, together with its fifteen hundred acres which he improved and enlarged. He bought other palaces for pennies, like the White Marble Palace, virtually stolen from the Firuz family, where he lived at the beginning of his reign. Then, using the simplest of expedients, he took over vast tracts of unowned land. At this time, Persia still had extensive tracts without owners. These were called *amlack* and covered about 60 percent of the country. The procedure for establishing ownership was first to dig a well. If during the next twenty-four hours, the well produced water, you had only to say *amlack* — which means "This land belongs to me" — and the land was yours.

The king collected most of his *amlack* lands around the Caspian Sea. He was soon in possession of almost the entire coast from Georgia to Ramsar. Moreover, since he owned the beaches as well, his acreage multiplied annually. The Caspian is eighty feet below sea level and drops about four inches a year. The beaches are almost flat, which causes rapid evaporation. The land on the southernmost end of the Caspian, where the bathing resorts are, is now worth up to a hundred dollars a square yard.

Riza Shah also confiscated the holdings of all the large landowners who refused to accept his absolute power. In Tehran, however, he bought little. The land there was useless for agricultural purposes, and no one was yet thinking in terms of urban development.

A master wheeler-dealer, the Shah was in large part responsible for his country's phenomenal economic development, and this in itself served to enrich him. In the Orient at that time (and not unknown today), the demarcation between public and private funds was very hazy. It was hard to tell where the state's treasury ended and the sovereign's personal fortune began. Even now, Kuwait's oil belongs to Emir al Saban and not to his country.

In May, 1931, Mohammed Riza had completed his elementary education. His father decided it was time to send him to Europe: it was very important that the crown prince make contact with the Occident and learn the way it lived and thought. At first, he considered a French boarding school. But on second thought, he was afraid this might look like a politically inspired move, and so he chose Switzerland, a neutral country. Besides, Swiss schools were well known for their high academic standards. An adviser was sent prospecting, and on his recommendation, the Shah chose Le Rosey near Rolle, between Geneva and Lausanne.

Mohammed Riza spent his last two months before leaving on the shores of the Caspian while his father made preparations for his departure. It was decided that his younger brother, Ali Riza, should accompany him, and so that the two boys wouldn't feel too lonely in a foreign country, their playmate Hossein Fardust was invited to go along. The retinue also included two tutors, Dr. Moadeb Nafissi to watch over their health, and a professor of Persian, M. Mostafar.

In early September, the whole Pahlevi family took off for the port of Enzeli (now Bandar-E-Pahlevi) on the Caspian. Queen Tadj-Ol-Moluk was on hand, as well as the princesses Shams and Ashraf and the four younger princes. Only Fatemed and Hamid were considered too young to go along. There were floods of tears, hugs and kisses, and everybody read verses from the Koran. Even the king was wet-eyed. He blessed his sons and, turning toward the two tutors to whom he was entrusting his most precious possessions, said: "Make men of them."

Mohammed Riza was twelve.

They boarded a Russian ship that carried them to Baku, where two days later, the five travelers took the train for Moscow, Warsaw, Berlin and eventually Switzerland. Postcards written in French arrived in Tehran every day. Shams and Ashraf translated them to their parents, then pinned them to the walls of their room.

The trip took three weeks, after which the four boys spent another three weeks in the Persian Consulate in Geneva. Then they were sent to Lausanne to take courses at l'École Nouvelle de la Suisse Romande which would prepare them for the entrance exams to Le Rosey. Fardust was a boarder, but the two princes were taken into a Swiss family named Mercier which had three sons and two daughters. The atmosphere was warm and friendly and the boys felt very much at home. Ten months later, the princes passed their entrance exams.

Mohammed Riza was on the brink of a new life and a number of surprises. He was no longer a "colonel" before whom everybody bowed, but a twelve year old much like any other.

Chapter 5

LE ROSEY, probably the best-known private school in Switzerland, is an ivy-covered Renaissance chateau reached by a long driveway which threads its way through a park thick with ancient trees. Lying between the shores of the lake of Geneva and the railroad tracks, the institution was founded by a Belgian around 1880, and for a long time, its students were mostly Belgian. When Persia's crown prince arrived, Henri Carnac, the son of the founder, was headmaster, although it was his American wife who gave the school its international dimensions. Not everybody who wishes to can get in; a boy has to be entered long in advance, and must pass the entrance exams as well. Its teachers are carefully selected, and its sports program is particularly outstanding. During the skiing season, the school moves to Gstaad in the mountains. Le Rosey, it goes without saying, is very expensive.

Frederick Jacobi, Jr., an eleven-year-old American student at the time, described Mohammed Riza's arrival in an article he wrote years later for *The New Yorker* magazine in its issue of February 20, 1949. (Frederick's father was a composer and his family lived in Switzerland.)

"The school was well known at the time as a haven for the male children of various categories of Americans in Europe — diplomatic and consular officials, businessmen, tourists who wanted to travel without their noisy sons, and semi-expatriates like us. Le Rosey was also a refuge for young royalty and nobility. Metternichs and Radziwills were enrolled, along with princelings from places like Annam, Baroda, Udaipur, Egypt and Iran. The Americans outnumbered the non-Americans by about two to one in an enrollment of a hundred boys. It seems almost unnecessary to point out that the sixty-odd Americans were not at all impressed by the thirty-odd non-Americans. In fact, the Americans seemed to make an indelible impression on the little rajahs, shahs, and princes. By the end of his first term, for instance, Butch Baroda spoke English like a Buckley boy, except that he used more dirty words.

"The *affaire Pahlevi* occurred the afternoon of my first day at school. We were both *nouveaux élèves*, Pahlevi and I. As a matter of fact, my parents had just deposited me on the steps of the Swiss Renaissance chateau that housed Le Rosey, my mother telling me to wear my rubbers, and take milk of magnesia, and I assuring her that I would, every day, when Pahlevi was escorted into the grounds by a retinue. He arrived in a canary-yellow Hispano-Suiza, which fifteen or twenty boys, most of us Americans, watched with fascination as it threaded its way up the cavernous, tree-hung driveway to the chateau. His entourage consisted of a chauffeur and footman, both in Park Avenue–type uniforms, and a spectacularly handsome, silver-haired old gentleman who carried himself straighter than any other man I had ever seen and who, I subsequently learned, was a Persian diplomat of high rank.

"Pahlevi looked, sixteen years ago, very much as his pictures show him today — wide mouth, angular chin, jutting hawk nose, piercing black eyes, and the kind of carefully tended black hair that is sometimes likened to patent leather. As he emerged from the Hispano-Suiza, he swept all of us with a stare that he must have intended to be regal. His efforts were lost on us, however, because we were busy examining the snakelike chrome tubes that coiled out of the hood of his car. He didn't say a word to us, and we were not really interested in greeting him. The headmaster and his wife, who never quite got used to having royalty around, bowed him to his quarters.

"He must have spent some time overseeing the unpacking of his impedimenta (such a collection of baskets, coffers, hampers, trunks, boxes, and suitcases can hardly be called baggage), because the rest of us had completed our inspection of the Hispano-Suiza long before he returned to the courtyard. By then, the afternoon was waning and the stone paving of the court was suffused with a red-gold September light. Some of us were sitting on a bench that ringed a dignified old tree—an oak, I think it was—that grew in the middle of the court. Charlie Childs, a boy of my age who had come from the United States only a month before, was trying to explain to me, more or less simultaneously, the mysteries of baseball, milk shakes, and the Baby Ruth candy bar. He was extremely patient about answering my questions, which must have been more than naive. So engrossed were Charlie Childs and I in our conversation that we didn't notice that Pahlevi had returned until we looked up and saw him stalking up and down like an angry tiger three or four feet in front of us. Apparently, he had been doing this for several minutes and nobody had paid any attention to him. Suddenly he stopped and, with a sweep of his right arm and a thrust of his chin, made a gesture intended to signify that we should all get up. None of us understood. We just looked at him in bewilderment until we concluded that he wanted to sit on the bench. As there was not a free place, we edged one way and the other and made a narrow space for him. Instead of placating him, this neighborly gesture infuriated him still more. Somehow he made it clear, in a mixture of French and Hollywood-gangster English, that people usually stood in the presence of the Crown Prince of Iran.

"What occurred next is not entirely clear in my mind. Somebody snickered, I think, and somebody said something. At any rate, all of us were soon roaring. Pahlevi's royal dignity was shattered. He flew at the nearest boy, who happened to be Charlie Childs, and seized him by the throat. Charlie was a couple of years younger than Pahlevi, and a little smaller, but he was wiry and agile. The next few seconds are just a blur in my memory, because the two bodies flashed around with the speed of those in a Disney cartoon. The next thing I knew, Pahlevi soon lay still and grunted for mercy. His black hair dank and falling over his eyes, his face scratched and bleeding, his shirt torn, he slowly got to his feet. His next move surprised us all. He smiled, shook Charlie's hand a couple of times, and patted him on the back.

"From then on, we had no trouble with Pahlevi. We accepted him as an equal."

From the first year on, the three young Iranians lived in the same room. According to his *Memoirs* and his official biography, Mohammed Riza's four years at Le Rosey were spent in exemplary attention to his studies, with gratifying results and the greatest possible success in everything, including sports, with the minor proviso that math gave the young prince a certain amount of trouble.

The testimony of his former schoolmates obliges one to revise the story somewhat. The crown prince seems in fact to have been a very average student who excelled in only one activity—sports. Sporting pictures and football trophies hung on the walls of his spacious room, but his bookshelves were almost empty—Mohammed Riza didn't care much for reading. There was little that was personal except for a photograph of his father. On the other hand, his clothes closet was jammed. He was something of a dandy, and his flashy taste in clothes astonished his schoolmates. He was particularly given to shirts with brightly colored checks and polka dots, and his haberdashery was eye-popping. He made frequent trips to his tailor in Lausanne, partly—to be sure—because he was growing in both height and weight, puberty and Swiss air aiding. Even though he remained a scrapper, the unfortunate incident of his first day was not likely to be repeated. His contact with Switzerland worked some kind of transformation in him, ridding him of his earlier stiffness and making him more democratic. He was full of common sense; the childhood visions were gone, along with any trace of his former mysticism. A nonpracticing Muslim, he said his prayers grudgingly and only at his Persian tutor's insistence. He had no intellectual bent; politics bored him. His only subject of conversation was football. He knew everything there was to know about football; he knew by heart the names of all the players on all the major teams of the day, the dates of the games, the scores, how the championships were proceeding, on what level, in what country.

On the subject of girls, he tended to be somewhat indelicate, assuming the tone of a Cossack. Of course it was only talk; he was still young. Not until he was seventeen, toward the end of his stay at Le Rosey, did he cause a flurry by getting involved with a chambermaid who was immediately fired.

The details are very vague, for the incident seems to have left no mark on anybody. That is unfortunate, for it was apparently Mohammed Riza's first amorous adventure.

When he talked of his father, it was with a mixture of admiration, respect and fear. He never mentioned his sister Ashraf. It wasn't until long after Le Rosey that his fellow students learned through the newspapers that he even had a twin sister.

His entourage lived in constant fear of an attempt on his life. They were afraid that the Qajar family might take advantage of his stay abroad to attempt to assassinate the son and heir of the man they considered a usurper. They saw a Qajar behind every tree in the school park, and the Persian embassy was constantly having the police comb the premises and harangue the headmaster, teachers and personnel. Of course nothing ever happened.

Ali was the despair of his older brother. A wild boy to begin with, his stay in Switzerland, far from the paternal rod, unsettled him completely. An unkempt and shameless clown, he yawned in class and invented one prank after another, disguising himself and disappearing, then returning as filthy as a bum to organize nightly escapades that woke the entire school. Conscious of their position, his brother tried to control him but it was beyond his power.

Mohammed Riza made two very close friends, one an American named Pierson, the other a Swiss by the name of Hubert Pictet who later became a journalist, then a banker. They were the ones most often in his room. He was very hospitable, his door was always open, and when he received a shipment of Persian caviar, he put on a feast for all who cared to come. He was no snob, he loved to laugh, crack jokes and make puns, and especially to exchange bawdy stories with his schoolmates.

Among his courses, math and French gave him special trouble. Luckily he had Hossein Fardust who was brilliant in math and always glad to help. His French teacher, M. Brunel, a former actor with the Pitoëff Company, soon gave up any hope of interesting Mohammed in literature. Then, suddenly, he began to show a decided improvement. He had made the acquaintance of Ernest Perron, and this marked the beginning of an extraordinary friendship. Ernest was not a student at the school. In fact, he was the son of the school handyman. Small and skinny, and ten years older than Mohammed, he helped his father around the school wearing a green apron and a large loosely tied bow at the neck.

With the unintentional cruelty of children, many of the students ragged him, his small size encouraging their bullying instincts. One day, Mohammed saw a student kick over the wheelbarrow full of compost Perron was pushing. He gave the culprit a beating and within a few days, the handyman's son and the son of the Shah of Persia had become intimate friends. Soon, Ernest had taken the place of Pierson and Pictet in their endless prebedtime conversations. But it wasn't football they discussed. No, they discussed literature. For Ernest had a secret vice: he was a poet. He wrote verses in bed at night. He showed them to Mohammed, who for the first time in his life, found himself reading poetry without his mind on the next football game between Le Rosey and Chataignerie—the neighboring school. And just as Mohammed became Ernest's god because he, a crown prince, had deigned to take notice of a poor servant's existence, so Ernest, because he was able to do something which seemed almost superhuman to the future Shah, became Mohammed's friend and inspiration. From then on, Mohammed was able to bring off the extraordinary feat of doing badly in his classroom French and superbly in his homework. The French teacher, who must have suspected something, looked the other way, especially since the relationship between the two was having such a marked effect on his student's French. Ernest was able to get him to read all of Chateaubriand and most of Rabelais—"my two favorite French authors," the Shah says today.

Unlike most school friendships, his relationship with Ernest Perron continued long after Le Rosey. In fact, the Shah had Ernest come to Iran where he remained the king's confidant up to the day he returned to Switzerland to die in 1961.

While Mohammed Riza was struggling over his math, playing football, and reading poetry with Ernest Perron, his father was trying to solve the vexatious problem of the feudal tribes. And he went about it in his usual way—by force. It is no exaggeration to say that had the Shah not succeeded, Mohammed Riza would today be one of the several exiled sovereigns haunting the jet-set, or perhaps, a few bones buried in a hole somewhere in the desert.

During the thirties, the feudal system in Persia was all-powerful. When Riza Shah came on the scene, Persia's situation was exactly that of France, Britain, and Germany in the Middle Ages. The feudal lords scorned the central power, and had their own armies or organized bands of warriors. Broken up into tribes, they were strong because they were nomads and fighters with independence in their blood. Almost one-third of the population—between six and seven million—belonged to a tribe. What made them particularly dangerous was that most had withdrawn toward the frontiers where their pasturage lay athwart the borders of neighboring countries. Hence they were very sensitive to foreign propaganda, and Iraq, Russia, Afghanistan and Turkey made the most of this precious asset to keep up the pressure on the new Shah who was showing a little too much enterprise.

But the real cause of their rebelliousness was not foreign influence; it was the kind of country the Shah was trying to create — a modern, industrialized and centralized Persia that would spell the end of their ancestral way of life and their mobility. They had nothing but contempt for urban Persians — shopkeepers, laborers and artisans. They saw them as fat lap dogs whose necks bore the mark of the leash.

The tribes were nervous from the start. They had a long acquaintance with Riza Maxim and many carried the memory of crushing defeats at his and his Cossacks' hands. So they prepared themselves by strengthening their control over their lands, recruiting, training and buying arms.

Riza, who knew all this, was as yet unable to move. It would be a major operation, and he needed time to prepare. He speeded up the reform of the army, increased its budget and matériel. "National Defense" was soon absorbing a quarter of the state's budget. Then he developed a *gendarmerie* and police that covered the country with tightly integrated fortified posts. He organized a police network in the cities. In Tehran, agents combed the city night and day. Then he cracked down on the people's freedom of movement. A permit was needed to leave Tehran, and once out, there was a road permit that needed constantly to be checked and stamped. Travelers had to submit to long interrogations when they entered a city. Foreigners were observed with special attention; any foreigner was automatically suspect. He was probably a political agent come to stir up discontent, deliver money, sell arms.

The Lurs, the Bakhtiari, the Kanders and the Qashqai were the most powerful tribes. The Lurs held Zagros in the west-center; the Bakhtiari were farther south, threatening Isfahan; the Kanders were in the northwest near Iraq; and the Qashqai occupied the south in the region of Shiraz and Firuzabad. The rest clung to whatever powerful tribe was nearest.

When he felt he was ready, Riza Shah declared war. It was almost as if he were taking advantage of his son's absence to put the country to rights. The hardest to bring to heel were the Lurs. This tribe, which lived south of Kermanshah in a region virtually unknown even at the beginning of this century, had mysterious origins. Some say it was the last survivor of the empire of the Medes, therefore the last of the absolutely pure Aryans. Others believe it was one of the "lost tribes" of Israel's turbulent history. It numbered about four hundred thousand and was known for its filth and the men's heavy beards.

It took Riza Shah ten years to pacify the region: each mountain, each pass, each rock had to be taken one at a time. And often, as in the days of Riza Maxim, he himself led his troops into battle. Twice, prisoners tried to kill him before they were disarmed. Both times, Riza Shah looked the man in the eye and asked: "Why have you done this?" then explained what he was trying to do, what he was hoping to make out of Persia. Both times, the would-be assassin fell on his knees and kissed his feet.

To help him in his mission, the king summoned Charles Banel. Banel was no longer alone; other foreign adventurers had joined him. But they still had only three broken-down old planes. Undaunted, the foreign mercenaries dropped their bombs as they hedgehopped over fortified camps or columns marching through the mountains.

One day, Banel saved a whole regiment from total annihilation. Entrenched inside a citadel, the Persians learned through a spy that a large troop was preparing to attack: the Lurs were advancing from every direction. There was no way out; they would all be massacred.

Panic-stricken, they telegraphed for reinforcements, even though they would come too late. So Banel, who was at staff headquarters, suggested a last-ditch strategy: the Persians should evacuate the city before the Lurs arrived and hide in the mountains. The Lurs would then enter the deserted city and while they were trying to figure out where the regular troops had gone, Banel would have time to act.

At dawn, as the Persians watched the Lurs swarm into the city from their rocky sanctuary, Banel came flying over with one of his accomplices and bombed the citadel. The Persians retook it in no time.

Riza Shah finally pacified Luristan just before the outbreak of World War II. The tribes were decimated, arms depots taken over, his *gendarmerie* in full control. Calm returned, although there were sporadic uprisings which Riza put down without mercy.

This left the Bakhtiari. Theirs was the land where the British made their first explorations for oil and from whom they won their first oil concessions. The Bakhtiari were even more nomadic than the Lurs. Over four hundred thousand strong, they moved with the seasons, living in tents and off their flocks. During the summer, they camped near Isfahan; in winter, they drove their flocks south, crossing several mountain ranges until they found grass. At the beginning of the century, the Bakhtiari played an important political role. They were ruled by two cousins, one of them—Sardar Assad—the grandfather of Soraya who was to become Mohammed's second wife. He had a private army, and had more or less given up the nomad's life to settle in a village south of Isfahan. The Karum, the country's only navigable river, flowed through his lands. He was a very rich man, and augmented his wealth by charging people for the privilege of navigating or crossing his river. Using sound business instincts, he took his toll money and converted it into suspension bridges and a road that funneled the caravans straight to his door. At that time, this was the only road between the Persian Gulf and the Indian Ocean. In return, Sardar Assad guaranteed the caravan's safety, he being the only person in a position to do so. The central government in Tehran had no desire to tangle with Sardar Assad.

The rest of the Bakhtiari did not get off so easily. Riza Shah invaded their territory, cut their chieftains' throats and the tribe never recovered. On the other hand, the Kurds, whose habit it had long been to poke out their enemies' eyes, put up a fierce resistance. Even Xenophon, two thousand years before, had spoken of their independent spirit. But, although Riza Shah fought them, he never tried to destroy them. As a result, theirs was the only tribe to preserve its heritage. (In the current maneuvering over oil, the present Shah has found it politically expedient to take the Kurds into camp—safely out of Iraq's reach.) The Qashqai offered the least resistance. Riza Shah disarmed them, decimated their flocks, imprisoned and killed their chiefs. Reduced to forty thousand families, the Qashqai quickly plummeted from wealth and pride to poverty and total dependence.

In the very different atmosphere of Le Rosey, Mohammed Riza was struggling with his Persian lessons. His old schoolmates remember well the pitiful expression that crossed his face when his tutor in Persian arrived for the evening lesson. For Mohammed, it was the hour of purgatory. He first had to take a reed and whittle it carefully, then his fellow students could hear the scratching of the pens as the two set to work, writing from right to left—only numbers were written in the traditional western direction.

Their father demanded a weekly and detailed progress report from the boys' tutor. If the report was late, a telegram from Tehran arrived, and if the boys had poor grades, there was a storm of recriminations from the East. But Mohammed always had football to compensate for his academic woes, as well as the hundred-meter dash, discus and weight throwing, tennis and sculling. On the subject of skiing, there is a small mystery. According to his official biographer, "the slopes of the Hornberg, Windspielen, Wasserngrat and Eggli held no secrets for the crown prince. . . . Two of his ski coaches, Freddy Pernet and Bruno Trojani, both of them Swiss champions, said of him: 'We've never seen anything like it, and God knows we've seen plenty of skiers here at Gstaad.'" And he went on to list the number of races won and prizes received, and the collection of trophies, medals and assorted trinkets that adorned the Le Rosey trophy cabinet. His biographer also noted his brilliance as an ice-hockey player. This fact seems to be confirmed by a photograph showing Mohammed Riza in his hockey uniform on the ice at Le Rosey.

But as for the skiing, André Choremi, a classmate at the time, has a quite different version. "His father absolutely refused to let him ski. He was terrified that this new-fangled and dangerous sport would be the end of his son. Mohammed protested violently, but his tutors were adamant. No skiing. So when we went off skiing at Gstaad, he would be left curling with his brother and Fardust."

Mohammed Riza later confirmed that he had not skied while at Le Rosey. "My tutor was terrified of an accident, so I was forbidden to ride a bicycle, swim, ski or play hockey — though I was allowed to practice hockey at school."

In 1936, three weeks before his final exams, Mohammed Riza was summoned back to what would henceforth be called Iran. As a result, he never got his *Maturité* — the Swiss diploma.

What memories of Le Rosey does the Shah have today? He

now speaks of it as the place where he learned "school spirit," how to get along with people, equality. "Had I stayed in Tehran, I would never have learned any of these things. I was surrounded by too much obsequiousness. Too many barriers, too much protection. This was both cruel and bad for me. My mind was broadened; I will always be grateful to Le Rosey for this, if for nothing else. But otherwise, it did nothing to change my basic character."

When Mohammed Riza returned to Iran, his father had not only pacified the country, he had launched an economic revolution. Out of a nation of small artisans, he was on the way to creating an industrial nation. He began by laying the foundation for a higher education where Iranians and not foreigners would be in charge. "Iranization" was everywhere in evidence. The king established an Iranian Academy and directed it to prepare a dictionary expunging all foreign words, especially technical ones. "Microscope," "cinema," "appendicitis," "siphon" were out. In their place, Persian words were made up, free of Greek or Latin derivations. The results were sometimes comical. For instance, the word "mechanic" was replaced by a Persian word. But the king had also set up registry offices which required the filing of last names, so all mechanics who had originally been named after their neighborhood or native village were rebaptized according to their profession—Mekaniki. So the word was illegal but the name had come to stay. Mekanikis today are legion in the garages of Iran.

The Shah's biggest venture, however, was railroads. Most of the revenue from the sugar monopoly and the oil from the Anglo-Iranian Oil company (heretofore a Bakhtiari possession) went into the construction of the Trans-Iranian railroad. The project was criticized; there were arguments about where it should go. But it was undeniably a colossal piece of work—

the first in centuries that had national scope and was done without external aid. The only foreign elements were the engineers, with sections parceled off variously to Germans, Belgians, French and Italians.

The line started at Bandar-Shah on the east coast of the Caspian near the Russian border, and ended at Bandar Shah-pur on the Persian Gulf. Covering 860 miles, it went through Tehran, Qom, Soltanabad, Dizful and Ahwaz. The first sec-tion between Bandar-Shah and Tehran was finished at the beginning of 1937 and was inaugurated in a frenzy of excite-ment. The second section from Tehran to Bandar Shahpur was completed three years later. A stunning piece of engineer-ing, it entailed 4100 bridges, and 194 tunnels totaling fifty miles.

Mohammed Riza and his brother Ali returned to Bandar-E-Pahlevi, their point of departure, in June, 1936. They barely recognized the place. Five years before, it had been a Persian village; now it was a European city.

The whole family was there, including naturally the old king who couldn't wait to get his hands on his son again. This took an interesting form. Once the family had settled into their summer villa on the Caspian, the king stood in the middle of the drawing room, undid his tunic and turned to his eldest son:

"You did tell me that you were the boxing champion of all the Swiss schools?"

"That's right, Father."

"Then come here."

And the old man took hold of his son and lifted him with one hand. Mohammed was not as big as his father, but he did weigh 165 pounds.

For one entire minute, Riza Shah held his son high in the

air, then letting go, caught him in midair and swept him under his arm.

"Your turn now," he said to Ali Riza.

The younger son ran to his father, who was still holding Mohammed tucked under his arm and now grabbed Ali as well, and with a whoosh, tucked him under his other arm. With tears of laughter, the old giant made the tour of the room like a circus juggler as the rest of the family stood in speechless wonder.

"Boys," he said as he let them go, "the days of tangos, tea-rooms and moonlit walks are over. From now on you're going to be soldiers."

That very evening, he fired his sons' tutors.

As soon as the summer holidays came to an end, Mohammed entered a military school in Tehran organized by his father with the help of French military advisers. He and thirty boys between the ages of sixteen and eighteen, all sons of top officials, were subjected to the most rigorous discipline: up at 5:30, exercises from 7:00 to 9:00, classes from 9:00 to 12:00 and 2:00 to 5:00, exercise from 5:00 to 7:00. For a change of routine, they made forced marches lasting several days with simulated attacks at night. It was a training for commandos.

Nor was this all. It wasn't enough that he go to military school; his father insisted that he get out and show himself to his people. So he inspected, visited, examined, and asked the suitable questions. And this experience began to pay off.

By 1938, he was commissioned a first-lieutenant assigned to military inspection. He didn't have a minute to himself. And to make sure he didn't, Riza Shah constantly summoned him to his side. When Mohammed wasn't off inspecting some garrison, he was ordered to appear a half hour before lunch

and again an hour after. He was kept informed about everything, and his father showered him with questions, set traps
for him. Soon, the king never appeared in public without him,
and together they traveled to the farthest reaches of the kingdom. Sometimes he asked his son's advice; sometimes he
even followed it. Riza Shah was preparing him for the succession.

The king was getting old, and he was sick as well. He had an
ulcer and was exhausted from the burden of work he had carried so long.

"One night," Mohammed wrote in his *Memoirs*, "we happened to be in Kalardachte in a magnificent valley a hundred
miles northwest of Tehran. We were walking back and forth
in a large tent, and my father was explaining to me how he
wanted to improve the administrative machinery of the country so that, when he died, current affairs could be handled
almost automatically — without need for a ruler's supervision.

"I was young, of course, and immature, so I took this as an
insult. 'What does he mean?' I wondered. 'Doesn't he think
I'm capable of succeeding him, of carrying on his work?' But
I said nothing."

Riza Shah had been observing his son since his return from
Switzerland, and he wasn't pleased. Mohammed didn't seem
sure enough of himself; he was too timid, too reserved. His
own embattled youth had taught him that pity and kindness
could be dangerous traps, that a ruler had to be hardhearted.
He also knew that once a course of conduct had been determined, one had to stick to it, even when the necessities of the
moment suggested compromise.

He had been preaching these precepts to his son for a long
time, but without success, he knew. With the enthusiasm of
youth, Mohammed still trusted people. The things he had
learned in Switzerland — the idea of equality, liberty for indi-

viduals and institutions, freedom of the press and the arts —
remained with him. They had left their mark. In a word, he
had become Europeanized.

Now, to the old man, this meant "softened." He became
obsessed with the fear that, after his death, his son would not
be able to govern. He saw him overwhelmed on all sides by
people who would realize very quickly that he was too weak
and too kind. In a few years, even a few months perhaps,
everything would come crashing down and Riza Shah's work
would be destroyed. Iran would return to the anarchy of the
Qajars.

What troubled him especially was that as soon as Mohammed
had finished with military school, he flung himself into Tehran's social life. He was always going to nightclubs, getting
into trouble, and disappearing for days in his newest sports
car. Was he about to equal the follies and excesses of the
Qajars?

Some people grow up very fast. Riza Shah had. And this
made it all the more difficult for him to imagine that his son
might develop more slowly. Was there anything he could do?
He could abdicate, and shock Mohammed into maturity by
putting him on the throne. He himself could always pull the
strings from behind until his son firmed up. Or perhaps he
could seek an amendment to the Constitution so that the
throne would not necessarily pass to the oldest son. Ali Riza,
Mohammed's younger brother, had not been Europeanized.
He was as tough, as intractable, as ever, like his father. In any
event, he decided to put off a decision for a few years. Then
he had an idea: wouldn't marriage be a good way to bring the
boy to his senses?

Chapter 6

AT NINETEEN, Mohammed Riza had become a playboy. Very handsome, a future king, and enormously rich, he had every girl in town at his beck and call, and no qualms about taking advantage of his position. He was one of those young men who succeed in everything, and during the last months of peace before the clouds began closing in, he made haste to indulge his appetites, passing from one pretty girl to another, according to the whim of the moment. Only two things occasionally distracted him from his love life: automobiles and horses. And so, to his female conquests, he added sports cars and thoroughbreds.

His father looked grim. What if his son fell in love with one of these girls? That would be out of the question. He must marry royalty — in other words, a political marriage which either strengthened an existing alliance or created a new one. And so he started looking around. He secretly sent emissaries to scan all the Muslim courts, for the future Queen of Iran had to be a Muslim. The people would accept no other religion. His envoys met, and examined, every marriageable girl in the courts of Afghanistan, Iraq, Arabia and the Magreb. They even screened the family of Constantinople's last Calif.

Finally, Riza Shah's choice fell on Fawzia, daughter of Fouad I, King of Egypt, and Farouk's sister. Fawzia was seventeen and the prettiest of the four sisters (all their names began with F, that being the good-luck letter of the dynasty.) She was so beautiful that Metro-Goldwyn-Mayer had made her an offer, an unspeakable affront which Fouad took weeks to get over.

When Riza Shah's envoy expressed his sovereign's interest in the girl, Fouad was at first indignant. How could a parvenu who hadn't even learned to read until he was thirty dare make such a proposition to him whose dynasty went back millennia?

But once he got over the shock, Fouad had second thoughts. He sent his own emissary to Tehran to take a close look at Mohammed Riza and report back to him with photographs. On further examination, he had to admit that things could be worse. He was particularly taken with the fact that Mohammed, like Fawzia, had studied in Europe. This was reassuring: the son of the old Cossack was apparently well brought up.

Secondly, there was the political aspect. Iran was fast emerging from the dark ages and could become dangerous. A blood relationship might serve as a safeguard.

By the end of January, 1939, when Fawzia returned from a skiing trip to Europe, the two kings reached an agreement. She was engaged, although neither she nor her "fiancé" had any inkling of it.

In early March, Riza Shah took his son for a walk in the hills above the palace. He suddenly stopped, plunged his hand in his pocket, brought out a photograph and handed it to Mohammed. His son looked at it and asked:

"Who is it?"

"Your future wife. Her name is Fawzia. She's Fouad's daughter. She is seventeen. You leave for Cairo tomorrow."

"Yes, Father," Mohammed stammered. The Shah hadn't even asked him what he thought of the girl in the picture.

The next morning, Mohammed Riza landed at Cairo airport and was immediately driven to the royal palace. Among the ladies-in-waiting and royal sisters gathered in the state drawing room, he soon recognized the girl in the photograph. She was looking at him with a timid curiosity which mirrored his own. Fawzia too had seen a picture of her fiancé only the evening before. Her father had said: "Take a good look so you can recognize him tomorrow."

In spite of everything, Mohammed was taken with her beauty and embarked on a tentative courtship—in other words, they exchanged banalities for an hour or so while drinking tea with members of the court. These preliminaries lasted several days—the time necessary to iron out the legal complexities. They were not left alone for so much as a moment.

The Cairo half of the marriage was celebrated in splendor eight days later. But the two participants were separated immediately after the ceremony: the Tehran half was still to come.

The next day, the royal plane headed for Tehran, followed by a second plane entirely taken up by Fawzia's trousseau: seven fur coats, a hundred afternoon dresses, as many evening dresses; two hundred trunks packed with lingerie, hats, all manner of finery, not to mention the priceless royal jewels. Her Paris wedding gown alone cost $20,000.

Riza Shah was waiting at the Tehran airport. As Fawzia descended from the plane, he took her in his arms and, pointing to Tehran in the distance, said: "My daughter, this is your country and these are your people."

The Shiite ceremony took place the next day in the great mosque in Golestan Palace and was no less splendid than the one in Cairo. For the first time in a long while, Riza Shah was relaxed and happy. He had brought off his alliance with Egypt.

The young couple left for their honeymoon on the Caspian and when they returned, took up residence in Saadabad.

On October 26, 1940, Riza Shah was again ecstatic: Fawzia was in labor. Mohammed had been born on October 26. The old king was certain this was a good sign. He broke into a Cossack song. Fawzia was about to bear a son.

The evening passed, and then the night, and still nothing happened. At last, in the morning, the doctor came out of the bedroom, a grim look on his face.

"My prince, it's a daughter," he said to Mohammed Riza whose head dropped.

"Her name will be Shanaz," he said. (Shanaz means "king's caress" in Persian.)

In his heart of hearts, Mohammed Riza was glad. He had wanted a girl, but he knew that his father would take the news very hard. And so he did. The old king went into a violent rage, sweeping everything off the desk with his steel-tipped cane, and locked himself in his study for the rest of the day.

When he finally emerged, he was heard to mutter: "It's a bad sign when a daughter is born before a son." In Iran's court, a girl had been born first for a hundred and fifty years. Wasn't that why no Persian Shah had ever died in his bed? All the Qajars had either been assassinated, poisoned or had died in exile.

The extravagant feasts that had been planned to celebrate the birth were all canceled. Wounded to the quick, Fawzia refused to see the king when he came to visit her.

The Shah with Princess Fawzia of Egypt, his first wife. *Svend Auge Nielsen*

To his son, he said: "You know what you have to do now. She must have a son as soon as possible."

But it wasn't all that easy. In less than a year, the marriage had begun to sour. And not only because of Mohammed's terrible father. Because of Mohammed himself. Although he was truly fond of the girl life had imposed on him, he was still very young and his attentions tended to wander. Opportunities were not lacking; affairs recommenced.

Fawzia, on her side, was not without guilt. She too had tried to play the game honestly, but she was accustomed to the luxury and refinement of one of the world's oldest courts, and of a sophisticated, glittering city. She couldn't get used to Tehran. At that time, it was nothing but an overgrown Oriental town, with coarse manners and stiff provincial receptions. She was bored and a little humiliated. She began to dream of Cairo.

The first crack showed a few weeks after Shanaz's birth. Shams, the Shah's second daughter, had decided to give a party. She and Mohammed's twin sister, Ashraf, spent the evening introducing the prettiest women present to their brother, and egged him on to dance, just as if Fawzia wasn't there. Fawzia stood it for an hour, pretending not to notice, then she abruptly got to her feet and, claiming a headache, left the party. When Mohammed came running to her, she waved him away. The party continued until dawn.

When he returned to his apartment in the Winter Palace at five in the morning, Mohammed Riza knew instinctively that something was awry. He walked through the drawing room, the dining room, finally to the bedroom. No one was there. Instead, there was a sheet of pink note paper on the round table in their small drawing room where he and Fawzia used to bill and coo over breakfast in the early days of their marriage. On it she had scribbled in French: "I've retired to my private apartment to find some peace."

Protocol dictated that Fawzia have an apartment of her own, but this was the first time she had ever used it.

Mohammed ran down the deserted hallways leading to the north wing. Total silence. All the doors were closed. He knocked, then he called, first softly, finally at the top of his voice. No answer. At last he decided to return to his own room and go to bed. But, unable to sleep, he got up very early, dressed and came back to Fawzia's apartment. She was already up, and before he could say a word, she announced:

"I've decided that from now on, I'm going to lead my life separately from yours. I don't wish to be humiliated. My European education has accustomed me to being treated with a certain respect. Last night, you offended me deeply. So I will continue to do my part at all official ceremonies, but that is all. You will live in your apartment; I will live in mine. Goodbye." And she slammed the door.

Stunned, Mohammed ran to his sister Ashraf and told her what had happened. Ashraf tried to mollify Fawzia, but to no avail. "If you try to put any pressure on me," Fawzia said, "I'll go back to Egypt and there'll be a scandal you'll never forget."

Ashraf was aghast. But the important thing was to keep Mohammed from doing something rash out of injured pride. So she distracted him with a giddy round of parties and excursions. Fawzia rarely left her apartment. She declined private parties and avoided Ashraf at all times. She knew who had set the Pahlevi clan against her. And the Pahlevi clan was a world unto itself.

In the Orient, the male is much less in command than Westerners think. Outside his house, Riza Shah stormed and made people tremble. At home too, he would bang on the table and make the big decisions, but there he had five females to contend with. Of these, the most fearsome were Tadj-Ol-Moluk, and the oldest daughters, Shams and Ashraf.

Riza Shah consulted the "queen mother" more than anyone realized. When he was considering Fawzia for the crown prince, he asked her consent before taking any action. To overrule her would have been out of the question. Sometimes he thought he listened to her too much. When he accused his son of having been "softened" by his four years at Le Rosey, Tadj-Ol-Moluk strongly disagreed.

"We are two unkempt bears," she told him. "Mohammed and Ali have to learn European ways. If some bad things rub off, we are strong enough to take care of it. Besides, you'll have plenty of time to harden them. The mixture can't help but be good."

At the start, her mother-in-law was pleased with Fawzia. Sitting in her Louis XV chair surrounded by her ladies-in-waiting, her piercing black eyes looked on the girl with affection. Then, two things happened to change her. First, there was Fawzia's rudeness. She was contemptuous of the old lady whose simple and old-fashioned manner kept peeping through the thin veneer of her recently acquired education. Fawzia knew all the courts of Europe; she had danced at Buckingham Palace and at fashionable charity balls in Paris. What could she possibly talk about with the wife of a Cossack?

One evening, she committed one of those tactless blunders that women don't forget. At a dinner for a group of ambassadors, Tadj-Ol-Moluk made a mistake in the order of precedence while seating her guests. Her master of ceremonies came and whispered in her ear, but in trying to correct her-

self, she only made matters worse. At this point, she heard a
snicker and looking up, she saw Fawzia choking with laughter,
a snide look on her face. She was only nineteen and too
young to control herself. Tadj-Ol-Moluk smiled but there was
murder in her eyes.

Everything might have been forgiven if Fawzia had done
what was expected of her: to give the crown prince a son. Instead she produced Shanaz. Then, soon after, came the dread-
ful evening at Shams's and Fawzia's temper tantrum. From
then on, hostilities were out in the open. Fawzia became "the
Egyptian," and the family gave her a hard time.

But why had Shams and Ashraf decided on their malicious
project? Was Tadj-Ol-Moluk also involved? Yes and no. Yes,
to the degree that she had been forewarned and had not discouraged the idea. Only what she had hoped would happen,
didn't. She had counted on Fawzia's being hurt to the quick,
and that instead of retiring from the field of battle, she
would go after her husband and tear him away from her adversaries. Who knows what might have happened then? Perhaps Mohammed's flagging interest in Fawzia would have
been rekindled, perhaps a son might have been conceived . . .

But Ashraf was the real instigator. She had a score to settle
with her brother. One day, Mohammed had summoned his
sisters to his study. There they found two young men they
knew slightly. One was Ali Ghavam, the other Ali Djam, both
from Iran's best families. (All this had been plotted by Tadj-
Ol-Moluk: Shams was to marry Ghavam and Ashraf, Djam.)
Ashraf was delighted with the arrangement; of the two young
men, she much preferred Ali Djam. Unfortunately, so did
Shams.

Now, Riza Shah had always had a soft spot for Shams: she
was the gentler, more malleable of the two girls. Two days
before the double wedding, Shams, without telling her sister,

went to her father. "I like Ali Djam much better than Ali Ghavam," she told him. "Can't Ashraf and I exchange fiancés?" "Nothing easier," her father replied. "I'll take care of it."

At the last moment, Ashraf had to cede her fiancé to her sister. She never forgot it, even though, as it turned out, both marriages ended in failure.

In the beginning, Ashraf was very hospitable to Fawzia. She seemed naive, hence not very dangerous. But there Ashraf was wrong. Fawzia was far from stupid, and as Ashraf began to realize this, she started plotting against her. After all, Fawzia would one day be queen and overshadow her. That, then, is what lay behind the disastrous evening at Shams's.

Mohammed tried to forget the whole thing with a series of new affairs and new sports cars. His brothers were equally feckless. Ali was always on safari, bringing home trophies from Afghanistan, India, Africa. Gholam, the only son by the Shah's third wife, an otherwise levelheaded boy, had one consuming passion: playing Zur-Khaneh, Iran's national sport. (Handed down from antiquity, it involves a series of very complex movements with heavy clubs, accompanied by the singing of old airs to the sound of a drum beating out the rhythm of rolling waves, galloping horses, the flight of birds of prey, and so on.) The three younger boys were at Le Rosey; only the youngest, Hamid, was still at home.

Then a new member came to join the family: Ernest Perron, the son of the handyman at Le Rosey whom Mohammed Riza invited to come live with him in the palace. Just as he had seduced the crown prince with his poems and gentle ways, so he soon won over the whole family. He made them laugh, he distracted them, and he soon found himself playing the double role of confidant and fool as in a medieval court. He was listened to, and his advice was often sought.

It wasn't long before the two young men's intimacy started tongues wagging. Those who knew about Mohammed's affairs smiled. The dozens of young Iranian and foreign girls who had the honor of submitting to his advances laughed out loud. And his tastes were becoming less indiscriminate. The girls he refers to to this day as his "shepherdesses" – following the tradition of one of his great amatory predecessors, Louis XV – were more and more often tall blond Europeans, especially Scandinavians.

Chapter 7

WORLD WAR II had broken out. Riza Shah, angered by his son's broken marriage and increasingly disturbed about the future of his country, was once again the irascible ruler of old. Mohammed, like the rest of the family, gave his fearsome father a wide berth. Politics interested him little, pleasure a great deal. And so he indulged himself.

A war pitting Britain and France against Germany was what the king dreaded most. In 1940, his kingdom was not strong enough to survive without Europeans. European engineers, technicians and diplomats were constantly crossing paths in his waiting room and could only function effectively if they cooperated among themselves. And now this delicate balance was on the verge of collapse. The embassies shut their doors, the engineers refused to work together and departed.

What made the situation particularly thorny was the size and activity of the German colony. This, too, was in imitation of Kemal Ataturk, whose pro-German sympathies were well known.

As a result, when World War II began, Germany occupied

far and away the most important role in Iran's foreign trade, well ahead of Britain and Russia, with the United States and France trailing far behind.

The German influence was crucial in Iran's army also. Its training may have been French, but its equipment and arms were entirely German. In addition, nearly five thousand German engineers and technicians were working in Iran. With the Trans-Iranian railroad finished, the king asked the Germans to extend it, build roads and bridges, construct factories. Rolling stock and aeronautical matériel, machine tools, pharmaceuticals, chemicals—most of these were German. And the only regular flights to Europe were operated by Deutsche Lufthansa. While a constant flood of experts arrived from Berlin, hundreds of Iranian students made the trip in reverse.

The University, the School of Agriculture, the School of Veterinary Medicine, all were run by Germans. The National Library overflowed with German books on culture in general and German propaganda in particular. There was even a center for Nazi propaganda in Tehran which flooded the newspapers with material, supplemented by Radio Berlin which was beamed into Tehran.

Mohammed Riza later told me: "My father didn't like Hitler. Dictators don't like other dictators, but everybody who was against the British and the Russians were our friends. But much as he admired Kemal Ataturk, Germany's handling of Turkey made him nervous. In 1941, Turkey had as many German experts as Iran, but Turkey had a strong army. That's why it wasn't invaded."

When Germany moved on Poland, Riza Shah immediately proclaimed his country's neutrality. In his speech to the opening of the Twelfth *majlis*, he repeated Iran's policy of noninvolvement, and stated that his one desire was that his country "continue to have friendly, profitable and lasting relations with both sides."

During the first few months—the period of the "phony war"—nothing changed much. Then, suddenly, the Germans marched into France and Hitler's invasion of England appeared imminent.

The British ambassador called on Riza Shah with a vigorous protest in hand. In British eyes, despite its declaration of neutrality, Iran had sided with the Nazis. This could not be allowed to continue. Riza Shah pleaded his case, protested his honesty and the integrity of his neutral stance. The British seemed satisfied—for the moment.

Autumn, winter and spring passed. Hitler had not invaded England and the war dragged on. Then, on June 22, 1941, came the alarming news that the Wehrmacht had marched on Russia.

"That evening," an old friend of the king's told me, "I saw something I never thought I'd live to see: there were tears in Riza Shah's eyes."

To the old king, everything was clear and everything was tragic. Once again, as in 1914–1918, Iran would become the bridgehead in the belligerents' strategy. Faster even than during the first war, the German armies were pouring across the Russian plains. It was obvious that Persia's old enemies, Britain and Russia, would once again unite against their common enemy. The front was in Russia, not in the West. Britain would come to Russia's rescue, and there were only two possible routes: through the north, by way of Murmansk, or the south, by way of Iran, where a beautiful railroad was newly finished, as if designed solely for the purpose of transporting matériel from the Persian Gulf to the Caspian Sea—in other words, to Stalingrad where the game would be played out.

The situation was so serious that the king summoned his son. From now on, Mohammed Riza must be kept informed about everything, including the worst. The old king put all his cards on the table; the time for self-indulgence was over. The boy must choose.

With the steel tip of his cane, Riza Shah outlined the situation on the world map pinned to his wall. It didn't take him long to convince his son that Iran was in peril. Mohammed's first reaction was to urge that the Iranian army be massed on the Russian frontier and along the coastline of the Persian Gulf. His father shrugged and, turning to his prime minister, asked him if he would please describe the size of the Russian and British armies to the prince. When he heard the figures, Mohammed's head dropped.

"You must be prepared," his father said. "In a year, I may not be on the throne."

For Riza Shah, the essential thing was to gain time. It was May, 1941. Germany still seemed invincible. If Russia were crushed, the war would end right there. A general equilibrium could be reestablished; the British and Russian threat would be over. And he would have succeeded in preserving his country's independence. Fearing British provocation, he prudently kept close watch over the Allies as well as the Germans. If, for example, a tunnel on the Trans-Iranian railroad were sabotaged, mightn't it be done by the British as a pretext for crying "German sabotage!" as a first step to taking over Iran?

For the same reason, he also doubled the surveillance of the giant refineries at Abadan, and anchored two gunboats between Bandar Shahpur and the coast, near eight German freighters that had arrived before the British blockade of the Mediterranean and Suez Canal. The German crews were forbidden not only to unload their cargo but even to go ashore.

There were rumors—started by whom? By the British, the Shah assumed—that these freighters were carrying arms, explosives and commandos whose mission it was to blow up Abadan and the oil wells.

In late June, Russian ambassador Smirnov joined Sir Reader Bullard in trying to convince Riza Shah that he must expel all German nationals and open the Trans-Iranian to the Allies. The Shah refused.

In mid-July, they tried again. And again in mid-August. Their notes became virtual ultimatums: open the Trans-Iranian or else . . .

Riza Shah held to his original position: Iran was neutral, the nation's soil was inviolate, and no foreign power on earth had the right to interfere in a nation's domestic affairs.

Some say that Riza Shah and his son were of different minds on this point, and had the old man listened to his son, things might have turned out very differently. To the crown prince, there was only one solution: side with the Allies. He pleaded his case day after day, but it was wasted breath. The king wouldn't listen.

At the age of twenty-one, Mohammed was for the first time showing his political acumen. And events were soon to prove him right.

In August, 1941, a violent campaign against the Shah erupted on the radio and in the press. The British radio in Baghdad attacked the king in Persian, accusing him of supporting the Germans, asserting that the Germans controlled all his troops, and had spies scattered all over the country. (In point of fact, two top German secret agents had arrived to set up a "fifth column" the previous October, followed in April by a third.) Anti-Shah articles began to appear in those Tehran papers subsidized by the British.

Prodded by the prime minister and his son, the old king

agreed to do something that pained him deeply: he called for help. Specifically, he called on Roosevelt to put pressure on the British to stop their propaganda.

Carrying the rubric "740.0011 European War 1939/1941 The Shah of Iran (Riza Shah Pahlevi) to President Roosevelt," the cable, in a curious translation, read as follows:

"Your Excellency has surely been informed that the Russian and British forces have crossed brusquely and without previous notice the boundaries of this country occupying certain localities and bombarding a considerable number of cities which were open and without defense. The old pretext which the Russian and English Governments raised consisted in the concern which those countries claimed to feel because of the sojourn of certain Germans in Iran, despite the assurances given by my Government that those Germans will soon leave Iran. No subject for concern could longer exist and I no longer can see for what reason they have proceeded to those acts of aggression and to bombarding without reason our cities. I consider it my duty, on the basis of the declaration which Your Excellency has made several times regarding the necessity of defending principles of international justice and the right of people to liberty, to request your Excellency to be good enough to interest yourself in this incident, which brings into war a neutral and pacific country which has no other care than the safeguarding of tranquility and the reform of the country. I beg Your Excellency to take efficacious and urgent humanitarian steps to put an end to these acts of aggression. Being assured of the sentiments of good will of Your Excellency, I renew to you the assurance of my sincere friendship.

RIZA PAHLEVI"

In a classic example of diplomatic circumlocution, Roosevelt answered a week later:

"I have received Your Imperial Majesty's communication regarding the recent entry of British and Russian forces into Iran. I have been following the course of events in Iran with close attention and have taken careful note of Your Majesty's remarks.

I am persuaded that this situation is entitled to the serious consideration of all free nations including my own, and Your Majesty may rest assured that we are giving it such consideration and are maintaining our traditional attitude with respect to the basic principles involved.

At the same time, I hope Your Majesty will concur with me in believing that we must view the situation in its full perspective of present world events and developments. Viewing the question in its entirety involves not only vital questions to which Your Imperial Majesty refers, but other basic considerations arising from Hitler's ambition of world conquest. It is certain that movements of conquest by Germany will continue and will extend beyond Europe to Asia, Africa, and even to the Americas, unless they are stopped by military force. It is equally certain that those countries which desire to maintain their independence must engage in a great common effort if they are not to be engulfed one by one as has already happened to a large number of countries in Europe. In recognition of these truths, the Government and people of the United States of America, as is well known, are not only building up the defenses of this country with all possible speed, but they have also entered upon a very extensive program of material assistance to those countries which are actively engaged in resisting German ambition for world domination.

Your Imperial Majesty's Minister at Washington is fully informed of this Government's views on the international situation, and of the great effort on which this country is engaged, and I am certain that he has transmitted this information, based on his discussions here, to Your Majesty's Government.

My Government has noted the statements of the Iranian Government by the British and Soviet Governments that they have no designs on the independence or territorial integrity of Iran. In view of the long-standing friendship between our two countries, my Government has already sought information from the British and Soviet Governments as to their immediate as well as long-range plans and intentions in Iran, and has suggested to them the advisability of a public statement to all free peoples of the world reiterating the assurances already given to Your Majesty's Government.

I desire to assure Your Imperial Majesty of my good will and to renew to you the assurance of my sincere friendship.

FRANKLIN D. ROOSEVELT "

Obviously, Roosevelt was not going to get mixed up in the affair. And Riza Shah got the point: Roosevelt was on the side of the British. In the end, all the king received from Cordell Hull, the American Secretary of State, was encouragement to give maximum collaboration to the Allies and to refuse all assistance to the Axis powers.

In August came the proclamation of the Atlantic Charter by which the United States gave all its support to the British. A few days later, the sky fell in.

Early one morning, Bullard and Smirnov handed two notes to the prime minister, Ali Mansur. The two countries found themselves obliged "to take unilateral and military measures against Iran, which would in no way endanger the country's sovereignty. Their only goal was to prevent any subversive activities on the part of the Germans.''

At about the same time, there was a radio announcement that Russian troops had crossed the Azerbaijan border and the British had entered from Iraq. Caught by surprise and bombarded in their barracks, the Iranian soldiers did not even have time to retreat. Their ships were sunk and their planes destroyed on the ground.

The old king filed an official protest, then gave in. There was nothing else he could do. He agreed to open the Trans-Iranian railroad, but only in exchange for a halt in the Allied troops' advance. He was told politely to go fly a kite.

It was a terrible blow. In a few days, Riza Shah had lost so much weight he was unrecognizable. The ulcer that had plagued him for years kicked up overnight, and the giant Cossack had become a shrunken old man with feverish eyes. At sixty-five he looked eighty.

In Azerbaijan, the appearance of the Red Army caused a panic. The people had not forgotten the invasions of the First World War, and because, between wars, Riza Shah had encouraged the dissemination of vicious anti-Communist propaganda, the people greeted the Russians as bloodthirsty monsters. There was a general exodus toward the south.

On August 27, Ali Mansur was forced by the British to inform all German nationals of their immediate expulsion; he resigned that evening. Riza Shah replaced him with Mohammed Ali Forughi, one of his oldest friends who had been his first government minister fifteen years earlier. The next morning, Forughi declared martial law and ordered the Iranian troops to lay down their arms.

Sitting down to lunch that day with his son, the king turned to him and said in a broken voice:

"Will you tell me how I, a reigning monarch, can accept orders from some little Russian or British captain?"

But he hadn't yet drained the dregs in his cup.

On August 30, the Russians and British — without so much as consulting him — divided Iran into three zones: the north went to the Russians, the south to the British, and the narrow band in the middle to the Shah. And they strongly advised him to cooperate or they would cut off all oil royalties and economic aid. In exchange, they promised to withdraw all foreign troops "as soon as the military situation warranted it." In other words, when they were good and ready.

Then he was asked to comply with a series of demands: that he close the German legation and all the German consulates, as well as those of the Italians, Hungarians, Rumanians and Japanese, that he renounce all indemnity for Iran's losses as a result of the Allied invasion, and finally, that he make an official declaration of war against the Third Reich.

September started calmly enough. Neither the British nor the Russians seemed to want to press any further. Reduced to a state of helpless waiting, Riza Shah spent more and more time with his family, as if he felt he might never see them again. Mohammed was always at his side, and the old king discussed endlessly the opportunities and dangers that lay ahead.

Then, suddenly, on September 13, the Russian and British radios renewed their attack on the Shah. Addressing the Iranian people, they told them they had a wicked king, that they had been exploited for years, that people were getting rich at their expense.

On the same day, Ambassador Bullard received a letter from Churchill which read: "If we don't obtain satisfactory results from the Shah, we will give chapter and verse on the deplorable way in which he governs his people."

What did they mean by "satisfactory results"? Total submission by the old king? Well, he refused. He had taken all he could stomach. First, he had believed that the Russians and British would never dare invade his country; now he believed they would never dare overthrow him.

He was king for only three more days.

And standing by him was his son, who, in a few weeks, had received the most profound political education a future monarch can have: adversity, including humiliation. The "playboy" had become a man conscious of his responsibilities. He had learned in the heat of battle to untangle problems, to put his finger on the key issue, to judge, to decide for himself.

September 15 was a humid day. It was siesta time in the prime minister's large house on Avenue Sepah. The family was resting on the second floor, the servants had retired to the basement. Foroughi was at work in his study; he was to meet with the king at the royal palace at four o'clock.

On the dot of three, the doorbell rang. Massud, the prime minister's younger son, who had gone downstairs to look for a book, opened the door and stood transfixed. Solemn and still, Riza Shah was standing before him in his uniform and boots, the steel-tipped cane in his left hand. Never since he had come to power had he gone to see anybody. People always came to him.

Riza Shah saluted the young man with a small smile.

"Take me to your father's study," he said.

Before the young man could announce him, the king had opened the door and marched in. Blushing with surprise, Foroughi jumped to his feet. Massud left them alone.

Riza Shah departed at four o'clock. He got back into his car and returned to the palace. No one had seen him go, for he had used a service car. A little later, he summoned a photographer to take pictures of himself with the crown prince strolling along the paths at Saadabad.

What had Riza Shah said to Forughi in the privacy of his study?

The morning of the fourteenth, Bullard and Smirnov had come to tell him that he must abdicate. The Shah had refused.

"Under these conditions," the two men replied, "we will have to do it by force. You would do better to be reasonable. Why don't you turn the throne over to your son. The only alternative for us is simply to abolish the monarchy and set up an Anglo-Russian duumvirate. If you haven't accepted by noon on September 17, our troops will enter Tehran that afternoon."

Early the following morning, Forughi drove to the palace and Riza Shah received him in his study. The king hadn't slept a wink and his eyes were bloodshot. Riza Shah took a rumpled piece of paper from his pocket—the draft of his abdication which he had worked on during the night.

"What do you think of it?" Forughi sat down, put on his glasses and began to read. Riza sat without moving, his fist resting on his right knee (a familiar gesture), his eyes fixed on the prime minister.

"Sire," Forughi said, "you have been too hard on the British and Russians. You must have the grace not to rub them the wrong way if you want the crown prince to have the throne."

"I thought you would say that. All right; you soften the language."

Sitting at the low table in front of the couch, Forughi took a sheet of palace stationery, picked up a Persian pen painted with birds and roses, dipped it in the ink pot and started to write. After the third attempt, Riza said:

"That one will do. Now sit at my desk and write up the final draft in your best handwriting." Forughi stared for a moment at the empty royal armchair.

"Get going, Hurry up!" Riza Shah prodded him. "I'm no longer king."

At 8:45, Forughi was finished. The Shah read the text slowly, got up, summoned his son, returned to his chair behind the desk and picked up the pen.

"It was the most dramatic moment of my life," Forughi said later. "The Shah carefully dipped his pen in the inkwell, tapped it on the side to shake off the excess ink, and approached the sheet of paper with infinite caution. I wanted to cry out: 'Sire, don't sign!' but I couldn't. Then he signed, very fast."

Forughi blotted the signature, reread the page, held it out to the king who also read it again. Then the Shah said:

"Take my car and go read this to the *majlis*, have them ratify it and come back immediately. Meanwhile, I have some things I want to say to my son." (Thirty-three years later, the present Shah remembered that it was a "terrible meeting. We had a hard time keeping our emotions under control.")

A little after 9:00 AM, Forughi, accompanied by Hadji Mohtachem Saltaneh Esfandiary, the President of the Chamber, climbed the five steps leading to the tribune and took the act of abdication from his dispatch case.

All the deputies were present. The minister of the interior had informed them the evening before that there was to be an important announcement and urged them all to be present. Neither he nor they knew what the announcement would be.

There was a deathly silence as Forughi announced the king's decision and began to read the text: "We, the Shah of Iran by the will of God and the Nation, have made the solemn deci-

sion to resign and abdicate in favor of our beloved son, Mohammed Riza Pahlevi . . ."

When he had finished reading, there was no reaction from
the deputies, or from the galleries where the Russian and British diplomats sat with stony faces. When Foroughi asked for
an immediate ratification, no one moved. A few deputies
wept openly while others launched into feverish discussions.
Esfandiary took the floor to announce that all doors to the
building had been closed and were guarded by the armed
forces. No one would be allowed to leave until the abdication
was ratified.

By 9:30, the ratification was completed.

The next order of business was to get a head start on the
Russians and British. There was no question that they had
wanted the abdication in favor of Mohammed Riza in order
to get around the old king. A complete overthrow of the
monarchy and its replacement by a puppet regime would
have suited them much better, allowing them to dismantle
the state apparatus and replace it with men of their own
choosing. However, if the people, and especially the bazaar
with its volatile emotions, learned of the Shah's abdication
without being told at the same time that his son had replaced
him, there might well be demonstrations, rioting and bloodshed. This would serve the British and Russians equally well,
for, under the pretext of restoring order, they could then
take over the city. This would indeed be the end of the monarchy.

It was therefore essential that Mohammed Riza appear before the *majlis* that very day to swear his oath of allegiance.
The news of the abdication had not yet leaked out. Like
everyone else, the British and Russians attending the session
were locked in. Therefore Bullard and Smirnov had no way

of knowing that the Shah had anticipated their ultimatum which wasn't to expire until the next day at noon.

When, at 8:45 AM, Forughi had finished writing the text of the abdication, the Shah had sent Nedjati, one of his guards, to seek out Mohammed Riza in the greatest secrecy. Nedjati picked an old Chrysler, and by a series of detours up the mountain and back, finally reached the White Palace. Since spies were everywhere, extreme precaution was essential. The prince's ceremonial clothes were packed in a suitcase which Nedjati placed in the trunk of the car. Then, while he took the palace guards aside under the pretext of discussing a change in their duty schedules, Mohammed Riza, wearing an ordinary suit, a beret and dark glasses, slipped into the car and crouched between the front and back seats. And so it was that the present Shah of Iran spent his first moments as king, hidden like a conspirator in a filthy old car. A half hour later, he was in his father's study where he learned the news and was handed the text of the oath he was to read before the *majlis*.

When Forughi, pale and visibly shaken by what he had gone through, returned to the palace about ten, he found the entire family from the Queen Mother down to Hamid, the youngest son, assembled in Riza Shah's study. Forughi announced that the ratification had been enacted; then Riza Shah turned toward his family and embraced each one in turn until he came to Mohammed Riza. To him, he said:

"My beloved son, you will soon be succeeding me. Love this country as I have loved it, and devote your life and those of your children to it. Continue my work with the help of your family." Then he waved everyone away, except for his oldest son and Forughi. Taking Mohammed by the arm, he led him up to Forughi.

"Mr. Prime Minister, I entrust him to you. Serve him as you have served me. He is all I have left."

The pitch of emotion was such that Foroughi broke into sobs and reached for the Shah's hand to kiss it. When he had regained his composure, the Shah asked them both to sit down, and looking in his son's eyes, said:

"If you are able to give your oath in time — and that's what is most important now — you must devote all your energies just to staying on the throne. They will try to push you off it. So you must be patient and bend with the wind. Eventually the war will end. You must still be king when it does. Then it will be time to raise your head."

Riza Shah emptied his drawers, took his cigarette case, one or two personal papers, his cane, rose to his feet and left the room without looking back. Mohammed Riza never saw his father again.

In Parliament, meanwhile, the deputies were becoming restless. Why were they being detained? The British and Russian representatives fulminated. Esfandiary tried to placate them: they were waiting for an important announcement and must be patient. But he was beginning to worry. What was happening? Why hadn't the crown prince arrived?

The reason for the delay was that, in anticipation of the next day's ultimatum, the Allies had secured the city with dozens of patrols stationed at every potential trouble spot. So Nedjati decided he would do better to wait until the patrols took up their positions and then figure out the safest route. It wasn't until 1:30 in the afternoon that he was satisfied that he had found a reasonably safe one.

At 1:45, with Mohammed Riza again crouched behind the front seat of the old Chrysler, Nedjati drove through the palace gates, gave the Russian and British patrol a casual salute, and took a right turn. For forty-five minutes, he wove in and out of side streets until he was finally ready to head for Parliament. He drove through the service gate which an orderly opened automatically. Why should anyone care about a dusty old Chrysler?

Nedjati parked the car near the service entrance which Foruhghi had managed to keep unlocked, and once in the narrow hall, the crown prince put on his ceremonial uniform. The last time he had worn it was for his marriage to Fawzia. He wrapped the sash of the head of state around his waist, and attached his father's gold and silver pommeled sword to his belt.

At precisely 3:15, Mohammed Riza appeared before the astonished *majlis*, marched into the semicircle and mounted the podium, with Forughi and Esfandiary at his side. Then, his face ashen and his voice trembling with emotion, he slowly read the sentence that his father had read in this very place fifteen years before: "Before God and the Nation, we Mohammed Riza Pahlevi, Shah of Iran, swear loyalty to the Nation and the Constitution."

As the ovation exploded, Forughi rushed out of the hall and down a corridor to telephone the palace. He knew the Allies had tapped all the phones, but he didn't care: He had brought off his coup.

When Mohammed Riza, now Shah of Iran, returned to Saadabad, his father was no longer there. Ten minutes before, his black Rolls-Royce had driven him, alone and without a suitcase, through the southern gates of Tehran toward Isfahan and exile.

In their respective embassies, Bullard and Smirnov were dumbfounded when they learned the news, and immediately realized it would already be on every wire service to the outside world. They were too late: the Pahlevis had saved their throne. The Allies had but one consolation: Mohammed was only twenty-one years old. He wasn't likely to be difficult to handle.

High in the hills in Saadabad Palace, His Majesty Mohammed Riza went looking for his sisters. They were all making ready to leave—all, that is, except Ashraf. Riza Shah had begged her to stay with her brother. At the very moment he most needed his family's support, they were all fleeing. Then, at eleven that night, the phone rang: it was the military governor of Isfahan to tell him that Riza Shah had just suffered a heart seizure.

The new king's first action was to plan his father's exile: in a matter of days, the old king had been reduced to the subject of a troublesome travel itinerary. Riza Shah wanted to go to Buenos Aires. Therefore passports were necessary for him and his party. Then, suddenly, Tadj-Ol-Moluk backed out. Her husband's abdication had been such a blow that she became ill, and they couldn't wait until she recovered. So passports were needed only for Ali Riza, Shams, Gholam, Abdul, Mahmud, Ahmed, Fatemed, Hamid, and Esmat, the mother of the five youngest. Malaki Turane, Gholam's mother, was divorced and had not been considered a member of the family for a long time. To this list was added Shams's husband, Ali Djam.

To organize the exodus, the new king needed a man he could trust. Finding one was far from easy. In a country under British and Russian domination, how could you be certain that a man who might seem the most devoted of servants wasn't in fact in the pay of the occupying forces?

He finally found his man in Ali Izadi, a lawyer who, in

1931, had joined the imperial court at the age of twenty-three. He had been named head of the crown prince's staff on the latter's return from Switzerland. The new Shah summoned him and charged him not only with all the formalities of the trip, but also to serve as the old king's secretary. When he took his leave, Mohammed said: "I entrust my father to you. Watch over him as I would if I were there. But while you're gone, remember me. Some day, I'll need you."

Two days later, all the arrangements were in order and the convoy of automobiles took the road to Isfahan where Riza Shah, although still very tired, had recovered from his attack. Then they left for Bandar Abbas by way of Kerman. Ali Izadi, who stayed behind to take care of the last details, joined them in Kerman. He had gone to the British to inform them of the old king's destination, and to ask them for transportation to Buenos Aires. They appeared to be very accommodating: "No problem. We happen to have a steamer in Bandar Abbas at this very moment, due to sail for South America by way of Australia. We will give the necessary orders to see that Riza Shah and his family have accommodations." When the travelers arrived in Bandar Abbas, they found the *Bandra* flying the Union Jack and a suite of cabins reserved in their names.

The departure was filled with drama. Before he agreed to go aboard, the old king asked Izadi to walk to the end of the wharf where the macadam stopped, dig up a handful of Persian soil and put it in a small bag. Izadi did his sovereign's bidding, and when he returned, Riza Shah was sitting slumped on a mooring bit, his eyes red with tears.

"Thank you," the old king said, slipping the small bag of soil into his pocket. "Now see to it that everything goes smoothly."

It was terribly hot on the sun-drenched wharf and Izadi

pleaded with his master to go aboard and find shade. Riza refused. He was going to stay on his country's soil as long as possible. Around him was posted a group of British sentries, their guns at the ready. Several Iranians approached and asked if they could pay their king a last act of homage. The sentries refused, but a British officer who happened to be passing by reprimanded them and allowed the Iranians to pass. One by one, they stepped forward and kissed the feet of their deposed king. Riza Shah straightened up, thanking and scolding them at the same time.

"I am no longer king," he muttered in a voice drained of emotion. "If you want to pay homage to the King of Iran and help him, it's to Tehran you must go. That's where he is, not here. I no longer need anything. But my son needs all Iranians."

Then he rose to his feet and strode down the quay the length of the boat. High up, leaning on a bulwark near the gangway, his family watched him silently. Finally a British officer approached him:

"Your Majesty, it's time to leave."

For an instant, Riza Shah stood motionless at the foot of the gangplank, then with slow deliberate steps and looking straight ahead, he went aboard.

"Where is my cabin?" he asked Ali Izadi when he reached the deck. "Have someone get out my civilian clothes. I won't be needing a uniform again."

As the ship got under way and headed out to sea, the entire family stood on deck, reciting prayers. Riza Shah remained behind, watching his country's coastline as it faded into the horizon.

In Saadabad Palace, Mohammed Riza was sitting for the first time in his father's chair. His prime minister, Forughi, stood nearby. Smiling, the Shah pointed to the couch. "Please sit down. We have work to do."

The first task was to make a tally of the faithful. The number was pathetically small. Most of Riza Shah's ministers had fled.

Twenty-one years old, in a country under foreign domination, alone on a shaky throne, with only an old man — Foroughi — to help him, Mohammed Riza felt profoundly discouraged. Then he thought of his father and his last words of advice, sent by telegram just before his departure: "Your Majesty, be afraid of nothing." It was for him to show himself worthy of Riza the Great and his inheritance, even if this inheritance had been reduced to a pittance.

When, a few days later, the *Bandra* arrived within sight of Bombay, its engines stopped and it dropped anchor in the middle of the harbor. Surprised, the old king asked the ship's commander why, and the latter said he had received orders to wait there.

"Wait for what?" Riza Shah thundered.

Embarrassed, the commander assured him that he didn't know either. Suddenly, a gunboat came steaming toward the ship, filled to the gunwales with Indian soldiers. No sooner on board, they closed off all the exits in first class. The British official in charge asked to be taken to Riza Shah. The old king was very short with him. What was the meaning of this? What right did they have to surround him and his family? "Tell those soldiers to leave immediately!"

The officer waited for the storm to pass, then explained that his men were there for security reasons. Riza Shah exploded: What security? Security for whom? Were they afraid that an old man and his family might round up all the weapons on board and open fire? Against whom and for what reason? Enough lying: what was the real reason for this intrusion?

"Forgive me, Your Majesty," the officer answered, fully aware of his duplicity. "But the trip to Buenos Aires has become too dangerous. You must resign yourself to going to Mauritius. The international situation is very tense. Britain doesn't wish to run any risks where Riza Shah is concerned."

White with fury, the old king understood: England had decided to take him prisoner. Just as in 1825, when Napoleon had trusted the British to take him to America and was left off at St. Helena instead, so he was being forced into exile on another British island—Mauritius.

Riza Shah ranted and threatened, but the officer could only repeat that he was terribly sorry, that there was nothing he could do; he was only following orders. A new steamer was expected at any moment and would take them aboard.

Two days later, the *Burma* appeared and tied up next to the *Bandra*. The transfer was expeditiously made and anchors weighed. Eight days later, in the freshness of an austral spring, Riza and his family arrived at Port Louis on Mauritius. The former king's exile had begun.

Chapter 8

ON OCTOBER 27, 1941, Mohammed Riza received positive proof that in the Allies' eyes, he counted for little more than a china doll.

On that day, Bullard and Smirnov came to him to explain, courteously but without circumlocution, that he must be a good boy and content himself with a secondary role. They would take care of everything.

The young king paled at the affront. It was that much harder, coming as it did the day after his twenty-second birthday, a bitter occasion which Ashraf and Tadj-Ol-Moluk "celebrated" by talking about their family in exile. Fawzia made no pretense of joining in the party.

Mohammed's first reaction was to bury himself in the far reaches of the palace. He didn't leave his apartment for two weeks as he brooded over his humiliation. He was absolutely powerless now. He was king, he had a prime minister who was devoted to him, but all important decisions were made elsewhere. British and Russian soldiers patrolled the city, occupied the key positions, garrisons, police headquarters, radio, the press. Their officials were in all the ministries.

They had listening posts everywhere. At the airport, top officials from Moscow and London landed by the dozens, accompanied by special agents, intelligence officers, and political and economic experts.

What resistance there was was led by Forughi. Without him, Mohammed Riza would probably have lost his throne very quickly. His youth and inexperience made it difficult for him to see through his adversaries' plots and left him in a state of total confusion. So, the old minister first set about galvanizing his sovereign's morale. Then he took Ashraf into his confidence. At his instigation, she tried to stiffen her brother's spine, tirelessly insisting that he mustn't give in, that the Russians and British were taking advantage of his youth and weakness for their own ends. Then Forughi took over, explaining that the king must extract an agreement from the occupiers: it was the only way to limit their reach. A precise text, clear and countersigned for all the world to see, would confine the damage and keep the Allies from extending their power too far.

Gradually, Mohammed Riza picked up hope. His sister's concern touched him; his minister's wisdom provided him with a tangible goal. He became convinced that Forughi's idea of an agreement was their only salvation. To everyone's surprise, the Allies speedily admitted that the project was sound. Moreover (as Forughi had anticipated), they were interested in it for their own private reasons. In other words, in the struggle already evolving between the Allied powers, this agreement would have the merit of clarifying their respective positions and would furnish them with a solid basis for discussion.

Things went very fast. The agreement was signed on January 29, 1942. Modeled on the Atlantic Charter (to which Iran adhered), it was called the Tripartite Treaty and contained nine articles of which the first seven were of prime importance to Iran's future.

In the first article, Britain and Russia assured Iran that they intended to respect its territorial integrity, sovereignty and political independence. (As things stood, these promises were laughable, but it was something just to have them on paper).

Article Two set out the terms of an alliance for mutual military aid. The third article guaranteed joint Russian and British aid to Iran in case of Nazi aggression, but the price the Shah had to pay was high: in case of conflict, the Iranian armed forces would be entrusted only with the country's internal security, the Allies deciding if they were needed against the common enemy. In addition, the Shah was to turn over absolute control of all communications — railways, roads, rivers, airports, ports, pipelines, telephone, telegraph and radio. In Article Four, the Allies reserved for themselves the power to decide the number of troops to be stationed in Iran "as long as the strategic situation demanded." The text went on to state: "It is of course understood that the presence of these forces on Iranian soil in no way constitutes a military occupation," which to Iranians, was a commitment that might come in very handy some day. The Allies also gave assurances that they would "interfere as little as possible in the administration and running of the country, its economic life, internal affairs, and the application of Iranian laws and customs."

Article Five was the key section as it dealt with the evacuation of foreign troops. If history had taught Iran nothing else, it had made one thing abundantly clear: that armies of occupation have a marked distaste for evacuating a country once they have taken it over. A vague Russian or British promise was not enough. Iran needed something very precise. And so it read: "The allied forces must leave Iranian territory six months after the end of hostilities between the Allied forces and Germany and its allies." (This sentence was to play a crucial role when Russia laid claim to Azerbaijan four years later.)

Article Six, which the Shah wrung from the Allies single-handedly, guaranteed Iran against any future partitioning between Russia and Britain. Article Seven committed the Allies to helping Iran solve the economic dislocation caused by the war.

Since the treaty was signed only by the ambassadors of the occupying forces, the Shah was naturally leery. He wanted a more ironclad agreement, and so he addressed himself directly to Stalin and Churchill, asking them to ratify the text with their own signatures. The two answers arrived on February first and both were affirmative.

For an added particle of assurance, the Shah also wrote Roosevelt. At first, the American President tried to dodge any commitment by having Cordell Hull answer lamely that "the Government of the United States has taken careful note of the Anglo-Soviet assurances." But the Shah persisted. He wanted more, and he got it.

On February sixth, Roosevelt sent him the following cable: ". . . I have taken note of this treaty and am gratified to observe among its provisions an undertaking by the Allied Powers to respect the territorial integrity, the sovereignty and the political independence of Iran, as well as certain undertakings of Your Imperial Majesty to cooperate with the Allied Powers in their struggle against cruel aggressors who seek to deny the right of free people to exist. . . ."

The Shah had few illusions about the worth of the treaty. But he had obtained something, even if many people in his country said it was only a piece of paper. And for him, that piece of paper was like a medical prescription, a shot in the arm to his self-confidence. True, he had given up much, but he hadn't given up everything, and that was already a large personal victory.

That much said, reality — as he had expected — soon confirmed his detractors' worst predictions. Shame and humiliation poured in on the Shah. The British and Russians behaved increasingly as if Iran were conquered territory. They fomented disorders to undermine the Shah's position, they imprisoned anyone they didn't like, and put pressure on the deputies and ministers. Forughi resigned; he was too old to cope. The Shah tried to dissuade him, but to no avail. Forughi became court minister, which he remained to his death. Squabbles between the Shah and the occupiers became more and more frequent. He deluged them with notes of protest but received no reply. The most painful humiliation concerned the printing of new money, a demonstration of the Allies' complete indifference to Iran's internal problems. In order to pay their troops, the Allies were using local currency. As a result, rials were soon in short supply and galloping inflation set in. Between June, 1940, and the end of 1942, the cost of living rose 400 percent. The reasons were obvious: the economy was disorganized; the wheat and rice from the north, essential commodities to the whole country, were requisitioned by the Russians and loaded onto trains destined for the Soviet Union; and the international blockade had cut off virtually all imports. All this was aggravated by the thousands of foreign soldiers and officials who blanketed the country.

To pay their nationals, the Allies were forced to speed up the printing of money. They knew the inflation would worsen, but they didn't give a damn. Since it was against the law, the Allies asked Ahmad Qavam, the new prime minister, to find a way around the law. Qavam replied that there was no way.

"Then change the law," Bullard and Smirnov demanded.

"Parliament will refuse," Qavam replied.

That very evening, Bullard swept into the Shah's study. He began by gently assuring the Shah that he had full confidence in Qavam, but since Parliament had rendered his prime minister powerless to act, there was only one solution: dissolve Parliament and call for new elections. It was a command.

The Shah paled at the insult and refused. Bullard stomped out of the room.

A few weeks later, an anti-Shah riot broke out in Tehran. The British, as expected, deployed their troops throughout the capital, "reestablished" order, and surrounded all official buildings. Each deputy was visited by a Briton who "advised" him to be reasonable.

The new law was passed; the printing presses went into action, and soon 700 million new rials were in circulation. Overnight, the cost of living went up 20 percent. A vast black market took over, enormous fortunes were made, poverty became widespread.

The Shah watched as his country disintegrated. Each day brought more bad news, and his pitiful victories could be counted on the fingers of one hand. He just did manage to keep the Russians from dismantling the ammunition factories his father had built and removing them to Russia; and he was able to hang onto the 105-millimeter cannon the British had surreptitiously planned to turn over to their own troops. In both cases, the violation of the Tripartite agreement was so flagrant that the Allies had to back down.

Meanwhile, ports, railroads and airports were simply annexed. What could the Shah do? It was in the treaty: the Allies were in control of all transportation. Day and night, convoys of freighters converged on Abadan and Bandar Abbas. Armies of dockers worked in temperatures that often reached 104 degrees in the holds. As soon as they were loaded, British and American locomotives and freight cars formed into convoys and chugged along the Trans-Iranian in a never ending line. In two years, the capacity of the railroad had increased tenfold.

Even though they were allies in the struggle against Germany, Russia and Britain had already begun to play private games with each other. Each country was eager to profit from Iran's general disorganization to establish its influence in anticipation of the future. And each decided that the best way to achieve this was by introducing a "fifth column."

At the very start of the war, the Germans had rushed dozens of special agents into Iran. But most of them had not had time to merge into the landscape, and were expelled along with the other German nationals. Only one was able to escape expulsion: an agent named Schulze managed to get out of Tabriz just ahead of the Russians and make it to Tehran. From the capital, he left posthaste with his wife for Afghanistan, disguised as a diplomatic courier. Arrested as he reached the border, he was sent back to Tehran and put in the German embassy under close surveillance, but he managed to escape — again with his wife — just before the embassy was closed. This time he headed south and settled in with the Qashqai where he was soon joined by another escapee from the German secret services named Mayr. Together, the two men tried various forms of disruption, but their efforts were not very effective.

The British, who controlled that zone, learned of their presence and seized the opportunity, not to expose Schulze and Mayr, but to shadow them. It was a perfect excuse for interfering in the region's affairs, and for watching over (while secretly encouraging) the development of a separatist movement which would be useful in undermining the central government.

The Russians adopted the same strategy in the north. Soon the other tribes began to stir. It no longer mattered that Riza Shah had disarmed them. Since rice, sugar and wheat were rationed, the Allies simply distributed ration cards to the tribal chieftains who sold them to buy rifles, and with these rifles, they launched attacks against the disorganized Iranian troops. In no time, organized bands were fanning out all over the country.

The Russians and British left them alone for a while. Then they went to the Shah and told him: "Let us restore order. Your troops aren't capable." And, little by little, the forces stationed in Iran became real armies of occupation, administering and policing the entire country.

The greater danger to national unity was in the north, for the Russians were far less restrained than the British. They expelled the Iranian governors and replaced them with their own men. Then they set their propaganda machines and unions to work establishing a party of "the masses" — the Tudeh — with their political commissars in charge. (The Tudeh was the same party that surfaced during the attempt on the Shah's life in February, 1949, and remained for years his principal enemy.)

In a matter of months, the entire Russian zone had become a separate region. Secession from Tehran was inevitably the next step. And after that, what? The Shah saw it all too clearly. As soon as the war was over, the Russians would begin moving south, and the British would find themselves hopelessly outnumbered. The very best the Shah could hope for would be a partition into two republics, one in Moscow's pocket, the other in London's. Iran would cease to exist.

Then, one day, Mohammed Riza heard a piece of news

which sent chills up his spine: the Allies were plotting to replace him with another more docile king. They had made contact with Prince Hamid Mirza, the son of the last Qajar crown prince. At an official reception at the British embassy, the orchestra had even struck up the Qajar anthem. The thought of a Qajar once again on the Iranian throne was too much to bear. It spelled the end of the Pahlevis. What would Riza Shah think when he learned that his son had been able to keep his throne for only a few short months?

Chapter 9

HIS SAVIOR'S NAME was Franklin D. Roosevelt.

Had Roosevelt not made the decision he did one day in the Oval Office in Washington, thousands of miles from Tehran, Iran today would be partitioned like Korea, like Vietnam before the Communist takeover. But thanks to Roosevelt, the equivalent of the Korean and Vietnam wars did not take place.

Why Roosevelt's sudden interest in Iran? Some said that he was only abiding by the terms of the Atlantic Charter. What appears more likely is that he too was looking for a foothold in Iran. To be sure, he would confine himself to economic aid. And so, as he had done for Britain and Russia before Pearl Harbor, he now opened the American cornucopia to Iran. A flotilla of freighters began to arrive at Bandar Abbas, bringing weapons, ammunition, tanks, locomotives, freight cars, trucks and planes. Such economic involvement naturally entailed a certain political interest, and as Roosevelt began to study the dossier on Iran, he saw exactly what was distressing the Shah: this country would soon be divided, with all that it implied for world stability. Most people were still too concerned with Hitler to think about the war's aftermath. But Roosevelt saw the Russian threat, and the importance of maintaining some kind of equilibrium in Iran — the bridgehead between Russia and the Persian Gulf, India and southern Asia. He also knew Britain's weakness. So it was up to him to get into the game.

A Persian Gulf Command was created, and during the course of 1942, nearly thirty thousand men — all noncombatants — arrived. The British and Russians were forced to make room, something they were not eager to do.

Under the direction of General Donald H. Connelly, who established his headquarters in a villa in Amirabad near Tehran, the Persian Gulf Command undertook to enlarge the ports in the Persian Gulf and Strait of Hormuz. The Command repaired existing roads, built new ones, constructed airports, modernized the Trans-Iranian. To placate its Allies, Qazvin became the northern rallying point for Russians and Americans; in the south, the British were asked to become a security force charged with protecting the American technicians. In less than a year, the machine was running at full speed.

The Shah has been greatly criticized in his own country for his complaisant attitude toward the occupiers. It is said that he was a mere plaything in their hands, and that it was a miracle that the country managed to preserve its independence. The truth is rather that the young king acted with intelligence and diplomacy. What good would it have done to bang his fists on the table and fly into a rage? The Allies would have laughed in his face and, had he persisted in being difficult, they would have sent him packing.

But by bending with the wind and accepting his many humiliations, Mohammed Riza made what was really his only realistic choice. He saw beyond appearances. To be sure, he now had three occupiers instead of two, but the newest arrival turned out to be a godsend: it counterbalanced the other two. And, for the time being, Roosevelt's interests and the Shah's converged. The only area of activity available to the Americans was the economic one, and this was precisely what the Shah needed the most.

The Shah knew that his calculations were paying off when he saw Bullard's and Smirnov's pinched faces as the Americans asked if they might assign one of their financial experts to Iran's finances. The Shah assented, at the same time congratulating himself for having already forced the Americans to agree to respect the terms of the Tripartite Treaty.

The economic expert turned out to be Dr. Arthur C. Millspaugh, a man not unknown to the Iranians, for he had been an adviser to old Riza Shah about twenty years earlier. The Millspaugh Mission received its authorization from the *majlis* on May 1, and its sixty experts quickly assumed their posts. It was a formidable team: Rex A. Pixley in Accounts and Administration, George T. Hudson in Public Domains, Bernard I. Lamb, Price Stabilization, Irving C. Hansen, Supply and Supervision, Esmond S. Ferguson, Distribution of sugar, tea and cotton goods, Floyd F. Shields, Transportation, Fred A. Schuckman, Transport Priorities, Dr. Albert G. Black, Cereals and Bread, with Dr. J. Forrest Crawford as his deputy, Harold Gresham, Customs, Melville Monk, Internal Revenue, Rex Vivian, General Inspection, Walter W. Harris, Industrial Supervision, W. K. LeCount, Treasurer-General, William Brownrigg, Personnel, and F. Kenerson Johnston, Foreign Trade Control.

Not unexpectedly, the Americans soon moved beyond the economic domain. They began with the army: General Clarence S. Ridley arrived with eleven officers and a contingent of military advisers. Then they took over the *gendarmerie*, and the Iranians were introduced for the first time to the man who was to play a crucial role in 1953 when the Shah won back his power from Mossadegh. Colonel H. Norman Schwarzkopf, a big strapping man with a thin mustache, was typical of those agents who turn up wherever there are intelligence networks to create and *coups* to mount. He had his hour of triumph at the time of the Lindbergh kidnapping in 1932 when, as head of the New Jersey State Police, he arrested the kidnappers. He arrived in Iran in 1942, officially authorized to reorganize the inept *gendarmerie*, but his actual assignment was much more than that. He had orders to measure the exact number of Communists in the Tudeh, and the extent of its Moscow connection. He was also to develop a network of his own agents.

The Central Intelligence Agency did not yet exist; it was the Office of Strategic Services (or O.S.S.) that performed those services. L. Stephen Timmerman was grafted onto the municipal police as an expert. Other Americans infiltrated Public Health (Dr. Bennet Avery), Irrigation (Luther Winsor), Agriculture (Harold B. Allen) and so on.

This was a particularly painful period for the Shah. No more parties at the palace, no more dances. The atmosphere at court was lugubrious. The Queen Mother kept to her apartments; Ashraf was on the rampage. The Shah himself roamed the corridors, a useless appendage. The Council of Ministers was in the doldrums, crushed and humiliated; their deliberations had no significance since all decisions were made elsewhere. Each week brought new affronts, new retreats, more bitter pills to swallow. Sometimes their meetings exploded in violent recriminations, and a few began openly to criticize the Shah for his weakness. Many of them had served under Riza Shah, following his orders without a murmur. Now they spoke out boldly, and the Shah alternated between fits of wounded pride and deep depression. He no longer knew whom to trust. He was suspicious of his closest advisers: how could he tell which among the faithful were in fact creatures of the Allies, and which ally — Russian, British or American?

So he formed a kind of parallel cabinet made up of the few men he was sure of, and set up his own network, placing his men in strategic positions. Through his informants, he learned that the Tudeh was everywhere. In Azerbaijan, there were cells in every town and village. There were Communist networks in Meshed, Isfahan, Kermanshah, Avez and even Abadan, the oil port the British were supposed to control.

But the Shah also learned that, however damaging to his pride, the American presence had its useful side. Friction between British and Americans was growing in the south. In the north, the Russians were sabotaging the work of Washington's envoys. They expelled Vivian from Azerbaijan, Gordon from Meshed, Nancarrow from Rezaiyeh. The United States retaliated by threatening to cut off military and economic aid. A precarious kind of balance came into being, with the Shah as the bond between the occupying forces. The ruckus over the Qajar prince was forgotten and passed into history.

The summer of 1942 provided the first real evidence that the young king was finally coming into his own. Prime Minister Churchill was on his way to Moscow to meet with Stalin. The only route possible was through Iran. So, Churchill stopped off in Tehran for a few days. It was natural that he should meet the Shah, but when they did, would the young monarch be able to stand up to the old British lion?

The meeting took place at the palace the day after Churchill's arrival. There was a large lunch, and the two men sat next to each other, each eyeing the other. The older man, by nature wily and suspicious, quietly observed the young man whose father he had deposed. For his part, Mohammed Riza did not want to seem too impressionable; on the other hand, he must not appear to be a cipher who didn't know how the cards were stacked. The man with the real power was the old politician from London, not the inheritor of Cyrus's throne.

He must have passed the test, for as he left, Churchill invited him to the British ambassador's summer residence at Zargandeh the next day. Nothing obliged him to do it. His courtesy call on the Shah would have been sufficient. When they met the following day, Churchill questioned the Shah at length and they covered a wide range of subjects. Pleased with the results, he asked if he might call on the Shah before his departure for Moscow.

According to the Shah, he conveyed to Churchill his fears for the future of the Tripartite Alliance, then, as the conversation turned to international matters, they exchanged views on the various plans for the Allied invasion of Europe. The Shah suggested they attack Italy first, then having consolidated their position, mount a massive attack through the Balkans. The Shah recalls the conversation with evident satisfaction: "Churchill mulled this over. There was a light in his eyes, but he said nothing. Later on, if you remember, he came around to the idea and started talking about attacking 'the soft underbelly' of Europe. Ah, if this plan had been followed, how different the history of Europe might have been!"

A little while later, the Shah had another visitor who made a lasting impression on him; General de Gaulle also stopped by on his way to Moscow. At that time, de Gaulle was little more than the leader of a group of exiles; he was under sentence of death in his own country, and fought daily battles with the Allies—especially the British—to preserve what official status he had. He found the young and threatened monarch very touching, caught up in a tangle of problems as insoluble as his own. "We must both be brave," he said as he was leaving. "If we don't give in, we'll win out in the end."

From one point of view, the Tehran Conference was the culmination of Iran's gradual rise in strategic importance. First the Persian Gulf Command, then the Millspaugh Mission, and on May 13, General Patrick Hurley recommended to the State Department that, in recognition of Iran's intention to declare war against the Axis, and the Allies' preempting of its roads and railways, Iran should be elevated from a legation to the status of embassy. England planned to follow suit.

It is equally true that Tehran was chosen to please Stalin because he wished to remain close to Russia. For Roosevelt, already a sick man, the long trip would be an ordeal, but he gave in, in part because Iran was looming ever larger in his eyes, flanking as it did Russia's southern border.

What was the purpose of the Conference? Essentially, the chiefs of state of the three great powers—Roosevelt, Churchill and Stalin—wanted to get together to formulate a common strategy, without intermediaries, for the final assault on Germany.

In the weeks that preceded the conference, Tehran became a hive of diplomats, generals, experts, and of course, spies and secret agents. The city was taken over by the Allies who kept it under tight surveillance night and day. The two meeting places were to be the Russian embassy on Hafiz Avenue and the British embassy on Ferdowzi Avenue, both south of the Shahriza in the center of town and separated only by one street.

The Iranians were wont to say that the handsomest houses

and the most beautiful gardens were those of the foreign embassies. This was particularly true of the British and Russian compounds. For the moment, however, they had become virtual fortresses. Patrols ringed the embassies twenty-four hours a day; the street connecting them was roped off and a closed passage—a veritable tunnel—was built to permit the participants to come and go without being seen. There was great fear that German agents had infiltrated Tehran for the purpose of assassinating Roosevelt, Churchill, and/or Stalin.

Roosevelt was to be put up in the American embassy on Takt-E-Jamahid Avenue, north of the Shahriza, hence at some distance from the other two. On the morning of November 28, Stalin conveyed his fears to the American ambassador, Averell Harriman. He thought the American embassy too far away. The three leaders would run too many risks getting there. Wouldn't it be better if the American President moved to the Russian embassy which had a separate house tucked away in its park? Roosevelt hesitated, considered moving to the British embassy, but finally accepted the Russian offer.

On November twenty-eighth the conference began. Mohammed knew nothing of what was going on except for the notes he was sent at regular intervals. But, as on so many other occasions, he swallowed his pride: the important thing was that he eventually meet the three men. But, adding insult to injury, when it came time to meet Roosevelt and Churchill, Iran's monarch had to go to them. To Churchill, he once again spelled out the terms of the Tripartite Treaty. To Roosevelt, he expressed the need for economic aid. "The conversations were conducted in the friendliest spirit," was all the official communiqué said.

On Tuesday the thirtieth, the Shah visited with Roosevelt a second time. Flanked by Hossein Ala, his Court Minister, Prime Minister Scheily and Foreign Minister Maraghehi, the

Shah came bearing a splendid Isfahan rug as a present for Mrs. Roosevelt. With the President were his close adviser General Patrick Hurley, his chargé d'affaires in Iran, Louis G. Dreyfus (whose remarkable wife was decorated by the Shah for her work in the Tehran slums), and his son Elliot. In his book, *As He Saw It*, Elliot Roosevelt gives a detailed description of the meeting. Prefacing it with the comment: "I had heard that the young Shah was quite a playboy; but for this occasion he was earnest, serious and intent." He then went on: "As ever, Father was interested in finding out more about the country, and in probing around for ideas that would help to solve its problems. He and the Iranian officials discussed the barren desert which made up such a great part of the country; they told him how, in centuries past, their land had been heavily wooded, and told him how it had become a dust bowl. This was a familiar subject to Father; warming up, he raised the question of a gigantic reforestation program; shifted from there to the plight of the majority of the Shah's subjects; tied the two things together; and was at length drawn by his visitors to a consideration of the economic grip which Britain had on Iran's oil wells and mineral deposits. Father nodded sympathetically, and agreed that steps should be taken to safeguard Iran's natural wealth." At the end of this conversation, the president asked that General Hurley "get to work drawing up a draft memorandum guaranteeing Iran's independence and her self-determination of her economic interests." In another context, Roosevelt made the observation: "An agreement from the Russians and the British guaranteeing Iranian sovereignty and political independence — it should be a good example of what we'll be able to accomplish, later on."

The Shah returned to the palace very pleased with the way the meeting had gone. Then Stalin made a move that put the young king's relationship with Roosevelt in the shade. Whereas the American President and the British Prime Minister had made the Shah come to them, the Soviet dictator appeared at his door without so much as a bodyguard. With him were his Foreign Minister, Molotov, and his chargé d'affaires in Tehran, Maximov.

Stalin's effect on the Shah was overwhelming. He gave the young king a bear hug and showered him with presents. They talked for two hours, during which Stalin offered him a regiment of tanks as well as a group of fighter bombers. For a moment, the Shah was tempted, then, his suspicions aroused, he thought better of it.

And for good reasons. When the detailed proposal arrived in January, 1944, it contained some very dangerous conditions: the arms shipment would include a covey of Soviet instructors, the tanks would be delivered to Ghazvini and the planes to Meshed, both cities—as if by chance—in the Russian zone. In addition, this matériel would be under the command of a Soviet general staff until the training period was over—and the length of the training period was left unspecified.

Before leaving Tehran on December 1, Roosevelt wrote the Shah a gracious note full of diplomatic flourishes, thanked him for the "magnificent rug," extended an invitation to visit America at some indefinite date, and sent him an autographed photograph of himself in a silver frame. The Shah answered in kind, but in his heart of hearts, he felt humiliated once again. In a country where the rituals of hospitality are sacrosanct, as in Iran, it was almost an offense on Roosevelt's part not to pay the Shah a farewell visit. Churchill did no better, and to the end of their stay, the young king hoped they would have the elementary courtesy of stopping by the palace.

Mohammed Riza eventually passed off the snub and he and Roosevelt exchanged many letters—mostly on the subject of reforestation—up to the time of the President's death. Roosevelt had become more and more determined to help Iran. The personal interest he took is demonstrated by a handwritten letter he sent his Secretary of State in January, 1944, in which he enclosed the report he had asked for from General Hurley:

". . . Iran is definitely a very, very backward nation. It consists really of a series of tribes and 99 percent of the population is, in effect, in bondage to the other 1 percent. The 99 percent do not own their land and cannot keep their own production or convert it into money or property.

"I was rather thrilled with the idea of using Iran as an example of what we could do by an unselfish American policy. We could not take on a more difficult nation than Iran. I would like, however, to have a try at it. The real difficulty is to get the right kind of American experts who would be loyal to their ideals, not fight among themselves and be absolutely honest financially.

"If we could get this policy started, it would become permanent if it succeeded as we hope during the first five or ten years. And incidentally, the whole experiment need cost the taxpayers of the United States very little money.

"Would you let me know what you think I should reply to Hurley? He is right that the whole Lend-Lease Administration should take complete control of the distribution of our own Lend-Lease supplies in the Middle East."

In a melancholy testimonial to America's mid-war idealism, Hurley stated in the preface to his report: "This plan of nation building may be improved through our experience in Iran and may become the criterion for relations of the United States toward all nations which are now suffering from the evils of greedy minorities, monopolies, aggression and imperialism."

This proved to be a very significant memorandum, not only because it demonstrated the sincerity of Roosevelt's intentions, but also because it became the basis for the policy on aid to Iran which Truman implemented as part of the innovative Point Four Program, continued to this day.

Everything seemed to be going well. Then one morning, the Shah found two telegrams on his desk, one informing him that a small tribe related to the Qashqai—the Boir Ahamadai—had decimated a battalion of regular troops, the other announcing that his father was gravely ill.

The stay on Mauritius had started auspiciously. The royal family had been installed in three separate villas in a park at some distance from the city. The governor of the island had paid his respects, as had the officer assigned to look after their needs. But within eight days, Riza Shah began to suffer a sea change. He lost weight and barely touched the meals prepared by his Iranian chef. He complained of stomach pains and the humid climate. But above all, he was bored—and worried. Although his son kept him informed of developments in Iran, the letters were late arriving. When his cardiac symptoms returned, an electrocardiogram was recommended, but there was no machine on the island. The British suggested Canada, but this meant going by way of Durban to pick up a ship heading for America. The family split up, some returning to Tehran, some making the trip with their father. But when they reached Durban, a British doctor diagnosed Riza Shah's illness as advanced arteriosclerosis. The journey must be abandoned. The doctor recommended the cool dry climate of Johannesburg, and the faithful Ali Izadi went in search of accommodations. In early March, the old king had another heart attack. Ashraf made the perilous voyage by sea to visit him. Then, to the old man's delight, Shams arrived in the middle of the summer. He looked much better than she expected, and he seemed to be revived by her presence and her store of fresh news. He had a good supper and told stories of the old days. The next morning, Riza Shah was dead.

His body was embalmed and dressed in his uniform, complete with decorations, Cossack sword and his little bag of Iranian earth. The British were asked to ship the coffin to Tehran, but refused for the usual reason—the danger of submarines. All they would be able to do was convey the royal remains to Cairo where they would have to wait until the end of the war.

In Cairo, the corpse was temporarily interred in the Rafai Mosque where it stayed until 1950 when Mohammed Riza was finally able to bring it home. The final interment took place with great pomp at Rey, a few miles south of Tehran, in a splendid white marble mausoleum built in a park carpeted with flowers and reflecting pools. The coffin was opened just before the ceremony. The old Shah's face was intact, features and expression were the same, but the decorations of gold, diamonds, rubies and turquoise, and the sword with its jewel-encrusted hilt, had disappeared. The tomb had been violated in Cairo—an old Egyptian custom. By whom? "Farouk," Mohammed Riza says. "He was a collector; he took anything that struck his fancy."

Chapter 10

WITH THE WAR coming to an end, the question haunting Mohammed Riza was whether the Allies would abide by their word and get out of Iran. The Shah had only two people he could really trust, his sister Ashraf and Hossein Ala. For the first time, the third daughter of Riza Shah was moving to center stage—a tiny woman, five feet two inches and weighing eighty-five pounds, but the glint in her eye, the set of her chin, her temperament and brains gave away the Cossack hidden inside the doll. Riza Shah, like most members of his generation everywhere, had always believed that girls were supposed to stay home. So, deprived from her earliest youth of any opportunity to make use of her abilities, Ashraf behaved outrageously and flew into a temper at the slightest provocation. She broke her dolls, she tore up her embroidery canvases. In short, she was a demon. Typically, one morning she caused a general panic at Saadabad, bringing the palace guards running to the far end of the park. She had stolen a lieutenant's revolver and was shooting at the dead leaves blowing about the lawn. Riza Shah was not amused.

The Shah's other bastion of support—Hossein Ala—was the

The Shah, in his twenties. *Henri Cartier-Bresson, Magnum*

Princess Ashraf, the Shah's sister. *Archives France-Dimanche*

son of a former prime minister under the Qajars, later court minister, and subsequently ambassador to Washington. Scrupulously honest and extremely cultivated, he held to the highest principles of service which, to him, meant unswerving loyalty to the king.

These two were to play dramatic roles, one in Moscow, the other in Washington.

With the end of the war in sight, the need for unified effort among the Allies subsided, and a host of enemies surfaced around the Shah. Outside the country, there were the British and the Russians—especially the Russians—though the Americans were also cause for alarm with Roosevelt gravely ill and his successor an unknown quantity.

Inside Iran, things were no better. The Tudeh party, with Russian encouragement, was taking an ever larger role, adding to its roster of students and workers, an odd coalition of intellectuals, supporters of the Qajars and large landowners. Then there were the Shah's traditional opponents: Mohammed Mossadegh, one of the old king's former henchmen—the *sayyid* Ziaeddine Tabatabai, and the *ayatollah* Abol Ghassem Kashani. Also a few small Fascist groups began to emerge.

Political unrest was endemic. The Tudeh were constantly organizing demonstrations, a particularly bloody one taking place in Isfahan. In late October, 1944, a huge crowd gathered in front of Parliament to demand oil concessions for the U.S.S.R., with Soviet military trucks forming a barricade around the demonstrators.

Under pressure from the Tudeh, Prime Minister Saed was forced to resign. Who was there to succeed him? Mossadegh was the obvious choice, but he agreed only on condition that he be allowed to regain his post as deputy in case the government fell. But the Constitution forbade it, so Bayat, a wealthy landowner and minister of state under Saed, was chosen instead.

Although he was able to tamp down the Russians' oil claims and managed to have the too-powerful Millspaugh dismissed, his government fell within a few months. Two more aging politicians followed, then the Tudeh triggered a general rebellion. Riots, mutinies, assassinations broke out in all the northern provinces with the quasi-open support of the Russians. Iranian and Soviet troops tangled in Tabriz, Meshed, Combaze-Ghavus and Firuz-Kuh. A local Parliament was set up in Tabriz, and "the Autonomous Republic of Azerbaijan" proclaimed.

By November, all communications between Tabriz and Tehran were cut. Mohammed Riza sent two battalions to Azerbaijan but the Russians stopped them at Qazvin. Six days later, Zanjan fell, then Takestan, then Astara on the Caspian, and the rebels were on their way to Guilan where the local bands welcomed them with open arms. Tehran was in a state of panic. Whereas the British and Americans, respecting their agreement, had started to evacuate, the Russians were not only hanging on but sending in Red Army reinforcements and marching on the capital. At this point, Britain brought its evacuation to a halt, and three troop transports on their way home turned around and headed back to the Persian Gulf. On November 28, three thousand American troops entered Tehran.

The Russians agreed to leave the capital, but that was all. Their control of the north was spreading, the rebels now straddling the pass of Ghaflan Kuh which commanded the route to Tehran. Within five days, all Iranian troops had laid down their arms.

That same evening, Jaffar Pishevari, president of the

Azerbaijan Parliament, gave a ringing speech in which he declared that he would stop only when he had conquered all of Iran. The rebels announced the formation of an army of a hundred thousand men and circulated petitions demanding that Azerbaijan be annexed to its Russian neighbor.

In Tehran, Mossadegh asked Prime Minister Hakimi to bring the question of Azerbaijan before the United Nations. Hakimi agreed, turned the mission over to his assistant, and immediately resigned. His successor, Ahmad Qavam, took off for Moscow three weeks later, on February 18.

Through his informers (paid for out of personal funds), Mohammed Riza began to collect evidence that Qavam was being manipulated by Stalin, even to plotting to oust his sovereign. What the Shah needed now was someone in Moscow to find out exactly what was happening and how far Stalin was prepared to go. He couldn't go, nor could anyone from his cabinet. He must be careful that Qavam did not feel betrayed and overreact.

Only one person could take on the mission—a person whose departure would raise no suspicions—Ashraf. She had all the qualifications. She was a woman, and a woman in Iran didn't meddle in politics. And in courage, intelligence and boldness, she was every bit as good as a man.

When this pint-sized woman of twenty-eight arrived in Moscow, it was at the height of the purges, the trainloads of deportees, the concentration camps, the cellars of Lubyanka. And not since 1917 had a member of any royal family set foot in Russia.

"When the Kremlin gates closed behind me, my heart sank to my boots," she said recently. "I was entirely alone. They had insisted on that. After a long wait in a sinister room, an officer finally appeared. 'Follow me,' he ordered. He took me down a long deserted corridor, then another, then still another. I thought to myself: 'Down there, at the end, they're going to arrest me and I'll disappear forever . . .' Then, suddenly, a door opened and I caught sight of a man with a mustache, standing with his hands on his desk. It was Stalin. I thought he would be big, broad, terrifying—a real Cossack. What a relief! Stalin was soft and fat, but above all, he was small!"

Ashraf bravely conveyed her brother's thoughts, the interpreter translating as she went along. She spoke with passion, her eyes glistening, her voice growing in assurance. She was a *pasionaria*, taking the astonished Russian ruler to task, telling him he had no business in Iran, that he was betraying the rights of people to self-determination guaranteed in signed agreements, that he was doing even himself a disservice. Minutes passed, then a first hour, then a second hour. Stalin continued to listen, silent. But when Ashraf prepared to leave, he said with a laugh that he was impressed, that he hadn't thought an Iranian capable of so much passion. When he rang for his aide-de-camp, he said: "Look at that tiny little woman! She's a real *pravda*!" ("a true patriot").

Before leaving Moscow, Ashraf received a magnificent fur coat—a present from Stalin to "Princess Pravda."

Whatever the benefits of his sister's trip to Moscow, the Shah learned soon enough that the Soviet Union intended to transform Iran into a Communist satellite. At a meeting with Stalin, representatives of the United States and Britain proposed to amputate three provinces—Kurdistan, Khuzistan and Azerbaijan—and convert them into autonomous provinces. The center—in other words the desert—would be left to the Iranians.

Stalin accepted the proposition at first. But after consulting his foreign minister, Molotov, he changed his mind. Molotov had pointed out that it would be foolish to let the British and Americans take root in Iran. Once Azerbaijan had become a Communist satellite, Russia would have a strategic base from which to launch the "satellization" of the whole country.

According to the Tripartite Treaty and the Tehran Conference, the British, Russians and Americans were to leave Iran six months after the cessation of hostilities, i.e., by March 2, 1946.

March 2 came and went. The Americans had pulled out on January 1, the British on the specified date. But the Russians, far from getting out, were digging in: they evacuated Sharud and Meshed but stopped seven miles away, and the troops stationed in Tabriz, instead of heading home, moved toward Tehran. At the same time, the Kurds erupted in western Azerbaijan, and the specter of separatism threatened the whole country. In his despair, the Shah appealed to Britain and the United States to put pressure on the Russians. Ernest Bevin, Britain's new prime minister, lodged a complaint on March 4, and on the sixth, the American chargé in Moscow, George Kennan, delivered a note to the Kremlin which stated: ". . . the decision of the Soviet Government to retain Soviet troops in Iran beyond the period stipulated by the Tripartite Treaty has created a situation with regard to which the Government of the United States, as a member of the United Nations and as a Party to the Declaration Regarding Iran dated December 1, 1943, cannot remain indifferent."

There was no official response, although the Soviet press remarked that the U.S. State Department was in error. On March 8, Washington asked Kennan to deliver a sharply worded cable asking for "information" about suspicious Soviet troop movements around Tabriz.

When the Russians continued to turn a deaf ear, Truman

wrote directly to Stalin. Truman later described his letter as simply a "blunt message." In reality, it was nothing short of an ultimatum. If the Russian troops did not begin to pull back within a week, and had not completed their evacuation in six weeks, the United States Navy would steam into the Persian Gulf and land American troops in Iran.

By using exact dates, Truman had closed all Stalin's escape hatches. And Stalin knew that Truman was a man of decision. He hadn't hesitated to drop the atom bomb on Hiroshima and Nagasaki. The State Department claimed — off the record — that Truman threatened Stalin with the atom bomb, but there has never been an official confirmation. And the exact text of the letter has never been divulged.

Emboldened by these expressions of support, Mohammed Riza saw that he had something worth exploiting and made the most of it. He instructed his faithful ambassador in Washington, Hossein Ala, to plead Iran's case before the United Nations Security Council. It was to prove the U.N.'s first success in the shoals of international diplomacy. Andrei Gromyko, the Soviet delegate, tried to prevent Ala's appearance, but on March 24, Ala won out, and spoke with such stunning effect that Gromyko was forced, five days later, to announce that all Soviet forces would be out of Iran "in five or six weeks if no unforseen circumstances occur." By May 9, they were indeed gone.

But Qavam had meanwhile acquiesced to the Soviet proposal for a joint oil company with the Russians holding 51 percent of the shares to Iran's 49 percent, and gave in to the Soviet demand that the revolutionary regime continue in Azerbaijan. Qavam also agreed to withdraw the Iranian case from the Security Council agenda, and when Hossein Ala refused, he demanded his resignation.

Although, to the British, the outcome spelled a Soviet victory, the Shah was able to tell his people on May 25 that western Khorasan, Gorgan, Mazanderan and Azerbaijan had been completely evacuated. Not a single Russian soldier was left on Iranian soil.

His appeal to Truman was clearly the most important act of his career up to that time. But thirty years later, that appeal is still a subject of debate. Many insist that the situation could have been salvaged without incurring such a huge debt to the United States. Perhaps so, but it seems more likely that it was the American response that prevented Iran from being partitioned, suffering the later fate of Korea and Vietnam. For the Shah, there were not one but two problems: to make the Russians leave, and to reclaim his power.

The reconquest of Azerbaijan was a bloody business. It took nine months, the last rebel giving up in Tabriz on December 18, 1946. When Mohammed Riza made his first visit to the province, he was greeted by scenes of collective delirium. Sheep, camels and bulls were slaughtered in his passage; an old man was prevented just in time from cutting his throat as a sacrificial gesture, and a peasant offered up his son clothed in white and crowned with flowers. But elsewhere the tribes remained restive and peace did not really come until the spring of 1947 when the Shah declared a general amnesty.

Meanwhile, Russia was accusing Iran of being tied hand and foot to the Americans, what with George V. Allen as the new U.S. ambassador, General Vernon Evans as chief of the military mission, and General Schwarzkopf in charge of the *gendarmerie*. The Cold War was on, and Truman was eager to reap the benefits of his opposition to Stalin. In his eyes, Iran was the West's first line of defense, and during that summer, Washington granted Iran a credit of $26 million to help arm its troops.

The Shah's popularity was at its zenith. His success at freeing his country from Russian occupation rallied the entire country behind him. With his renewed confidence, he was able not only to carry on full-time political activities, but to resume one of his favorite pastimes — the pursuit of the ladies.

Chapter 11

ONCE AGAIN, limousines glided silently up to the palace, delivering handsome women with heavy makeup and calculating
eyes. Other times, discreet factotums went to the airport and
returned with splendid creatures who were driven straight to
villas in Shemiran where they barely had time to repair their
faces before being introduced to the royal embrace. (According to a one-time "employee" of Mme. C., one of the better
known Madams in Paris, the Shah was a somewhat timid
lover. In any event, he appears to have had perfectly normal
if expensive tastes. These importations are said to have cost
him as much as $10,000 each.)

While, in Azerbaijan, two hundred people were dying of
starvation every day, the king was buying still more sports
cars, spending whole days on horseback and evening after
evening in nightclubs. When he felt tired, he would summon
a few friends and play cards for high stakes until dawn. (Fawzia had returned to Cairo for good, taking Shanaz with her.
She asked for a divorce and received it in 1948.)

Then, to women, cars and cards, he added a fourth passion:
airplanes. He had long since learned to pilot a plane, usually

the Hawkers and Hurricanes of the Iranian Air Force. Now he wanted his own. He first bought a Beechcraft, but it held fuel enough for only five hours' flying time. Then one day, he noticed a B 17 belonging to Trans World Airlines in a hangar at Tehran Airport. It was an old World War II bomber converted into a cargo plane. When the Shah learned that its range was fifteen hours, he decided he must have it. To teach him to fly the plane, T.W.A. offered him the services of a pilot who had a record of seventy-five hundred hours of combat flying, a thousand of them in a B 17. But before the pilot took on the mission, the American embassy warned him that under no circumstances was he to take any chances with his precious cargo.

According to the pilot, he was summoned to the palace within twenty minutes after his arrival at his Tehran hotel. Since the palace was only two blocks away, he decided to walk, and, passing the royal garage, saw scores of cars: Buicks, Cadillacs, a Mercedes Benz, and six Rolls-Royces, not to mention the jeeps. An automobile enthusiast, the fascinated pilot forgot all about his appointment and spent the afternoon in the garage with the mechanics.

The next morning, he was to meet the Shah at the airport. When he arrived, the king was already there, waiting impatiently with his brother-in-law, Ahmed Chafik, Ashraf's second husband. They got into the B 17 and the Shah took the controls. The takeoff was rather bumpy—normal for a first attempt—but as they reached cruising speed, the Shah began to fly the B 17 as if it were a fighter. He would dive toward the mountains and pull out just in the nick of time, then weave back and forth through the valleys.

Hoping to teach the Shah a lesson, the pilot remarked that he might have even more fun with one of the engines cut. He cut the outside left engine but, undeterred, the Shah continued his tricks on three engines. The pilot said nothing. Finally, they headed back to Tehran. The Shah fouled up his landing approach and had to pull back up. The pilot inquired how he proposed to make his approach this time. The Shah replied, laughing, that he had no idea; he had never landed a B 17 before.

The next try was successful. The Shah bought the B 17, but the pilot emphatically refused to give him another lesson.

It was easy enough to understand how, after the tensions of the war and its trying aftermath, the Shah might abandon himself to pleasure — the more dangerous the better. His awakening was brutal but salutary. The five shots from Fakhr Arai's pistol on the steps of the University of Tehran brought him up sharp and reminded him of his duties.

During the few days of February, 1949, that Mohammed Riza spent in bed after the assassination attempt, he experienced a profound change. The playboy, woman chaser, sports car buff and daredevil pilot had for the first time felt his mortality. He became a king again, with the power to punish and to forgive. He would start by punishing.

The target was the Tudeh Party, for he was convinced that it was they who had put the gun in Fakhr Arai's hand. But as the investigation got under way, some very curious anomalies came to light. Fakhr Arai's permit had been signed by the newspaper *Partcham Islam*, an organ of various right-wing religious groups. Its director, Faghidi Chirazi, whose signature was on the permit, was one of the most active members of the religious sect closest to the royal family. On the other hand, Fakhr Arai's companion was an extreme leftist. A former deputy's son, with a doctorate in science, he was in charge of Tudeh youth propaganda. And Fakhr Arai himself apparently belonged to the Tudeh.

So the question arose: Why did the right-wing Dr. Chirazi agree to endorse a known Communist? During the investigation, he claimed that the young man had fooled him by pretending to be a free-lance photographer and promising him exclusive rights to his pictures of the ceremony. However, certain elements in the religious parties, particularly the ambitious army chief of staff, Hadj Ali Razmara, had been seriously considering an attempt on the Shah's life. So there was at least a possibility that the extreme right had manipulated the left to make the latter seem responsible for the assault.

Meanwhile, the Shah, who was still fuming over the fact that Fakhr Arai was dead and would therefore never be able to talk, decided to take advantage of the situation to finally rid himself of all his opponents.

An hour after the Council of Ministers met in extraordinary session, a court communiqué came out, quoting the Shah: "Those few bullets were of no importance when one is serving one's country and beloved fatherland. As far as We are concerned, Our will in this area remains unshakable." Read: to serve one's country and fatherland at this particular moment means obliterating the opposition.

At seven-thirty, a second communiqué announced the imposition of martial law and a curfew beginning that very evening at ten o'clock. Drivers returning to town after a weekend in the country were astonished to find police barricades barring their way. (Two hundred and thirty-six arrests were made that first night.) Knowing nothing about the assault on the Shah, they were equally unaware that the elimination of the Tudeh was under way. The first arrested were the Czech student who had tried to rescue Fakhr Arai, and all the photographers present at the ceremony. Soon after, the police arrested Dr. Chirazi of *Partcham Islam*, the *ayatollah* Kashani, twenty-odd agitators who had been under surveillance for some time, a dozen members of the Tudeh, several union members, and the publishers of various left-wing newspapers. By morning, many more members of the opposition had been picked up and put behind bars, and during the next few days, hundreds of arrests were made all over the country.

For the Communists, the time had come to go underground —where they still are.

Having liquidated the problem of the Tudeh Party, Mohammed Riza turned to his second act: clemency. Many of those arrested were freed, and he had the sentence of others reduced. He even refused to allow the arrest of Ahmad Qavam, the former prime minister suspected of taking part in the plot. As the police were making ready to arrest him, he managed to telephone the Shah and ask his pardon.

Meanwhile, crowds poured into all the city's mosques to thank Allah for their sovereign's narrow escape. All the various religious communities celebrated the miracle: the *imam* Djumeh delivered an impassioned address in the bazaar, a Te Deum was sung in the Catholic Church of the Consolata, another Te Deum in the Greek Orthodox Church, and prayers were said by the Armenian bishop as well as in all the synagogues.

The Shah took advantage of this wave of enthusiasm to make a series of political moves designed to consolidate his power. To the *majlis*, he presented a law limiting freedom of the press which stated that henceforth, any insulting remark about the king or any member of the imperial family would be considered a misdemeanor; the police would immediately confiscate the newspaper and arrest its publisher and those reporters involved. Naturally the newspapers raised a hue and cry: "No criticism of any kind will be possible" . . . "the end of all freedoms of expression" . . . "a violation of the Con-

stitution . . ." The law passed, but slightly diluted: no confis-
cation of newspapers; instead, prison sentences of one to
three years.

In another buttressing of royal prerogative, the Shah directed that the Senate, the Parliament's hitherto inactive
chamber, henceforth be made equal to the first—the *majlis*.
But whereas the *majlis* were elected, half the Senate would
be appointed by the Shah. Furthermore, he would have the
right—by a simple *firman* (decree)—to dissolve both houses,
singly or together. The amendment to the Constitution was
passed on May 8.

The king justified this curtailment of parliamentary powers
on the grounds that foreign influences were too strong on
Iran, especially where the delegates who chose the representatives for the *majlis* and Senate were involved. And, although
Parliament had never had complete control over such matters
as the choice of a prime minister (they could only recommend
to the king by a procedure called "inclination"), the king had
nonetheless often felt himself forced to accept politicians
whom he suspected of being "elected" by foreigners, if only
to avoid the risk of a political crisis or open conflict. This
he would no longer be obliged to do.

The Shah made a rapid recovery. Two days after his near
assassination, he was on the radio thanking his people for
their expressions of sympathy. Four days later, the newspapers published a photograph taken during his talk, showing
him in pyjamas in bed, a large bandage between upper lip and
nose. His face was a little swollen, but otherwise he looked
well and his voice was clear and steady. Ten days after the
first photograph, another was published, with the Shah in a
loud checked suit, hands behind his back, his face in three-
quarter profile. A small scar was clearly visible near the right

dimple, and a white spot in the mustache he had grown indicated where a bullet had been removed.

The curfew was revoked in early March. Order had been restored. Then the Shah made his third move: on March 8, the *Journal de Tehran* published a postscript to the attempted assassination which read: "Today, matured by his trials, and having demonstrated to his people the clarity of his thought, and the extent of his patriotism, the Shahinshah is initiating a series of social reforms which will make Iran a prosperous country. . . . Iran is now entering a revolutionary phase in the social and economic area."

Every other day, the newspapers announced the arrival of foreign experts—mostly Americans—and shipments of munitions—also American. The name "Overseas Consultants Incorporated" began to crop up, affixed to the names of new American arrivals in Tehran. When the Shah went to visit Truman the following November, it was revealed that "Overseas Consultants Incorporated" was an umbrella for eleven American enterprises involved in helping Iran realize a seven-year plan of recovery costing 700 million dollars.

The Shah could take much of the credit for this. The attempt on his life and his personal bravery had made a deep impression on the Americans. In addition, the suppression of the Tudeh, the recovery of his power, and even his exercises in clemency had not been lost on Truman and his Secretary of State, Dean Acheson. Instead of a spoiled playboy, they were dealing with a man of energy and guts. At long last, out of that brawling mass of rapacious Iranian politicians, a strong man was emerging whom the Americans could trust.

At the age of twenty-nine, the Shah had taken his country in hand.

Chapter 12

GENERAL HADJ ALI RAZMARA was a career soldier and an alumnus of Saint-Cyr. Small, physically powerful, all muscle and nerves, he had the reputation of being unscrupulous and cruel. During the conflict in Azerbaijan, he was said to have boiled his prisoners alive, and it was claimed that the trees were so overloaded with men he had hanged that their branches snapped. And again, when he was fighting against the Kurds, he extracted 20 millions rials ($200,000) from Mohammed Qazi, the leader of the Kurdish republic, in exchange for letting him live — and executed him two days later.

Razmara was immensely ambitious, hence he was widely suspected of having been involved in the attempted assassination of the Shah. Why, then, did the king name him prime minister? For one thing, the Shah needed a strong man, and for another, Razmara had the support of the Americans who were disturbed to see Iran, which they were showering with dollars, sink into corruption, extortion and trafficking for the sole benefit of the "one thousand families" — the promoters and businessmen who were making vast fortunes. The Americans liked Razmara. So they put pressure on the Shah to appoint him, even though he feared the results. And with good reason: no sooner was Razmara prime minister than he began preparing a military coup d'état. The Shah knew about it but decided to bide his time.

Razmara had frequent contacts with the American embassy in Tehran. The Americans wanted a strong anti-Communist and a man sufficiently corrupt to be malleable if anything untoward happened to the king. They had liked the way he boiled the Communists in Azerbaijan, and furthermore, the attempt on the Shah's life had made them nervous.

One American faction supported Razmara all the way. Its chief protagonists were Edward Wells, director of the United States Information Agency in Iran, and Gerald Dooher, whose activities on Razmara's behalf became so blatant that they seemed to have gone well beyond the State Department's instructions. As soon as Razmara was named prime minister, the American embassy was promoted from Class II to Class I which gave it the right to a more prestigious staff, a company of marines, higher pay for the new ambassador, Henry F. Grady, and more attention from Washington.

However, despite the flattering articles about Razmara in the *New York Times*, the State Department did not entirely share its embassy's enthusiasm for the new minister. In fact, six months after his appointment, Razmara, who had asked the Americans for a loan of $100 million annually, received only one-quarter the amount and with very disadvantageous financial conditions. But he did better elsewhere. He established warm relations with Britain, anticipating the unpleasantness that was sure to develop over oil rights with the Anglo-Iranian Oil Company. He even went so far as to disavow any interest in nationalizing Iran's oil. With Russia, he renewed the trade agreement of 1940. And to keep the Tudeh quiet, he freed a few of its imprisoned members. But he was equally adept at creating enemies, including Mossadegh, an ardent believer in the nationalization of oil, the Imperial Court which found him a little too aggressive, and the *mullahs*, who resented Razmara's adoption of Western ways.

Meanwhile, Ashraf was trying to find her brother a new wife. The young woman in question must have four qualifications: she must be very pretty, to distract Mohammed Riza from his "shepherdesses"; titled—and a good title; Muslim—that went without saying; she must help forge an important alliance. And time was of the essence. The Shah still had no heir.

The family had trembled when, during his trip to America in 1949, the Shah had met and apparently fallen in love with an American—a foreigner and an infidel, both. She was twenty-three, with the slim body of a girl and large green eyes set in a tiny face. She belonged to one of San Francisco's oldest families and she was a painter. They became inseparable. The American press began to talk of marriage. Princess Ashraf cabled her brother to return home immediately. The Shah paid no heed. Ashraf sent emissaries to Los Angeles. In the end, Mohammed Riza gave in.

On his return to Tehran, his sister produced a photograph. "This is the girl for you. She's a Bakhtiari." Then Ashraf ticked off the virtues of the match: she was from an excellent family, she was nineteen, brought up in Europe, and willing. Besides, a marriage into one of the more troublesome tribes would be good politics.

Mohammed Riza agreed that it made sense, then replaced the photograph on the table with the remark: "She's too fat."

Determined to win out, Ashraf said: "Let's ask Perron what he thinks." Ernest Perron always gave sound advice. So he was summoned. He looked at the photograph and came to the same conclusion: the Bakhtiari girl was indeed too fat.

One September afternoon in 1950, in the bedroom of a small family boardinghouse near St. James's Park in London, a young Iranian was trying on the dress she planned to wear to a cocktail party later that day. In London to learn English, she was chaperoned by her Aunt Chokat. Her name was Soraya Esfandiary, she was eighteen, tall and dark, with beautiful almond-shaped green eyes.

There was a knock on the door. It was her cousin Gudard, Aunt Chokat's son, also in London to study English.

"Can you spare me an hour? I want to take some pictures of you."

"Again? You've already taken two lots this week."

Her cousin smiled, a look of embarrassment on his face.

"My aunt has written from Tehran asking for pictures. All she has are old ones. She'd like something more recent."

Soraya looked skeptical and Gudard ended by telling her the truth: "The Queen Mother is looking for a wife for her son. The Shah has seen some pictures of you and wants to see some more."

Soraya burst out laughing: "You must be joking!"

Soraya Esfandiary was a member of the Esfandiary tribe, a satellite of the Bakhtiari. The two tribes had made common cause in the struggle against the central power in Tehran and had suffered the fate of the vanquished. Ruined by that war together with the spendthrift ways of his guardian, Khalil Esfandiary, Soraya's father, exiled himself to Berlin in 1924 at the age of twenty-two. The following year, he met a pretty sixteen-year-old schoolgirl with blond hair and green eyes. Her name was Eva Karl, and although German, she had been

Former Queen Soraya in 1953. *Wide World*

born in Moscow. In the aftermath of the revolution, the family found refuge in Berlin. It was said that because of the Karls' financial straits, Eva had had to work evenings as a waitress in a café.

Fifteen months after their first meeting, Khalil and Eva were married in a Muslim ceremony. They lived in Berlin for two more years while Khalil finished his studies in economics, then moved back to Isfahan. Soraya was born on the sixth anniversary of their marriage, June 22, 1932. Eight months after her birth, Eva, fearing that her child might catch one of the skin or eye diseases common to Persian babies at that time, returned to Berlin without her husband. Four years later, mother and child were back in Isfahan where Khalil was the director of a professional school. When Soraya was fifteen, Eva urged her husband to return to Europe and they settled in Vollishofen on the outskirts of Zurich. Soraya attended a boarding school in Montreux, then Les Roseaux in Lausanne. In 1950, she was sent to London to learn English, being already fluent in German, French and Persian.

Two weeks after her conversation with her cousin Gudard, Soraya received a letter from her father. He had been asked by another cousin, on behalf of the Shah, to present her at court as soon as possible. "Since the invitation commits us to nothing, I accepted," her father wrote.

After that, everything moved very fast. Shams arrived in London with her husband. They invited Soraya to tea at Claridge's, together with the Iranian ambassador. Shams inspected her closely, then suggested: "Before you go back to Tehran, why don't you come to Paris with me for a few days. I have some shopping to do." Shams reserved two suites at the Crillon and the young women did the Paris shops. After a couple of days of amiable chatter, Shams put the proposition to Soraya in the middle of the Rue de Rivoli. She had received an answer to the report she had sent to Tehran. They were walking under the arcade when Shams stopped suddenly and started talking about her brother, how lonely he was, how much he needed a family of his own. "How wonderful it would be," she exclaimed, "if a girl like you would be willing to share Mohammed Riza's life!"

Soraya laughed; she still couldn't take the idea seriously.

A few days later, Shams and Soraya met Khalil in Rome and together they took the night flight to Tehran. Just before leaving, Soraya read in an evening newspaper: "The young Persian student, Soraya Esfandiary, is in Rome. It is rumored that she is to be the Shah of Iran's new fiancée." When they

arrived at Tehran Airport, Soraya was the last passenger
the plane. That very evening, she was summoned to Tadj-Ol-
Moluk's. "Just a friendly little dinner for the women." She
would meet the Shah the following day.

As soon as they were seated, the Queen Mother started
questioning her closely, with particular emphasis on the state
of her health. Soraya was not surprised, for it is a Persian
custom to ask after a person's health immediately after the
introductions. Then, suddenly, a servant came in and announced: "His Majesty, the Shah!" Soraya almost turned
over her teacup as everyone rose to their feet. Smiling
broadly, the Shah stood in front of her, in the full-dress uniform of a general of the Air Force. There were bows and
greetings, a spate of small talk, then dinner was announced.
The Shah had Soraya sit next to him, even though it was
against protocol. Their conversation quickly turned to the
subject of Switzerland which they both knew well, but the
general atmosphere could hardly be called relaxed.

When Soraya was later asked what her first impressions of
the Shah were, she said that she found him attractive and intelligent, but that "it was hardly love at first sight."

It was for the Shah, however, although he tried not to show
it. The guests moved into the drawing room and the tension
eased a little as they embarked on parlor games—a favorite
pastime at the palace. Two games the Shah particularly liked
were one involving a trial, the other an orange. In the first,
the accused chose his counsel from among the guests, and
counsel had to plead his case before the "jury," in other
words, the guests. If he failed to acquit his "client," he had
to pay a forfeit by walking around the room on all fours singing "Il pleut bergère," or sewing his pockets together, etc. In
the orange game, the guests formed two parallel lines, with a
referee in the middle. An orange was given to the first person

in each line, the player placed it between his feet and had to hop to the end of the line and back without letting go of it. If the orange fell, the guilty party had to pay a forfeit.

They played until eleven o'clock, the Shah participating with a boyish enthusiasm which Soraya found astonishing. As they made ready to leave, she saw the Shah take her father aside. When they arrived home, her father asked her: "Do you like him?" Soraya said, "Yes." Her father persisted: "I mean, enough to marry him?"

"Do I have to decide right away?"

"I think you'd better. The Shah wants an answer tonight. As soon as I have it, I am to return to the palace."

"All right then, the answer is 'yes.' But go tell him quickly; I want to go to bed." She was exhausted by the long flight and the strain of the evening.

The next morning, her photograph was in every newspaper. The official betrothal was celebrated three days later and the wedding set for December 27.

Meanwhile, Razmara had suddenly tightened his grasp. His political police were tracking down the Fedayeen of Islam, he was having the *mullahs* shadowed—especially Kashani. His plan: to eliminate the sects, dissolve Parliament, and send Mossadegh into exile together with the top members of the opposition. His men in the army and the police were ready. The only problem was the Shah. Razmara's plan was to dispose of him without actually doing him any harm. Either he consented to being a figurehead, or he would simply increase by one the number of kings in exile.

The palace was increasingly anxious. To counter Razmara's upsurge and to increase his own popularity, the Shah placed his hopes on his marriage. Once that was behind him, he would have time to cut the general down to size. Besides, he was infatuated with Soraya and was impatient to marry her.

They saw each other almost every day. They rode horseback, he took her up in his plane. Together they visited his new palace at Echtessassi—a large modern villa he had built in 1937. Soraya was greatly relieved, for she had found the other palaces intimidating, with their marble and mirrors everywhere and no creature comforts. Saadabad had exactly one bathroom and no central heating. Behind its high stone walls, Echtessassi was a two-story building with a marble facade, and at one corner, a tower supported by columns with a hanging garden on the roof. Around it were lawns, beautiful trees, carefully trimmed hedges. But even though its sanitary facilities were far superior to those of the other palaces, it had a look of neglect. The chairs were worn, curtains and draperies torn, the kitchens lacked equipment, the servants' quarters were rudimentary.

"Don't you think your house needs a little renovating?" Soraya asked the Shah.

"What do you mean? Don't you like it?" he asked with some surprise.

Soraya told him what she thought needed doing, and the Shah agreed to send for Jansen, the Paris decorator. When he submitted his plans and the estimate, the Shah blanched and said the project could wait. The contentious Razmara was too much on his mind. By way of apology, he said to Soraya: "Don't think I'm offering you an easy life. I hope you have no illusions on that score."

Then disaster struck. On the eighteenth day after her arrival, Soraya returned from a horseback ride with a high fever. She had contracted typhoid. She became delirious and for two weeks, her life hung in the balance. The Shah was devastated.

He called in the best foreign doctors; he found her the best nurse in the country, trained in America. He showered her with flowers and records, and installed a movie projector in her hospital room. All the while, her doctors were fighting over the best treatment to follow, and in the end, it was the Shah's own physician, Dr. Karim Ayadi, who saved her life by sending to America for the recently discovered drug— Aureomycin. By the end of the month, she was on the road to recovery. But a wedding on the twenty-seventh of December was out of the question, and from mid-February until May was a period of religious mourning when no marriages could be performed. So the choice fell on Monday, February twelfth, allowing Soraya the longest possible convalescence. And the priests were unanimous: "The stars are particularly favorable to Your Majesty on that day," they told the Shah.

Then Soraya, her recovery barely under way, did an incredibly foolish thing. Some Swiss friends had sent her a box of chocolates from Sprungli's in Zurich. Although she knew perfectly well that typhoid was an intestinal disease, and that diet was all-important to her recovery, she couldn't resist the bonbons and ate the entire box. The next day, she suffered a relapse, aggravated by lung congestion. Her temperature shot up to 105 degrees and for three days she was given up for lost.

When her fever finally subsided, the Shah consulted with her doctors. They were very pessimistic: Soraya wouldn't be well by the twelfth of February. Yet the wedding must take place that day. So a compromise was reached: a much simpler ceremony, without the banquets, balls and dinners that were to continue for four days, and not at Golestan Palace—which couldn't be heated—but at the Marble Palace where workmen immediately started installing heaters.

The twelfth of February dawned very cold. Tehran was deep in snow. At four o'clock, Princess Shams came for Soraya. The bride was very pale, her eyes bright with fever, but she welcomed Shams with a smile. "It's going to be all right," she said. Then she nearly collapsed under the fifty pounds of lamé and silver brocade that Christian Dior had used in her wedding dress and its interminable train. Over the gown, she wore a luxurious sable coat, a present from Stalin, and around her neck, an emerald necklace and diadem from the crown jewels. And, under all that shimmering glory, a pair of woolen stockings to keep her warm!

Shams's car, its heater on full blast, conveyed the two women through the snow-banked streets, with an escort of lancers front and back. When they arrived at the foot of the main staircase, there was panic: the little bridesmaids were not strong enough to hold up the train. Valets had to be called in to help.

The Shah was in a navy blue uniform with gold epaulets he had designed himself to resemble an eighteenth-century hussar. Flanking him were his entire ministry, court dignitaries, members of his family, priests and the diplomats assigned to Tehran. The Aga Khan and the Begum were the only foreigners invited.

To keep Soraya from getting tired, the ceremony was reduced to the bare essentials. The couple were seated on a sofa. Before them on a gold cloth lay eggs, herbs and the Koran—symbols of health, prosperity and happiness. Presiding over the *mullahs* was the young *imam* Djumeh with his long beard. When, according to the time-honored formula, he asked Soraya if she agreed to take the Shah as her husband, she said nothing and looked away. He put the question to her a second time, and again she turned away without answering. The third time, she said "Yes." The demands of the Muslim ritual had been met.

All the witnesses, including the *mullahs*, broke into applause and the company moved to an adjoining room for the presentation of gifts. The Shah's present to Soraya was an emerald necklace, bracelet, earrings and clips set in platinum. Soraya grew pale and seemed about to faint.

"Cut off the train!" the Shah ordered, and a maid-of-honor came running with a pair of scissors and cut off about ten yards of cloth. Then came the banquet, its menu: "pearls" from the Caspian Sea, consommé Imperial, cold salmon Ambassadeur, saddle of lamb, assorted vegetables, Chirine polov (a sweetened rice) with pheasant, asparagus with Hollandaise sauce, Glacé Madeleine, oranges, tangerines and apples. The beverages included gin and Persian vodka, French vermouth, red and white Rhine wines, and champagne.

After the banquet, Soraya almost fainted again and had to be supported to her car. But she recovered enough to attend the dinner for three hundred guests that night.

While the ceremonies pursued their sedate course at the palace, Tehran was celebrating with abandon. There were fireworks in the public squares; a circus the Shah had flown in from Rome performed in front of Parliament. Free meals were distributed to the poor, and young people collected donations from the rich whom the Shah had "requested" to support various charitable activities.

The next morning, the Shah and Soraya left for Balbosar, his father's villa on the Caspian. Their plan was to stay two weeks, until the queen was completely well. Then they would set off on a round-the-world honeymoon.

At the rear of a gallery in the Tehran bazaar, a puny young

man with shaved head and long beard worked from morning until night making crates for shopkeepers. His name was Khalil Tahmassebi and he held a grudge against the entire world, especially foreigners who sprayed mud on him as they drove by in their shiny cars. He had naturally fallen in with the Fedayeen-Islam, and was proud to say that after a year's trial, he had been initiated into the sect.

At the beginning of March, 1951, Khalil abandoned his crates for mysterious meetings in the back rooms of small cafés in the bazaar. His fanaticism rivaled that of the *mullahs'* partisans, and he and they were united in their hatred of Hadj Ali Razmara. Even though the prefix "Hadj" indicated he had made the pilgrimage to Mecca, the *mullahs* still regarded the prime minister as a threat to the state religion, and the word "assassination" began to crop up in people's conversations. the *ayatollah* Kashani, whose supporters were everywhere in the bazaar, believed that the only solution was to bring Mossadegh to power. But in a legal way. He was afraid of the reaction that might follow a coup or assassination. Not that Kashani was timid. He had had a violent loathing of foreigners ever since the British executed his father; he had plotted against them during the war, going so far as to preach a holy crusade among the Kurds in Iraq. On numerous occasions, he barely escaped the "executioners" of the British Intelligence Service. But when Mojtaba Navab Safavi Seyeb, the young chief of the Fedayeen, came to him one afternoon with a proposal that Razmara be assassinated, Kashani counseled prudence. If they failed, he pointed out, the repression that was bound to follow would be sure to crush them all. Safavi left in a rage, but he didn't abandon his project. A few days later, Khalil Tahmassebi learned that he had been chosen by the Fedayeen to assassinate General Razmara. He felt very proud.

It was scheduled for March 7, in Masjed Saltaneh, the bazaar's great mosque. An important religious ceremony was to take place, which the prime minister was duty-bound to attend. And if it happened in a sacred place, the traitor's death would have an even greater impact: it would seem to come straight from the hand of Allah.

On March 4, the king returned from his honeymoon at Balbosar to find his desk piled high with the reports of his secret police. Two days later, he asked Razmara to represent him at the following day's ceremony. Early the next morning, Razmara replied that he was very sorry but he didn't have the time—couldn't someone else take his place? After all it was only a run-of-the-mill ceremony. But the Shah insisted. He dispatched one of his most loyal advisers, Assadollah Alam, to the prime minister. Alam succeeded in persuading Razmara to appear at the mosque.

At 10:30, with Assadollah Alam at his side, General Razmara crossed the court of the mosque. The crowd was so dense that the prime minister's guards had trouble clearing a path for him. Khalil Tahmassebi was there, his hand clutching the pistol in his pocket. As Razmara passed, he elbowed his way behind him and pulled the trigger four times. Two bullets hit the prime minister, one in the neck, the other in the back. He died in the hospital an hour later, without regaining consciousness. He was forty-nine years old.

Khalil Tahmassebi tried to turn the gun on himself, but he was immediately surrounded, disarmed and thrown into prison.

The Shah was at breakfast when an aide ran in to announce that General Razmara had just been killed. As soon as the news spread to the city, there were explosions of joy, crowds filled the streets, and processions of cars raced in every direction, horns blaring.

All the newspapers came out with special editions. One banner headline read: "Iran has proved that it is still very much alive." Another produced a montage showing Razmara wiping away tears of blood on the Union Jack, in the middle of which George VI was shown smiling, while an extended arm waving a revolver jutted out behind the jeering figure of Churchill. Every newspaper carried the picture – to prove he was indeed dead – of Razmara lying half naked on a hospital bed, mouth open, eyes closed, gashes in his head and torso, surrounded by doctors and nurses.

Two questions remained unanswered: did the Shah know about the plot? And, if not, why did he insist that the prime minister attend the ceremony?

Twelve days after Razmara's murder, the minister of education, Azam Zanganeh, was also killed, by a fanatic in the mosque at the University of Tehran. And in the months that followed, the fanatics continued to strike down all those they thought too lenient. One thing, however, is certain: Khalil Tahmassebi had relieved the Shah of a powerful adversary.

But the favor he had done the Shah was soon to prove a poisoned pawn. That pawn's name was Mohammed Hedayat, called Mossadegh – meaning "the valorous."

When, five days after Razmara's murder, it was learned that the Shah had appointed Hossein Ala as prime minister, the bazaar exploded. Eighty thousand people crowded into the square in front of Parliament – Tudeh supporters, members of the National Front, but mostly the undecided, waiting to see which side could yell loudest.

The *ayatollah* Kashani announced: "We want no part of Hossein Ala!" Fatemi, one of the most influential National

Front deputies, also expressed his opposition. The crowd applauded and started chanting: "The oil belongs to us!" "Shove the British into the sea!" "Down with foreign colonialism!" Inside the Parliament building, the deputies trembled with fear. But the crowd hesitated, uncertain what to do, then dispersed after breaking a few windows.

On March 15, the *majlis* were forced to approve a plan for the nationalization of oil, hurriedly thrown together by Hossein Ala. But when the British ambassador, Sir Francis Shepherd, was informed of the project, he rejected it out of hand. Demonstrations broke out everywhere, with several dead, including three British. Mossadegh's name was shouted day and night. Hadn't he been demanding the nationalization of oil for years? He naturally became the standard bearer.

The Shah too was convinced that Iran had to nationalize its oil. But he also knew that for the time being, his hands were tied. He was still too dependent on the British and Americans. It would have been better to put the whole matter off for a while. But now they were forcing his hand; he must act, and quickly.

He summoned Mossadegh and offered him the post of prime minister on condition that he exercise prudence and tact with the foreigners whose loans were so vital to Iran. Mossadegh agreed with enthusiasm. So the Shah placed his name before the *majlis* and he was confirmed on April 29. Nine days later, he won a vote of confidence, 99 against 3, and a two-month period in which to study the problem of nationalization.

The Mossadegh era had begun. And the Shah's honeymoon with Soraya came to an abrupt end. It now included a third party—his new prime minister. But Mossadegh was not going to be an easy partner.

Chapter 13

MOHAMMED HEDAYAT MOSSADEGH was born sometime around 1881. His father was finance minister under the Qajars for thirty years; as his mother was a Qajar princess, he was raised in the imperial court.

At the age of fifteen, Mohammed was sent into the provinces with the title of Inspector of Finances. He did so well that, on his return, the Shah gave him the surname "Mossadegh," signifying—more or less—"He has been tried and proven valorous." Whetted by his success, Mossadegh began plotting a small-scale palace revolution, apparently more for the fun of it than for any real reason. The fledgling plot was exposed and the Shah exiled him to Paris. By this time he was eighteen, and he entered the university where he discovered socialism and became a militant in the thin ranks of Persian students. Already in poor health, he soon developed an ulcer, aggravated by nervous disorders. His distraught mother threw herself at the Shah's feet and asked for her son's pardon, which was granted. Back in Tehran, Mossadegh entered politics. As under-secretary of finance, he launched a campaign against the corruption of the petty officials (whom he considered too numerous anyway), and barely missed an assassin's bullet. Undaunted, he turned to the problem of oil.

The extent of Britain's control over Persian oil offended him deeply, and he was soon stirring up violent attacks against the "occupiers." Once again he was exiled, this time under British orders. A year later, he was pardoned again, but dispatched away from Tehran to serve as a provincial governor. He was soon back, however, and by 1922, he had made the giant step to minister of finance.

His first act was to cut by half the salary of every official, deputy and minister, starting with himself. The personal sacrifice was hardly overwhelming, as he was one of the richest landowners in the country with a fortune estimated at 800 million rials (approximately $10 million). This had two results: he was almost assassinated again, and he was elected to the *majlis*.

In 1928, on the day Riza Shah seized the throne, Mossadegh rose in Parliament to denounce the coup. But the Shah took no action against him and proceeded to leave him alone for three years until his patience finally gave out and he ordered the pint-sized troublemaker to get out of politics.

Mossadegh complied for three years, then, using his retreat in Karpur Abad, seventy-five miles from Tehran, as headquarters, he began another campaign. So, one morning, as he was walking in his garden with his seventeen-year-old daughter, Riza Shah's secret police suddenly appeared and, without a word, hauled him away. The poor girl was so frightened that she had a nervous collapse from which—it is said—she never recovered.

When Mossadegh was released from jail five years later, he couldn't walk. It took weeks of exercises before he was able to take a single step. Already ill before his arrest, his health was now permanently impaired. But he resumed his attacks on Riza Shah and was again arrested in 1938. It was on this occasion that the present Shah, feeling sorry for the ailing man, interceded with his father and had him pardoned.

Mossadegh spent the war years trying to regain his health. In 1944, he surfaced again, to propose a law forbidding any new oil concessions without a parliamentary vote. This move was triggered by the news that the U.S.S.R. had just obtained concessions to drill for oil 120 miles from Tehran. He was immediately accused of being in the pay of the British — a ridiculous notion since he was far too rich to be for sale.

Having taken on the Russians, he went after the British. He denounced their hold on Iran and demanded their departure. Going one step further, he formed the National Front. And despite the fact that the new party had only nine deputies, this handful of men, on the day after Razmara's assassination, was able to impose the law nationalizing oil. The chronic invalid, whose imminent death from starvation had been forecast for years (he subsisted on tea, milk and cookies), had risen like a phoenix from the ashes his opponents had heaped upon him.

Mohammed Riza, who thought he had appointed an old man ready for the grave, found himself faced with a whirlwind of energy. What had caused this new explosion? Oil, of course. And the stakes were enormous.

As early as 1870, the British had begun wooing the Shah, the tribal chieftains, and anyone else who was ready to sell Iran's soil to pay off his debts. In 1901, the Australian prospector William Knox d'Arcy won from the Shah the rights to all the oil in Iran — except for the Caspian provinces and Khorasan — for a period of sixty years. In other words, until 1961. In exchange, he paid 200,000 gold francs (about $40,000) and 16 percent of future profits, keeping the lion's share for himself. But at that time, oil meant nothing to the

Shah and the Persians. If those crazy British were willing to put up the money, it was proof of just how crazy they were. Besides, d'Arcy was unpleasantly surprised to find that when he started to prospect in the region his geologists claimed to be potentially the richest, he found that these lands were really under the control of the local chiefs, where his agreement with the Shah meant little or nothing. So new negotiations had to be started all over again.

The First Mining Rights Exploitation Company was formed in 1903. The initial wells were dug near Shashtar, as much because of the presence of "eternal flames" in the rudimentary wells dug by *naphtha* worshippers at the now ruined temples, as from any geological studies.

In 1904, d'Arcy sent George Reynolds to prospect in Bakhtiari country. D'Arcy had just lost £170,000 on dry wells in the northwest and was in desperate need of something productive. Near Masjed Soleyman, a village in the vicinity of Solomon's ancient temples, his geologists found what appeared to be good oil producing land. The region belonged to Soraya's grandfather, Sardar Assad, and Reynolds proposed to him that he be allowed to drill ten wells. He also wanted Assad's assurance — as he was the only one who could give it — that his engineers and workmen would be protected from brigands and looters. Sardar Assad, who knew something about Westerners, went him one better: he would offer him not only protection, but an association providing him 10 percent in royalties. But in 1904, the Europeans were still masters of the world. Reynolds refused the offer. After conferring with his superiors, however, negotiations were resumed two months later on the basis of Assad's 10 percent.

Unfortunately, Assad died the following year before the agreement could be signed, and his many sons (he had nine) could not agree on a common front. The British hardened their position and offered 3 percent. The agreement was signed and d'Arcy set up the Bakhtiari Oil Company with a capital of £400,000.

In 1909, the British Admiralty, which was responsible for the ships bringing equipment and for the security of its nationals, demanded and obtained the merger of all the prospecting groups into one company. This marked the birth of the famous Anglo-Persian Oil Company which in time became the Anglo-Iranian Company. It included d'Arcy's concession, 450,000 shares in the First Exploitation Company, and rights in the Bakhtiari Company by now allied with the Shell Transport Company. The wells near Shashtar were soon turning a profit where two hundred highly productive wells would be dug over a period of twenty years. Two of these became famous: F 7, disgorging—without pumping—7 million tons between 1911 and 1925, and B 17, producing one million tons in the first year of its exploitation.

The refinery at Abadan started functioning in 1911, thirty-six miles from an arm of the sea whose territorial waters were under Iraqi jurisdiction. By 1936, it was capitalized at £26 million, and in twenty years, its production increased from 43,000 tons to 7 million. By 1931, the Anglo-Persian Oil Company was realizing profits of £7 million of which the Iranians received a mere 16 percent.

Riza Shah, who had long been accusing the oil company of out and out robbery, suddenly demanded a revision of the contract. There were meetings, discussions, frayed tempers. But, as the Wall Street crash spread to Europe, the pound was devalued and Anglo-Persian's profits plummeted to £4 million. So, in 1932, Riza Shah went ahead and revoked the treaty of 1901. A new agreement was signed in 1933. The Anglo-Persian, now the Anglo-Iranian, had its concession extended to 1993, but its land was reduced by half, and the

Iranian share in the profits was raised to 20 percent, not counting the £1 million Iran received on signing the contract.

By 1936, production had passed 8 million tons, or 3.6 percent of world production, and the Iranian government was pocketing £3 million a year. This was manna for the construction of the Trans-Iranian railroad and the modernization of the country.

During this period, the northern provinces were under Russian influence. In March, 1916, Akarius Mefodievitch Khochtarian, a Georgian, had turned up in Tehran to ask for the northern oil concessions, and a contract was duly signed. In 1920, Khochtarian, who stubbornly refused to nationalize his holdings for the U.S.S.R.'s profit, sold his concession to Anglo-Persian which formed an affiliate, the North Persian Petroleum Company. In 1921, the Russians responded by signing a treaty which forbade Iran to sell former Russian concessions — retroactively — without the express permission of Moscow. The Anglo-Persian Company replied that this was irrelevant since Khochtarian was not a Russian but a Georgian, and Georgia had declared itself an independent republic. Soon after, Moscow annexed Georgia. That was the end of that. Khochtarian and the Armenian Calouste Gulbenkian, the notorious Mister Five Percent, became associated and founded a Paris company — with Moscow's authorization — to exploit the oil in the north.

One zone remained unclaimed: Khorasan in the east. Standard Oil won the race and bought the concession in 1921. The British were outraged and threatened to break off diplomatic relations. Very cleverly, the Americans — whom the British had bested at Mosul in Iraq — countered that they deserved compensation. So they cut the cake in two equal parts: The British would share the American oil in Khorasan, and the Americans the British oil in Iraq. Apparent reconciliation only. The British, refusing to admit defeat, talked the Iranian government into revoking the American contract.

The next year, there was a new development. Harry S. Sinclair, head of the Sinclair Consolidated Oil Corporation and chief competitor of Standard Oil, arrived in Tehran to have a look. His trump card was his excellent relations with the Russians. For $10 million in cash, he appropriated the concession which Anglo-Persian and Standard Oil thought they already owned. Such cheek called for the abandonment of all scruples. And, curiously enough, when Sinclair returned to America, a malodorous political-financial scandal broke over his head. The Persian government responded to this by declaring that it had been taken in by an unprincipled adventurer; it revoked the contract but kept the money. Sinclair wisely retreated to the wings, but again curiously, the American vice-consul, Major Robert Imbrie, was assassinated in the middle of a Tehran street. He had been seen making up to the Shah at the time of the Sinclair scandal.

That same year, the Americans returned to the fray in Baluchistan in the southeast, but under Russian pressure, the *majlis* passed a law forbidding all foreign concessions.

As the spirit of nationalism took hold, it naturally affected oil. In 1949, for the first time, Iran envisaged a national company – the Iranian Oil Company. At the same time, Anglo-Iranian was going into high gear. By 1950, seventy-five wells were producing an average of a thousand tons a day. Since 1911, Anglo-Iranian had extracted 250 million tons of oil from Persian soil; in 1950, it reached 30 million tons a year. Iran was now fourth in world production, after the United States, Venezuela and the U.S.S.R.

From this liquid gold, Iran earned roughly £16 million a

year. And by buying its own oil at a very low price, it was able to realize another £7 million in savings. Oil now represented almost half the annual budget. The revenues from Anglo-Iranian were five times that; in taxes alone, it provided Great Britain with £40 million.

Anglo-Iranian's shameless exploitation infuriated the Shah. But after a decade of unending struggle, he had learned that, first and foremost, a head of state must observe prudence and moderation. Of course he wanted to get back what the British were brazenly stealing, but it had to be done with tact and by working on the susceptibilities of a still powerful England.

When he made Mossadegh prime minister in 1951, the Shah exacted a promise that he would be prudent. Mossadegh complied, but in reality, he was determined to strike boldly and without advance notice. The day after his investiture on April 29, 1951, he pushed through the nationalization law. From that day on, all oil fields would belong to Iran. End of British domination.

Chaos was around the corner.

Chapter 14

THERE WAS NO OFFICIAL REACTION from Mohammed Riza after the vote. To condemn publicly something he privately approved of would be awkward. But to support Mossadegh openly might tie his hands in the future.

There was no lack of reaction from other quarters, however. The military, in particular, streamed into the palace, giving voice to their fears of Mossadegh. The Shah's regime was their natural ally, and they were afraid of an old democrat like Mossadegh. So Mohammed Riza decided to bide his time.

In Britain, the announcement of Iran's nationalization was greeted with shock and disbelief. "They can't do that to us!" the British ambassador to Iran exclaimed indignantly to a group of foreign correspondents. And, not surprisingly, the British decided to restore order with a show of power. The *Daily Express* headed its story: "Mossie takes over British petrol but the Navy comes to the rescue."

Too bad for Britain. Times had changed, and in Tehran, Mossadegh laughed with glee – which didn't prevent his fainting in the middle of Parliament. He was pummeled and given smelling salts, and when he came to, he announced: "I don't budge from here until I've won total victory."

A bed was installed in the committee room; he was brought his indispensable boxes of cookies, tea and bottles of milk. Iran was thrilled to discover that its hero was even more heroic than it thought. Mossadegh's star was rising to its zenith and the Shah began to grow uneasy.

There were exaggerations on both sides. In London, a kind of racism reared its head and people asked how anyone could take this crazy old fool seriously. In Tehran, it was a holy war against colonialism. Discussions flared into insults, threats into violence. The *ayatollah* Kashani rushed to support Mossadegh, summoning newsmen and announcing prophetically the birth of Pan-Islam and the creation of a Muslim army of 20 million men of which he would be the leader.

Doing him one better, Safavi, chief of the Fedayeen-Islam, woke up the foreign correspondents in the middle of the night and solemnly informed them that he had just finished a census of the men ready to die for him and they numbered 5123. He went on to organize meetings to prepare a crusade-in-reverse against London. He was particularly irate with Kashani whom he accused of betraying the cause of Islam, and let it be known that he headed the list of men to be liquidated.

Once again, the Shah had been overtaken by the Right.

Mossadegh and Kashani dispatched Safavi and his chief supporters to the dungeons of Ghars prison, north of Tehran (Escape from Ghars is impossible; Riza Shah saw to this when he had it built. His son still finds the prison useful.)

Once Safavi was out of the way, Mossadegh and Kashani found themselves faced with a Parliament sunk in gloom after its earlier euphoria. Had they gone too far too soon? To restore their spirits, Mossadegh hit on an inspired idea. He had one of his men break into Anglo-Iranian headquarters in Tehran and steal a list which its British director had kept scrupulously up to date. The list comprised the "gifts" made by Anglo-Iranian to a number of deputies, ministers and other Iranian politicians. It even included names of people close to the Shah. Parliament was once again united behind Mossadegh.

With the Labor Party in power in Britain, Iran's act of nationalization was accepted with a certain equanimity. Nationalization, after all, was a tenet of their party platform. As the Iranian flag was being hoisted over Anglo-Iranian headquarters in Khorramshahr near Abadan, the company made a peace offering: why not form *two* companies, one — an Iranian one — to oversee production in the fields, the other — Anglo-Iranian — to operate the refineries and the distribution of oil products. It proposed an immediate payment of £10 million, a monthly payment of £3 million from then on, and the transfer of its assets to the national Iranian company. Mossadegh called this flagrant robbery and brought negotiations to a halt.

Unable to suppress its colonial habits, Britain sent paratroopers to Cyprus, British troops based in Iraq massed on the Iranian border, the cruiser *Mauritius* dropped anchor off Abadan, while all tankers moored in the harbor were given orders to turn back, unload, and head for the open sea.

To make up for this return to gunboat diplomacy, Britain at the same time asked the International Court of Justice in The Hague to appoint an arbiter in the oil dispute. After two months of fruitless talks, President Truman sent Averell Harriman to Tehran to see if he could get the negotiations off dead center. As if to celebrate his arrival, the Tudeh party came out of hiding and staged a mammoth demonstration to protest America's intervention in the dispute. Between the airport and the city, Harriman's car was surrounded by a crowd armed with sticks, chanting anti-American slogans. A poster proclaimed "Ahriman Go Home!" Stunned by this reception, the American ambassador made straight for Mossadegh's yellow brick house two blocks from the royal palace. The prime minister received him on his famous iron bed with the red sheets, and burst into sobs.

Soon after, Richard Stokes, Lord Privy Seal and minister of supply in Britain, joined in the talks, arguing once again for the original proposal. To force Iran's hand, Britain withdrew all British personnel from Abadan. By the beginning of October, not a single British technician was left at the refineries and production had ceased. To make matters worse, Britain slapped on an economic blockade as well.

In the hope that another diplomatic arena might bring forth better results, Britain appealed to the United Nations and on September 30, the Security Council voted to examine Britain's complaint against Iran. Sir Gladwyn Jebb gave the British side: that Iran should be instructed to abide by the provisional ruling of the International Court which stated that the *status quo* must be observed pending a final settlement. What would Iran's argument be? Mossadegh announced that he would come and deliver it himself.

Many an expert in Iranian politics believes to this day that the Shah should not have let him go, and that the moment had come — together with a good excuse — to put an end to Mossadegh's capers. Why didn't the Shah act? Did he really lack the power? Or was he taking a calculated risk? Impossible to know. As with so many incidents in Iran's recent past, any discussion of the subject is taboo.

During this period, the Shah was politically inactive. Whether by choice or force of circumstance — the circumstance being Mossadegh — is hard to say. By way of compensation, he had Soraya. He was deeply in love, and even if she had not yet borne him a son, they were young and she had been a long time recovering from her typhoid. To make her happy, he finally accepted Jansen's plans for the remodeling of the palace, and she was delighted with the results. All the paneling, which had made the public rooms look like so many steamship cabins, was removed, and the walls were painted and decorated in Louis XVI style, as were the dining room, the three drawing rooms on the ground floor, and the two drawing rooms, two bedrooms and the Shah's study on the second, with of course a profusion of superb rugs.

To Sita, her wolfhound, and Tony and Pucky, two Skye terriers, was added a seal which a Caspian fishery gave her as a present.

"Where are we going to put the animal?" the Shah asked with some concern.

"Oh, very simple. We'll put it in the fountain in the conservatory," Soraya said.

"But that's fresh water. Seals need salt water."

"I'll fix that." And she emptied a salt shaker into the fountain.

Every day at noon, Soraya fed the seal herself, handing it fresh fish from the end of a fork. It got to the point where the seal would follow her through the palace, sliding on its wet fins. "After a while, the seal began to upset my sense of order—what there was of it," Soraya admitted. So a swimming pool was built expressly for the seal.

There were teas, cocktail parties and dinners. Their intimate circle was very gay. And always the jokes and games. When movies were being shown in the private projection room, Mohammed Riza liked to do imitations of dogs barking at the most touching moments in the film. When he was playing bridge, he slipped toy spiders and frogs into his partner's lap.

And he adored fancy dress balls. One night, he decided to go disguised as a lion. Soraya announced she was going as Madame de Pompadour, but at the last minute, without telling anyone, she changed costumes with a friend and went as Joan of Arc. During the ball, everyone bowed before the woman they took to be the empress. Only one man paid "Joan" any attention, and he flirted with her so boldly that she began to be annoyed. It was, of course, the Shah. Only he had recognized her.

Mossadegh's performance in New York was to be one of the most extraordinary ever recorded in the annals of international diplomacy.

The trip from Tehran to New York gave the tone for what was to follow at the United Nations. At seven AM on Sunday, October 7, Mossadegh and twenty advisers left the capital on a K.L.M. plane. A swarm of supporters crowded the airstrip chanting "Allah Akbar" (God is Great). The prime minister looked thinner and yellower than ever, and his nose kept running but he made no attempt to wipe it. Once in New York, Mossadegh was taken off the plane on a stretcher and placed in an ambulance which sped to New York Hospital on the East River.

On the seventeenth, Mossadegh was still unwell. On the nineteenth, the Security Council voted to postpone consideration of Britain's request until the International Court had ruled on its competence in this area. In other words, a clear rebuff to the British. Then, suddenly, "Old Mossie" was fully recovered, and pranced before a group of journalists assembled for a press conference.

Four days later, Mossadegh had lunch with President Truman in Washington, and then met with the Secretary of State,

Mohammed Mossadegh, then Premier of Iran, in New York, 1951.
Larry Morris/NYT Pictures

Dean Acheson. What did he want? Money of course. But all
he got for his pains was a measly loan of seven and a half
million dollars—a pittance. By now, the situation in Iran was
catastrophic. Government officials had not been paid for
weeks, the military's pay had been reduced to the equivalent
of $40 a month. The Iranian employees of Anglo-Iranian had

been laid off, the country was on the verge of bankruptcy. On October 31, new disorders erupted in Tehran.

Mossadegh had to return. (The American doctors had found him in excellent health except for shortness of breath.) So he packed his bags at the Shoreham Hotel and was carried to the airport. But when he caught sight of Dean Acheson among the officials come to see him off, he ran to him with the agility of a goat.

On his return to Tehran, he was greeted with hysterical joy. Then began an insoluble imbroglio: to find money, Mossadegh floated a loan of 2 billion rials and started printing money. Bills in circulation rose by 14 percent. More inflation. Yet his popularity was undiminished. The *majlis* were reelected, with a plebiscite scheduled for early 1953. And he made the most of his victory. He asked for six months of absolute power to put the country back on its feet. This was granted him. But when, to make his position unassailable, he demanded in July the portfolio of War Minister, the Shah saw that at last he was in a position to fling a noose around his intractable prime minister's neck. He refused. Mossadegh threw a fit, fainted, came to, went into hysterics, and fainted again. The next day, he resigned.

The Shah immediately called in Ahmad Qavam who had the *majlis*'s backing. Qavam asked for the army's support and the Shah promised him he would have it.

Unfortunately, he had underestimated Mossadegh. (Not for nothing had *Time* magazine named the prime minister "Man of the Year" for 1951.) He too had been preparing his next move. For three days, Tehran was overrun by rioting mobs. While Kashani was launching an attack on Qavam in the press, the army went into action. There were pitched battles all over town and tanks gunned down the mob. Dozens were killed, hundreds wounded. Making improvised flags out of the bloodstained shirts of the dead and wounded, the people shouted for revenge and the return of Mossadegh.

After four days of pandemonium, Qavam offered the Shah his resignation, and the next day, the *majlis* voted Mossadegh's reinstatement by a vote of 61 to 3. When they emerged from Parliament, the crowd broke into wild applause.

Mossadegh immediately set off for the Shah's summer palace where a tense interview took place. The prime minister made little effort to hide his joy. The *Journal de Teheran* reported laconically: "Dr. Mossadegh has agreed to form a cabinet and offered the king his views on the country's affairs." The extent of the Shah's defeat was reflected in his message, delivered that same evening over the radio:

"I congratulate the Iranian nation with my whole heart for our success at the Court of The Hague. I wish to express my gratitude and thanks for the efforts of His Excellency, Dr. Mossadegh, the President of the Council, and the entire Iranian nation which collaborated in the affair. This victory is an important step toward our eventual success and the realization of Iran's national goals."

The newspapers, which had been throwing bouquets at Qavam, now did a quick about-face and accused him of pro-British and anti-Iranian sympathies, and of firing on innocent people.

Mossadegh lost no time. He named himself war minister, exiled Djamal Emami, president of the *majlis* and replaced him with Kashani, and he pardoned Khalil Tahmassebi, Razmara's assassin, "for ridding the country of a traitor." Then he purged the army, cashiering ninety top-ranking officers, outlawed Qavam and confiscated all his possessions. Finally, emboldened by Naguib and Nasser's ejection of Farouk from the Egyptian throne, he turned on the Shah. He began by taking over the crown's budget and helping himself to the revenues owed the Pahlevis. Next, he exiled dozens of the king's friends and—supreme outrage—exiled the Queen Mother, Shams and Ashraf, and the Shah's brother Ali Riza. Then he moved on the Shah himself, infiltrating the palace with informers and tapping the king's telephone. "I've muzzled him!" he announced triumphantly. And when Truman and Churchill (the Tories were back in power) offered to ease the terms of the oil settlement, Mossadegh's response was to break off diplomatic relations with Britain and ask for a payment of £49 million.

Never had Mohammed Riza been so close to the abyss. He was virtually a prisoner in his palace while Mossadegh alternated between fits of depression and explosions of rage. Everyone trembled before him.

Then, suddenly, the Shah's luck began to turn. Painful as it had been to see an Iranian play the clown in New York, the king was in a way secretly relieved. The more ridiculous Mossadegh appeared, the better he himself looked. And it seemed that the Iranian people were beginning to grow weary of "Old Mossie" and his ways. In addition, Kashani was finding the Tudeh far too meddlesome, the perilous financial situation was causing great unrest in the business community, and the bazaar was once again at the boil. And the oil problem remained unsolved.

Mossadegh tried desperately to break the British oil blockade and to get the wells and refineries going again. The storage tanks at Abadan were full to the brim, but nobody dared tap them. Anglo-Iranian was too powerful. Only the Italians challenged the blockade, but after Enrico Mattei, head of Agencia Italiana dei Petroli, met with Lord Strathalmond, president of Anglo-Iranian, he abruptly changed gears. Rumor had it that his palms had been well greased.

One small Italian company forced the blockade and filled

two of its tankers at Abadan, but the first ship was stopped at Aden and the second at Naples. After that, nothing moved.

The truth is that international oil circles had learned that there was no point in challenging the British. England could get along very well without Iranian oil simply by increasing production elsewhere. The Near-East — Kuweit, Saudi Arabia, Iraq and Bahrain — would produce 135 million tons in 1954 to Iran's 88 million in 1950.

His back to the wall, Mossadegh turned to Calouste Gulbenkian. This was licking the enemy's boots. Gulbenkian had strongly advised the Iranians not to nationalize Anglo-Iranian; in retaliation, when he came to power, one of Mossadegh's first acts was to withdraw Gulbenkian's diplomatic passport. But such was the prime minister's need that he asked Gulbenkian's son, Nubar, for help. "Early one morning at the Ritz," as Nubar tells it, "I received a telephone call from Tehran asking me to take charge of the sale of the whole of the Iranian production. The caller offered me almost any financial inducement or social advancement I might care to name. . . . I promised to consider the offer. . . . I went on 'considering' it for some three years until Mossadegh was finished, the Shah was back, the consortium had been formed and oil was flowing again, by which time, of course, the offer was void."

The last straw was when General Eisenhower, the newly elected American President, sided with Britain and announced that Iran would not get a dollar until "a reasonable and judicious agreement was reached between Tehran and London on the subject of oil."

Mossadegh panicked. For weeks he tried to find some way out, and not finding it, now resorted to a last-ditch effort to arouse popular opinion. He decided to exile the Shah. On February 26, 1953, he went to the White Palace and ordered the king to leave the country — with an allowance of $11,000 for traveling expenses. The Shah had to give in. Mossadegh was still too popular and so was the nationalization of oil. Officially, the Shah would be leaving "for reasons of health."

On the eve of their departure, a messenger from the *ayatollah* Kashani came secretly to Soraya, saying, "Your Majesty, the *ayatollah* begs you to use all your influence to make the Shah change his mind about leaving."

When Mossadegh arrived the next day to bid the king goodbye, there was a sudden commotion outside the palace. Everyone ran to the windows. Thousands of people had gathered below, some even clinging to the branches of trees.

"Please leave the palace as quickly as possible," Mossadegh told the Shah with ill-concealed delight. "It's too dangerous for you here."

Suddenly, the crowd broke into a chant: "Long live the Shah! Down with Mossadegh!"

Mohammed Riza was astonished. Mossadegh began to tremble . . . then fainted.

When he came to, Soraya took the old man by the arm.

"Follow me," she said, leading him to a back door. "You can reach the street by crossing the property next door. No one will see you."

Once Mossadegh was gone, the Shah asked for a loudspeaker and went out on the balcony to address the crowd, most of them supporters of Kashani. His voice hoarse with emotion, he promised to stay.

"Practical as always," Soraya said later, "I was wondering what was to become of our luggage which I had sent to the border by car." (They were to travel by land to Beirut, then by plane to Europe.) "Fortunately, the car returned the next day. It had run into a blizzard and been forced back. 'You see,' the Shah said to me, 'even the skies meant us to stay!'"

Mossadegh got his revenge two days later. He organized a counter-demonstration and arrested seventy officers. In a radio address, he renewed his attacks on the Shah, stating that he would let him rule but not govern. Rioting immediately broke out between supporters of Mossadegh and the Shah. The new military governor of Tehran was kidnapped in the middle of the night, his mangled body found the next morning in a cemetery on the outskirts of the city. General Zahedi who was accused of instigating the massacre, sought asylum in the Senate, proclaimed his innocence and disappeared. Mossadegh promptly dissolved the Senate.

Chapter 15

ON JULY 6, 1953, a tanned, thirty-seven-year-old American presented himself to the customs officer at Qaar-E-Shirin on the border between Iraq and Iran.

Kermit Roosevelt did not try to hide his identity. He presented his real papers, although the son of the former U.S. President Theodore Roosevelt and cousin of Franklin D. Roosevelt was in fact an agent of the Central Intelligence Agency. (The C.I.A. had been organized under Truman in 1947 at the start of the Cold War for the purpose of setting up intelligence services throughout the world.) Kim Roosevelt was a specialist in Middle-Eastern affairs and had just been given an assignment by Allan Dulles, head of the C.I.A. and brother of the secretary of state, John Foster Dulles. His mission was to get rid of Mossadegh. The United States had made its choice: it would back the Shah.

The decision to intervene was based on the theory, developed by C.I.A. agents in Iran, that if the country and the army found itself in a situation where it had to choose between the Shah and Mossadegh, it would choose the Shah. The C.I.A.'s mission was to create that situation.

Churchill and Eden were consulted and gave their approval. The C.I.A.'s idea was not to mount a military operation but to organize and coordinate resistance to Mossadegh. Its role was made easier by the fact that the Soviets seemed to be improvising in Iran, rather than following an established plan.

Perhaps Kim Roosevelt was taking a chance by using his real name. But he knew that Iranian customs were not very exacting and, furthermore, he noticed with some amusement that the confused inspector had mixed up two lines: where he should have written in Roosevelt's name, he inscribed "scar on the left cheek," and since the Iranian form had no line for "physical characteristics," his name was never entered.

A few days later, Kim Roosevelt went to work in his hide-out in Tehran. Only three people knew where he was: General Zahedi, his son Ardeshir, and the Shah. Zahedi and the Shah had already agreed on their plan of operation: for the time being, the Shah would stay in the wings and let Zahedi act for him. Mossadegh was watching him too closely, but Zahedi could act because he was still operating underground.

Roosevelt's initial meeting was with Zahedi, who arrived at his house crouched behind the back seat of a car. The first thing he wanted to know was what armed forces the Shah could count on. Very few, Zahedi was forced to admit: The army was increasingly infiltrated by Mossadegh's men, and dozens of officers belonged to the Tudeh. Roosevelt asked for a census of the loyalists. They were pathetically few: maybe fifty officers at the most, and as for the rank and file, not more than eight or nine hundred men.

Applying the techniques of wartime resistance groups in Europe, Roosevelt decided that he himself would see only a very small number of people. These would then work on their friends in ever expanding circles, so that no single link would know any but the one directly preceding him. It was slow and laborious work, but it finally began to bear fruit. By the end of the month, Kim felt he could count on a small nucleus. They would even have some tanks, if it came to that.

The next step was to convince the Shah to make the first move. In other words, to remove Mossadegh by *firman* — which was perfectly legal — and to name Zahedi in his place. But even though this was exactly what the Shah had long wanted to do, convincing him to take the step turned out to be very difficult. He was in a very depressed state, taking barbiturates to help him sleep, his hair was turning white, he had stopped eating. He was smoking three packs of cigarettes a day and his hands trembled visibly. The truth was that he was in no condition to make a decision. He didn't trust the people around him, and even Soraya found their life in Tehran hardly worth fighting for.

As he sat brooding in his study, his reluctance to act was part mystical, part calculated. If he waited, perhaps the people would turn against Mossadegh on their own initiative. Anyway, what would happen would happen, so why interfere? Roosevelt kept protesting America's unconditional support and promising new floods of dollars the moment Mossadegh was removed. But the Shah's intimate circle kept warning him to trust no one, that he had too often been betrayed.

Zahedi, who knew the Shah well, also knew that the only person he would listen to was his sister Ashraf. He was certain that the mettlesome princess would do anything to help restore the Pahlevis' power. But unfortunately, Ashraf was still in exile, currently in Cannes with her husband. She must be made to come to Tehran, but how? In addition to sending her into exile, Mossadegh had made her return virtually impossible by accusing her of owing the Agricultural Bank 5 million rials — which, with interest, had increased to 6 million.

"No problem," Roosevelt told Zahedi. "Once she's back in Tehran, all she has to do is say she's here to sell off some property to pay off her debts . . ."

So Ashraf arrived on July 25 in an Air France plane as Madame Chafik — her married name. She went straight to her younger brother Gholam Riza's house, and appeared at the Shah's that same evening. The meeting was stormy; outside the study, people could hear brother and sister screaming at each other. The next day, they were at it again. That same day, Allan Dulles, who was in Switzerland on vacation, told newsmen that the Communist threat in Iran was growing to alarming proportions. As if to bear him out, the new Russian ambassador, Anatoly Laurentiev, who had just arrived in Tehran, was known to be a hard-liner and was used in situations that called for toughness rather than subtlety. He had been ambassador in Belgrade when Tito had his first brush with the Kremlin, and his offensive manner had made him very unpopular with the Yugoslavs. A Yugoslav diplomat later asked Molotov: "Why did you send us such a stupid brute as ambassador?" To which Molotov replied: "Laurentiev may be stupid but he's a very good Bolshevik."

Five days after her arrival, Ashraf left Iran for Geneva. Short though her stay was, she had managed to bring her brother around. So Kim Roosevelt decided to seize the opportunity and sent for his "bulldozer," General Schwarzkopf.

The general was no longer in Tehran, his work with the *gendarmerie* having long since terminated. But he was close by, traveling in Libya, Syria and Pakistan on what was officially termed a "pleasure trip," and was ready to come on short notice. Schwarzkopf was very close to Zahedi, having worked hand in glove with him for many years. He also knew the Shah well.

He arrived on August 1, "just to see a few old friends," he told the press, which was perfectly true, his old friends being Zahedi and the Shah.

He found the king's state bewildering. Momentarily buoyed by his sister's visit, the Shah had sunk back into a deep depression as soon as she left. "Everything is finished," he told the general. "Your coming is a welcome expression of friendship, but I have no illusions. I'm a beaten man."

Schwarzkopf spent two days trying to shore up the Shah's morale, but he finally gave up and left for Pakistan. Now Zahedi and Roosevelt had only themselves to count on.

As soon as Laurentiev had presented his credentials to the Shah, he was summoned by Mossadegh to begin discussions on a political and commercial treaty between Russia and Iran. The Tudeh gloated, while Kashani's supporters cried treason. The usual demonstrations and scuffles broke out. Mossadegh's position worsened. He changed his mind about the treaty and called Laurentiev back.

Later versions had it that Mossadegh was in cahoots with the Russians, and that because of his hatred of the British and Americans, he was ready to throw his country into the maw of the Soviet wolf. This was not entirely true. Even though he flirted with the Tudeh, Mossadegh was afraid of the Russians. So he negotiated lamely while waiting for the referendum he had demanded to decide the fate of Parliament. When the results were in, the vote in Tehran alone was 155, 544 to 115 in favor of dissolving Parliament.

Both sides took this as a hopeful sign: to Mossadegh, it meant that he might now get a new chamber totally subservient to him; to the conspirators, the vote revealed a profound dissatisfaction with the status quo. For the Shah, it was like a shot in the arm. And there was even better news to follow. Kim Roosevelt informed him that General Gilhenshah, chief of the air force, had come to offer his services unasked. Gilhenshah was a prime acquisition: not only were his pilots of unswerving loyalty, but he had great influence at the officers' club and in the capital's drawing rooms. Getting him was as good as having half the army.

Then Mohammed Riza's informers brought him the heady news that the bazaar was becoming critical of Mossadegh and his flirtation with the Russians, and that disenchantment was growing in the salons, the chic bars, even at the two reigning dressmakers — Marthe's and Ninon Harainan — hotbeds of society gossip.

Finally the Shah decided to act. On August 10, a communiqué from the Ministry of Foreign Affairs announced that Soviet-Iranian discussions had resumed. The next morning, Mohammed Riza and Soraya took a plane to Ramsar on the Caspian Sea from which they intended to go to Kalardachte in the mountains, the excuse being Soraya's delicate health — which was always plausible in her case.

In his pocket, the Shah had a *firman* that Zahedi and Roosevelt had pressed on him. The decree would remove Mossadegh and replace him with Zahedi. He was to give the decree to Colonel Nemetollah Nassiri, the commander of the Imperial Guard, once they arrived in Kalardachte, and the colonel would deliver it to Mossadegh in Tehran. As the Shah was out of the city, Mossadegh would have difficulty arresting him. And Zahedi, who had installed himself in a suburban house guarded by armed supporters disguised as water carriers and grape peddlers, would use Mossadegh's moment of indecision to prepare his coup.

Everything depended on the element of surprise. Then, somewhere along the line, there was a leak. Mossadegh was informed of the plot. On the evening of August 15, the drama unfolded as loyal officers arrested the foreign minister and minister of transport, occupied the central telephone exchange, arrested two generals. But what they did not know was that at five o'clock, Mossadegh had summoned General Riahy to inform him that an attempt at a coup was imminent.

As a result, when Nassiri arrived at Mossadegh's house at ten-thirty PM, decree in hand, he found himself face to face with the commander of the Second Alpine Brigade who promptly arrested him. The coup was over.

Warned in time, Zahedi managed to escape, but by dawn, most of the conspirators had been caught, including Ernest Perron whom the Shah had left behind at the palace to serve as his eyes and ears.

Early the next morning, Mossadegh went on the radio and, his voice quavering with emotion, announced; "Last night, a coup d'état was launched against the regime. Most of the traitors are now behind bars. Only Zahedi and a small group of men got away. I offer 500,000 rials for Zahedi's capture. Death to all traitors!"

With that, the entire press came down on the Shah, with the evening paper, *Bakhtar-Emruz*, setting the tone: "The Shah is of the same stuff as the fifty or sixty rajahs the British created in India when they occupied that country. He is for sale to foreigners. His court surpasses anything in Farouk's court. It is the enemy of all free men and patriots and all those struggling for freedom and independence."

There was panic at Kalardachte. Just before he was arrested, Ernest Perron had called the Shah and advised him to flee as quickly as possible. With what little luggage they had brought for their short stay in the mountains, the royal couple returned to Ramsar where the Shah's Beechcraft—if it hadn't been seized by Mossadegh's men—would be waiting for them. Happily, it was still there, with its pilot and two aides.

"It's all over," the Shah told them. "We have to leave immediately. Destination Baghdad." And they took off, leaving one aide behind to arrange for their possessions.

On August 16, in the blinding light of noon, an unidentified twin-engine plane appeared above the airport at Baghdad. It did not announce itself and made no attempt to communicate with the control tower. The airport was crowded, for the young king of Iraq was expected home any minute from a tour of inspection.

The Beechcraft made a rapid descent and taxied to a far corner of the airfield. A jeepful of angry police raced over, then sped back, squealing to a stop in front of the airport manager's office. An employee leaped to the phone and called the *sayyid* Khalil Kenna, the foreign minister, who was at the airport to greet the king. Breathless with excitement, the employee told him: "Excellency, an Iranian plane has just landed. There are three men and a woman in it. None of them will give us their names. But when they learned His Majesty was expected, they said it was very urgent that they speak with him. What should I do?"

Khalil Kenna jumped into the jeep with the manager and they in turn raced over to the plane. When the minister looked in the door, he was flabbergasted: the man sitting next to the pilot was the Shah of Iran.

"I request asylum in your country," the Shah said, "but only for a few days. I have not abdicated." And he introduced his pilot and aide. Then, in a weary voice, he added: "My departure was entirely unplanned."

Glancing toward the back of the plane, Kenna could see that it was indeed true. Clothes had been thrown over the seats, Soraya, in a brown linen dress, sat slumped in a corner seat looking pale and exhausted, and in the rear among some suitcases, he recognized a large diplomatic pouch and a jewel case.

"So Mossadegh has won," Kenna said to himself. But as a good diplomat who knew that, regardless of who was in power, his country must remain on good terms with its neighbors, he respectfully inquired after the Shah's wishes.

"Should I inform your ambassador in Baghdad?"

"No, thank you," the Shah replied, knowing that the Iranian ambassador to Iraq was one of Mossadegh's men.

"May I offer your Majesty Rihaab Palace during your stay? It is the official residence for government guests."

"Whatever you say," the Shah said with a shrug.

An hour later, the fugitives left the airport in an official limousine accompanied by a motorcycle escort. On their arrival, they were greeted by an honor guard. Two hours later, King Faisal was announced. Soraya turned to Kenna. "How can I receive the King looking like this, without a hat or gloves?"

Kenna reassured her: "His Majesty knows you haven't come from a fashion show."

The following day, it was all over the world press: "End of the monarchy." "The fall of the Shah of Iran." "The Shah has lost his throne."

Chapter 16

IT WAS A VERY NERVOUS AND ANGRY SHAH who addressed the reporters filling the reception room at Rihaab Palace. He almost shouted: "No, I have not lost my throne. No, Mossadegh has not won."

But the reporters were skeptical. They could already see him joining King Farouk on Capri. But he didn't go to Capri, he went to Rome. He had hoped to stay longer in Baghdad, but the Iranian ambassador demanded his extradition. The king refused to grant it, but when the Shah learned of his ambassador's treachery, he decided to leave Iraq. Before going, however, he revealed what was not yet known in Tehran: that he had dismissed Mossadegh and replaced him with General Zahedi.

Zahedi was almost totally unknown outside Iran. But now his photographs were in all the papers, and something of his background began to come to light. A tall robust man with a craggy face, he was a rich landowner, great hunter, horseman, poker player, and spoke fluent English, French and Turkish. He had been in the Cossack brigade and had lost four ribs fighting the rebels in Azerbaijan in 1921. His bravery was brought to Riza Shah's attention and he promoted him to brigadier-general at the age of twenty-five. A year later, he captured an elusive Kurd outlaw and was rewarded with the order of Zolfaghar (the Sword of Ali), Iran's highest military decoration which only three men have received—one of them the Shah. Riza Shah then appointed him military governor of Isfahan until his pro-German sympathies caused him to be arrested by the British. When his house was searched, Fitzroy MacLean, the British agent, found a collection of German automatic weapons, opium, an impressive array of silk shirts, letters from German agents who had parachuted into the area, and a file—complete with photographs—of every prostitute in Isfahan.

Freed after the war, Zahedi held various provincial posts, then became minister of the interior under Mossadegh. But Zahedi's passionate anti-communism was bound to collide with Mossadegh's pro-Tudeh acrobatics. When the inevitable rupture came, the general began his clandestine activities on behalf of the Shah.

On the night of the abortive coup, Zahedi escaped to Kim Roosevelt's house in Shemiran. The atmosphere was gloomy. Zahedi announced: "We're finished." But Roosevelt was not the kind to give up easily. With his long experience as a secret agent, he knew how often even the most desperate situations could be reversed.

Their first step must be to regroup the conspirators, then keep a sharp eye out for anything they could turn to their advantage. And Zahedi knew that Mossadegh's skittishness might well lead him to commit some blunder. Meanwhile, Roosevelt asked Zahedi to give him the Shah's *firman*. He would have thousands of copies printed and distribute them at the opportune time.

August 16 was the decisive day. First, the Tudeh papers

threw off their masks and proclaimed: "We are in power . . ." "Mossadegh will not betray us . . ." "We demand the immediate establishment of a republic and the public trial of the Shah." Then, rumors began to spread that Mossadegh was seeing too much of Laurentiev. Desperate to hold on to his power, the old man seemed ready to sell out to the Russians to escape the Tudeh's embrace. And when Loy Henderson asked to be received by Mossadegh, he was sent packing. This caused further consternation among the prime minister's moderate supporters.

Then came a spate of really good news: four hundred cadets at the military academy in Akdassieh announced they were going on a hunger strike to protest the insults to their king; in the bazaar, the *mullah* Bebamani, an assistant to Kashani, was going around inveighing against the Red peril and the imminent death of Islam; and lastly, the chief of the garrison in Kermanshah, one Teymur Bakhtiar, indicated he was ready to move on Tehran to help Zahedi.

The following day, a piece of information came to light which Mossadegh had tried to suppress, namely that two days earlier, Riza Shah's tomb at Rey had been desecrated. In the wake of this revelation, Tudeh militants were beaten up, and the priests in the mosques consigned the authors of the sacrilege to eternal damnation.

That afternoon, Roosevelt was visited by an arresting young man who went by the name of "Brainless." A powerfully built athlete, he was the leader of a group of young roughnecks who divided their time between playing Zur-Khaneh and roaming the streets looking for trouble. "Brainless" was soon to prove that his nickname was undeserved. After some obligatory hand-wringing over the fate of his beloved sovereign, he quickly came to the point: he and three or four hundred of his buddies were at Roosevelt's disposal; they would go after whomever they were told to, even with guns if someone provided the guns. On condition, of course, that they were properly rewarded.

The bargain was quickly sealed, Roosevelt taking a large bundle of rials out of his special funds, the remainder to be paid after the victory. "Brainless" immediately set off for the southern end of town to conscript his troops. That same evening, Zahedi was assured that he could count on enough soldiers and tanks to make another attempt. The coup was scheduled for two days later.

During the interval, there was work to do. Henderson took on the assignment of stirring up a wave of popular enthusiasm for the Shah. On the morning of the eighteenth, he drove to the Bank Melli—the state bank—in a car stuffed with dollars, estimated to be $400,000. The Bank Melli, being very uneasy about Mossadegh's relations with the Russians, was eager to oblige. On the return trip, the dollars had been replaced with rials and tomans (ten-rial notes).

On that same day, the Shah and Soraya arrived in Rome in a private English plane chartered in Baghdad. They looked worn and disheveled, and when they saw the mob of newsmen bearing down on them, Soraya fought her way through them, while the Shah told the reporters he had nothing to say. He would call a press conference at a future date.

The Iranian ambassador in Rome took the opportunity to go for a swim at Ostia, not even leaving the keys to the Shah's own car, left in his care on a previous visit.

When they arrived at the Hotel Excelsior, a burly policeman was waiting by the elevator. He bowed and said he was responsible for their security. Khatami, the Beechcraft's pilot, helped with the bags, the Shah carried four tennis rackets and a pair of shoes, and Soraya two large alligator handbags and some underwear slung over her arm. Her first act on reaching their room was to telephone a couturier and order a dozen summer dresses.

Reporters and curious bystanders waited in vain for the king to come down. He had dinner sent to their rooms, and spent the evening listening to the radio: Fatemi had given an inflammatory speech and the crowd had booed at the mention of the Shah's name; he called for the hanging of all Pahlevis and the proclamation of a republic. Then thousands of demonstrators surged through the streets, breaking into shops and throwing pictures of the Shah on bonfires.

"This time it's really over," the Shah said to Soraya. (He was saying little else these days.)

"Where will we go?" she asked.

"To America. We'll all go. I'll buy a farm."

At almost the same moment, Loy Henderson was on his way to see Mossadegh once again. This time the old man received him in bed with a weak smile.

"All right," Henderson said, "call in the Tudeh. You know what that means." The American ambassador reminded the prime minister of the risk he was running. Did he really want to see Russian tanks in the streets of Tehran? If that were to happen, the three thousand American advisers would leave Iran immediately. The old man, already worried, was easily brought around. He agreed to one last gamble: he wouldn't tell the Tudeh about the projected coup (he had no idea it was scheduled for the next day) and let the devil take the hindmost. If the conspirators were beaten without Tudeh help, then Mossadegh would have won out against both the Shah's supporters and Russia's. If he lost, well, he lost.

Not long after Henderson's departure, Mossadegh's telephone rang. It was Laurentiev. His spies had just informed him of his American colleague's visit. What had transpired? What did Henderson want? He was disturbed, and his questions were searching.

Mossadegh was evasive — it was nothing important.

Back at Kim Roosevelt's, Henderson told him the results of his visit and the two men added up their assets. This time, they could move. Zahedi arrived, and he agreed. His emissaries left to give the go-ahead to the men in the loyalist barracks. "Brainless" was told to be ready.

Now there was nothing to do but wait — and hope.

The next morning, while preparations for the coup were under way, Radio-Tabriz broadcast the astounding news that the Shah had dismissed Mossadegh. The fat was in the fire. And the Tudeh must not be given time to gather its forces.

As embassy officials, most of whom lived in Shemiran, started for town, they were surprised to see small groups of Iranians, young people mostly, slipping ten rial bills bearing Mohammed Riza's portrait under the windshield wipers of passing cars as they shouted "Hurrah for the Shah!" People began to cluster about them, their hands outstretched.

"Shout with us, 'Hurrah for the Shah!'" Those who did received a bill.

Within an hour, all the avenues converging on Parliament Square were swarming with excited people waving ten-rial bills and shouting to the Shah's glory. Members of the Tudeh grappled with the demonstrators, snatched the bills and tore them up. Fights broke out between the Shah's supporters and Mossadegh's, the latter carrying rifles, with the guns of their tanks and machine guns trained on the crowd.

At about ten o'clock, a weird procession came marching out of the bazaar: three to four hundred men — mountebanks, jugglers, wrestlers, clowns — wove through the crowd as they made for Parliament. Then they suddenly formed into small groups, removed their disguises, took out guns, revolvers and clubs, and bore down on the ministries where they attacked officials and guards, forced their way into buildings and occupied offices, shoving their occupants out and locking the doors.

Mossadegh's forces were soon alerted and fanned out into the city. While newly fledged orators climbed on the pedestals of vandalized statues and called on the people to rise up against Mossadegh and bring back the Shah, others argued with the soldiers, begging them not to betray their oath of loyalty to their king and to lay down their arms.

Suddenly, a tank appeared rumbling through the crowd. Which side was it on? The answer came quickly as a man climbed through the hatch and down onto the street. It was Zahedi—in full dress uniform. The crowd separated into two groups, each facing the other: on one side, Fatemi, surrounded by his soldiers and the police, on the other, the people to whom the C.I.A. rials had been distributed, watching, as ready to follow Fatemi as Zahedi.

Zahedi walked slowly into the no-man's-land, with only his son Ardeshir at his side. The rifles and machine guns were pointed squarely at them as, step by step, he approached the soldiers. The only sound was the distant sputter of gunfire. All of a sudden, close to Fatemi, an officer threw his cap in the air and shouted: "Hurrah for Zahedi! God protect the Shah!"

Five minutes later, Zahedi was being carried in triumph through a mob in which soldiers had merged with demonstrators, both shouting slogans for the Shah. He was carried to staff headquarters where his first act was to order the arrest of Riahy. Fatemi had meanwhile disappeared.

On that same August 19, the Shah and Soraya went shopping on the Via Condotti. He bought some sport clothes, she ordered three dresses at Emilio Schuberth's and went to several shoe stores. At one o'clock they returned to the Excelsior and had lunch in the dining room: shrimp cocktail and cold chicken. They were drinking their coffee when a young man charged up to their table, waving a piece of paper. He was a reporter from the Associated Press and he had news for the Shah. He handed the king the telex he had just received which read: "From Tehran: Mossadegh defeated. Imperial troops in control of situation. General Zahedi named Prime Minister on Shah's orders."

As he read the telex, the Shah grew very pale. Soraya rose to her feet to read it over his shoulder and promptly burst into tears. At long last, the Shah looked up and, taking in the dozen people who had gathered around the table, said in a voice choked with emotion: "I knew they loved me!" and he added: "It's a revolution, but a just and honorable revolution. At last we have a legal government. Everything will be better from now on."

Then he turned to his wife and said with a smile: "We can go home now." And they went up to their rooms.

Later in the afternoon, Ashraf blew in in a state of wild excitement. She had been at Juan-les-Pins when she heard the news of her brother's flight. There was a general strike on in France—no planes or trains were moving. But she managed to cajole a young Frenchman into driving her to Rome. When she arrived at the border, she realized she had left her passport behind, but made such a fuss that customs let her through.

Yet, despite the good news, the Shah remained reserved. To the reporters he had admitted to his apartment, he said, passing his tongue over his dry lips:

"I wanted you to come so that I could thank you for the sympathy you have shown me during these critical hours. I am now awaiting an answer to the cable I sent General Zahedi. As soon as I receive it, I will be leaving." He stopped for a moment, then continued: "I know I haven't played much of a role in the struggle. I was far away and under surveillance. I wanted to avoid bloodshed. That's why I left my country."

In Tehran, the loyalist troops were taking command, meeting almost no opposition as they spread out through the city. Everywhere the royal flag was being hoisted and pictures of the Shah put back in place. The army had carried the day; the mob had only added a note of spontaneity to what was essentially a military exercise.

The C.I.A. analysts took the view that Mossadegh's government was disintegrating of itself and that their intervention had only speeded things up. But there was always the chance that the Tudeh might have seized power. (The C.I.A.'s role in the coup was to remain a secret for many years and became known only through the indiscretions of certain top men in the agency.)

Not surprisingly, Mossadegh still refused to admit defeat. In his frustration, he turned his house into a fortress, and when an emissary from Zahedi arrived carrying a white flag to ask Mossadegh to give himself up, he was greeted with a salvo of gunfire. At 2:00 in the morning, Mossadegh went in search of Fatemi, but he had fled. At 3:00 AM, the battle began in earnest, and continued, with casualties on both sides, until the house was completely surrounded. Inside, his officers urged Mossadegh to surrender. He refused. When an officer tied a white shirt to a broom and held it outside the window, Mossadegh yanked it away.

"I didn't ask you to surrender," he said. "I only wanted you here to make sure they didn't loot my house when they entered." Then he ran back to his room and flung himself on his bed.

Not long after, two Sherman tanks pulled up and started shooting at the house. With a theatrical gesture, a deputy friend of Mossadegh put his revolver to his temple, but the prime minister snatched it from him. Then he asked for his coat, put it on over his pyjamas, went down to the courtyard behind his house, climbed the wall with the help of a ladder, ran across the garden of the house next door, and kept on running until he reached the cellar of the minister of posts' house.

The Shah had to wait until dawn for Zahedi's telegram. Yes, the king could return, but Soraya was advised to stay in Europe until things calmed down. Later that morning, the Shah took her to a jeweler's and bought her several diamonds.

When he got back to the hotel, the Iranian ambassador was waiting, full of contrition. The Shah refused to see him. Then he paid his hotel bill (he did not need to use the blank checks endorsed by a rich Jewish businessman from Tehran who had given him the keys to his car as well). The next morning, he left on a chartered K.L.M. Constellation. It had taken him twenty-four hours to find a plane. No one was willing to fly the Shah to Tehran. Too risky.

Once in the plane, he relaxed and sat in his shirtsleeves among the reporters he had invited to accompany him. Over Greece, they opened bottles of champagne. This time, in Baghdad, the Iranian ambassador rushed to pay homage. Leaving the Constellation to the press, the Shah spent the night in Baghdad. The next morning—it was now August 22 —he put on his air marshall's uniform (he had it sent expressly from Tehran), and took the controls of his Beechcraft for the flight back to the capital.

By 9:00 AM, the army had surrounded the airport and lined the entire length of the route to the palace. Stores and stalls were sealed off, as well as all windows facing the street. Soldiers were posted every fifty feet, with bayonets in their rifles, wearing heavy duty helmets and campaign gear on their backs. Some even carried rolled blankets over their shoulders. Alternately one soldier faced the road, the next faced toward the buildings, his eyes carefully scanning the windows. Armored cars stood at every intersection. The heat was so intense that a man was dispatched to take glasses of water to each soldier. Workmen had hurriedly erected triumphal arches crowned with portraits of the Shah and Zahedi, and draped rugs over the vandalized statues.

At 10:45, three army planes took off to escort the Shah's Beechcraft home. As the Shah stepped out of the plane at 11:00, the orchestra struck up the national anthem, while General Daftari and several ministers threw themselves at his feet and kissed his shoes. The Shah walked up to Zahedi, embraced him, and saluted everyone in sight—among them Ernest Perron. Then he stepped into his armored car and set off through the cheering, flag waving crowds. By noon, he was home. For Mohammed Riza, the nightmare was over. For Mossadegh, it was time to pay the piper.

Five days later, Mossadegh telephoned Zahedi at the Officers' Club and offered to give himself up. Early that evening, an old man in pyjamas presented himself at the door of the club. A guard pulled out his revolver, but Ardeshir Zahedi took it away in time.

Panting and trembling, Mossadegh was a pitiful sight. Ardeshir led him into his father's study where his staff was assembled—among them Teymur Bakhtiar (himself soon to be heard from).

Suddenly, Mossadegh broke into sobs, threw himself at Zahedi's knees and tried to kiss his feet.

"No," Zahedi said, pulling him up. "I won't accept that."

Then Mossadegh took his hand and covered it with kisses.

"Solh ba shoma (peace be with you)," the general said. "I wish you no harm. You will have a fair trial."

The old man was taken away, not to be placed under house arrest as his advanced years might have suggested, but into a barracks cell with a pickpocket and a Communist for company.

The Shah showed his gratitude to "Brainless" by giving him a magnificent gymnasium and assigning him to train his shock troops. To Kim Roosevelt, he gave his friendship. Every year, when he goes on his skiing holiday to Switzerland, the Shah invites Kim Roosevelt to join him, all expenses paid. As for the conspirators, many of them hold important posts today. Ardeshir Zahedi is Iran's ambassador to Washington; Ovessi is chief of staff of the army; Khatami commands the air force, and Atabai and Amir Motaghi are vice-ministers of the Court. Nassiri is chief of SAVAK, the secret police.

As for Laurentiev, the big loser in the Mossadegh stakes, he sealed the doors of his embassy in the wake of the prime minister's arrest. After several days, an Iranian official telephoned the embassy and was told: "Didn't you know the ambassador tried to commit suicide?"

Apparently Laurentiev was so terrified of Moscow's reaction to the American triumph that he even tried to seek asylum with—of all people—Loy Henderson. His own men stopped him before he could get into his car and he returned to his room where he swallowed a cup of poisoned tea. But the dose was not strong enough and, after a thorough stomach pumping, he survived. Thereupon he disappeared and has never been heard from since.

Meanwhile, at the American embassy, Henderson and Roosevelt drew up their accounts. Putting the Shah back on his throne had cost exactly $390,000, a small price for a strategic position right on the Russian border. For the Shah, it was not only a political victory but a psychological turning point. As he told a press conference a few days after the coup, "I feel that I am starting a second reign." Until then, he had always felt that it was the British who had placed his father on the throne and thus were responsible for the Pahlevi dynasty. But the role played by the army and the people during the coup gave him the sense that he had been "elected." His attitude toward his role changed, and he put a stop to the vacillations that had so often been the despair of his supporters. But in the end, it took him two years to consolidate his newly acquired confidence.

Chapter 17

AT THE SHAH'S THIRTY-FOURTH BIRTHDAY PARTY, General Teymur Bakhtiar, thirty-nine and six feet two, made quite an impression with his thick black mustache and white uniform à la Russe. Bakhtiar aroused both fear and respect. As a reward for his help during the coup d'état, the Shah had named him military governor of Tehran—in other words, one of the most powerful men in the regime. And it was his particular job to track down those of Mossadegh's supporters who had managed to disappear after their leader's downfall.

Why did the Shah choose Bakhtiar? Some said it was because he was related to the Shah through Soraya—and the Shah was a strong family man; others said it was because he was a man without pity. The latter seems the most likely reason.

Teymur Bakhtiar (the name means "friend of good fortune") was a born killer. An impassioned anti-Communist, he had fought in Azerbaijan, and later against Mossadegh. Born in 1914, he had his military training at Saint-Cyr and was known for his bravery as well as for his cruelty to prisoners.

He wasted no time with Mossadegh's partisans. Emptying

Teymur Bakhtiar. *Gamma*

the prison at Ghars of all its civil prisoners, he filled it with Mossadegh's former ministers, opposition deputies, and Tudeh members whom he interrogated, beat up, and tortured. (The Shah later admitted that 640 officers were arrested, but the actual figure is thought to be closer to 3000.) Bakhtiar's efforts also demonstrated the extent to which the country had been endangered. In Tehran alone, his men turned up forty-two wheelbarrow loads of Red propaganda with 2000 photographs of Stalin; six secret arsenals, one cache alone containing thirty-five bazookas, two crates of hand grenades, one of revolvers and ammunition, and fifty cases of dynamite. In another arsenal, they found dozens of drums of sulfuric acid and nitric acid, and in a cellar, automatic weapons made in Czechoslovakia with over a thousand clips. Most dramatic of all, one September night at the air base in Ghalamorghi, a lieutenant happened on a Bickford fuse sputtering in the dark. Luckily, he managed to put it out with the heel of his shoe, thus saving twenty-six F 47 Thunderbolts from destruction. . .

By October, Bakhtiar had identified most of the 7000 card-carrying Tudeh members and placed 800 of them behind bars. He imposed a curfew and harsh restrictions on consumer goods. (Curiously enough, the only merchandise in plentiful supply were Kleenex and condoms.) Otherwise, people were dependent on the black market and parcels from abroad — if post office employees didn't get to them first.

With Bakhtiar in charge of the repression, the Shah was free to pick up his new broom and put his country's house in order. There was much to do: the state was again on the verge of bankruptcy and he must act quickly. He immediately appealed to President Eisenhower for emergency aid and was granted $45 million. But that was only a drop in the bucket;

he needed hundreds of millions: to compensate Anglo-Iranian for nationalization, $300 million; to put the Iranian economy back on its feet, another $200 million; to hire new engineers and oil technicians, $30 million. And that was only a beginning. So he turned to the Americans again, and the Americans sent him Herbert Hoover, Jr., a State Department expert and son of the former President. He arrived in October and was soon shuttling between Tehran, London and Washington, but it was months before the Shah saw any results.

To buttress his power at home, the king replaced almost everybody in the ministries and the administration. In foreign affairs, he undid "Mossadegh's ravages"—as he called them—by reestablishing diplomatic relations with Britain, and started negotiations to replace the Anglo-Iranian Company with an international consortium. But it would be a year before the accord was signed with American, British, French and Dutch companies. (These included Anglo-Iranian—now changed to British Petroleum—Gulf, Socony-Vacuum, Standard Oil of California, Standard Oil of New Jersey, Texaco, the Compagnie Française des Pétroles, and Royal Dutch Shell.) Meanwhile, the tankers were back at Abadan filling their holds, and gradually money began to flow again into the state's coffers.

Fortunately for the Shah, Soraya had been able to return in late August, accompanied by her young brother-in-law Hamid Riza, in Europe for dental work. Everyone was at the airport to greet her: her husband, the entire family, General Zahedi, and all the top dignitaries. Of her homecoming, she later observed: "I noticed that there was a good deal more fervor in the hand-kissing and bows than before the crisis."

Mossadegh's trial was due to begin on November 8. The old man was up to his old tricks, so it promised to be quite a show. During his prison stay, he had prepared his cell mates' defenses, and had done so well that when the pickpocket and the Communist appeared before the tribunal, their arguments caused many a juridical headache.

He was moved to the Officers' Club — next door to Zahedi — where he complained of stiffness in the joints. Doctors were summoned to his bedside, but he himself decided on the treatment to follow: to limber up his legs and loosen his joints, he must have his tricycle. From then on, the ecstatic former prime minister spent his days — and nights — riding up and down the corridors of the Officers' Club.

During the month preceding the trial, he had been offered various lawyers to take charge of his defense. "I don't want any," he said, "and besides, I have no intention of defending myself." A few days before the trial was to start, he changed his mind and announced he would plead his own case. When the prosecutor visited him to ask a few questions, Mossadegh shouted: "I refuse to be interrogated by you!" pedaled off to his room and crawled into bed, saying, "I'm tired."

He was permitted to see only his guards, the prosecutor, his wife, daughter, and nurse. Then suddenly, he demanded to see his friends. He had few left, he was told, and those he had were either exiled or in prison.

"All right," he said, "in that case, I shall go on a hunger strike. It won't take me long to die." He made a great show of not touching his lunch, but when evening came, he devoured his dinner. "I need rich food to conserve my strength," he explained. "From now on, I want a thick soup with every meal and three roast chickens a day. And for dessert, I must have lots of cakes."

That same night, he summoned the captain of the guards and announced: "I'm going to throw myself out the window."

The captain went to the window and opened it: "My orders

forbid me to let you see your friends, but I have no orders that forbid me to let you jump out the window."

Two hours later, the captain came back to check on Mossadegh. The old man was sitting, sulking, his back to the window.

Early in November, in the state reception room of the old Qajar palace in Soltanabad, a shriveled old man of seventy-four wearing three frayed dressing gowns over a pair of striped pyjamas, shuffled into the presence of five judges, the prosecutor, the six lawyers assigned to his defense, twenty officials and over sixty journalists.

He was no sooner seated than he collapsed. Various people rushed up to him. Just as suddenly, Mossadegh straightened up, made a grimace at his would-be helpers, and started speaking.

"I wish it to be known," he said in a surprisingly loud and firm voice, "that even if the Shah grants me a pardon, I will refuse to accept it. Only traitors are pardoned; I was merely a victim of foreigners."

Then, from the several pockets in his dressing gowns, he extracted rumpled pieces of paper, sorted them, and launched into his defense. Using all the tricks of the ham actor, he developed the theme that a military court was incompetent to judge him. At the end of five hours, he was still talking. At that point, the harassed president of the court told the exhausted audience that the session was adjourned.

The accused protested vehemently: "But I haven't finished my preamble. I still have forty-five pages to read!" (He had read only five.)

The spectacle went on for days, Mossadegh venting his wrath on everybody — Iranians, Russians, British, Americans. He poked fun at his judges and was contemptuous of his law-

yers. When a colonel tried to get a word in edgewise, Mossadegh spat out: "Get away from me, you dog. You're not my
lawyer!"

He complained of the cold, so an electric heater was brought
in. He had heart palpitations; a military doctor gave him
medicine. Sometimes, he simply went to sleep. On waking, he
would take a chunk of bread from his pocket, munch on it,
and turning to the newsmen, ask plaintively: "Doesn't anybody have a cigarette for an old friend?"

One day, he talked for ten hours without a break. When he
finally stopped, he said: "Whew, I'm tired. But I hope I've
made it clear to all of you that the Shah is a phony and that I
am still prime minister."

A few days later, when the prosecutor asked for the death
sentence, Mossadegh shouted: "Shut up, you! You're nothing
but a clown!"

On December 21, after seven hours of deliberation, forty-
three days of trial and fifty-three hearings, the tribunal gave
its verdict: "Mossadegh, for all the crimes you have committed, you are condemned to die according to the law, but
through the intercession of the Shah, your sentence has been
commuted to three years in prison. ("After all, I wasn't going
to make a martyr of him," the Shah said later.)

When he had served his sentence in 1956, Mossadegh retired
to his house in Karpur Abad. Now nearly eighty years old, he
set about growing pumpkins. Tight surveillance kept people
from getting near him, but one day, an enterprising American
reporter cadged an invitation to hunt in the region, pretended
to get lost, and tried to enter Mossadegh's house. That very
evening, he was on a plane bound for New York.

In January, 1967, Mossadegh developed cancer of the
throat and was allowed to go to his son's clinic in Tehran for
surgery. He died two months later at the age of eighty-seven.

Mossadegh was finished, but not the Tudeh. One morning in March, 1954, two policemen patrolling the bazaar noticed a woman hurrying along with a market basket, her *chador* hiding all but her eyes. What puzzled them was her oddly unfeminine walk. The police called to her, but when she didn't stop, they ran after her and pulled off her veil. It was a man with a two-day growth of beard and in his market basket was a stick of dynamite. It was Fatemi. Like Mossadegh, he was sentenced to death, but he received no pardon.

On August 19, the first anniversary of the C.I.A. coup, some Tudeh survivors organized a new plot but it was swiftly and brutally put down. After a second attempt that autumn, all the remaining Tudeh leaders were shot and the lesser members imprisoned. The Shah then embarked on an ingenious strategy of seducing the left-wing intellectuals—mostly students, young civil servants, doctors, engineers and lawyers. He agreed to forget the contents of their files if they would collaborate with him in the country's reconstruction—and he promised generous salaries. Many allowed themselves to be tempted, among them Amir Abbas Hoveyda, then a student of political science in Paris, today Iran's prime minister.

Also that autumn, the Shah was finally able to announce, after five months of negotiations, an agreement on oil. An International Consortium would take over the distribution of Iran's oil, guaranteeing the shipment of 30 million tons annually from Abadan. British Petroleum would earn 40 percent in royalties, the other countries dividing the rest in equal shares. All installations, wells, equipment, etc., were recognized as the property of Iran—as was originally provided for in Mossadegh's nationalization law.

The Consortium agreed to furnish the National Iranian Oil Company with the technical means necessary to operate these installations, and contracted to buy 15 million tons of crude in 1955, 30 million in 1957, plus (but no guarantee here) 6.5 million tons of refined oil in 1955, 10.5 million in 1956 and 13 million in 1957.

The oil problem seemed finally to be solved.

Chapter 18

ONE STORMY OCTOBER DAY in 1954, the Shah's brother, Ali Riza, took off from a tour of inspection in the Caspian to fly home for the celebration of the king's thirty-fifth birthday. He never arrived. Six days later, the wreckage of his plane was spotted on a spur of the Ebruz Mountains, forty miles from the capital. Ali Riza's funeral was held on November 3. That same day, Parliament voted a law requesting the Shah never to fly his own plane again.

Why this summary reaction? Because Ali Riza's death abruptly brought into the open what until then had only been whispered: after two years of marriage, Soraya had still not produced a child. And with Ali Riza dead, the Pahlevi dynasty no longer had a crown prince, since, according to the Constitution, Riza Shah's five other sons had no rights to the throne. Their mother was a Qajar.

For the Shah, the problem of succession was made all the more difficult by the fact that he was truly in love with his wife. There was no question about it: their honeymoon was now in its third year. He was full of little attentions, going out of his way to please her. They had secret hideaways; they rode horseback together, they skied together. Together they discovered the joys of water-skiing during the course of a cruise on the *Shah Savar*, the yacht Riza Shah had had built in Holland. To gratify Soraya's passion for the sport, he had a villa built near Ramsar with a launching dock under the drawing room. Sometimes they drove through the desert in the Shah's Mercedes at 120 miles an hour. Other times, they broke speed records in his private plane. In Tehran, they would drop into the various nightclubs and dance, clinging to each other, whispering and giggling like a pair of lovesick adolescents.

But even though the Shah adored her, Soraya was not an easy woman to get along with. She often quarreled with Shams and Ashraf, and detested the Shah's daughter Shanaz; she also had it in for Hossein Ala, the court minister, and especially his scheming wife. But above all, she hated Ernest Perron. This strange and mysterious person was everywhere, knew everything. Having the title of private secretary, he spent long hours with the Shah, and was often delegated to make secret contacts with the British and American ambassadors when the Shah wished to avoid official channels. But what irritated Soraya most were his prying questions into their conjugal life. Nevertheless she was forced to put up with him; the Shah refused to dismiss his old friend.

If Soraya had troubles with her husband's entourage, she herself was not entirely blameless. She was self-indulgent in the extreme, and something of a birdbrain. Her temper tantrums were notorious: priceless china, bibelots, jewels, anything that came to hand were hurled out the window. Then there was her mother, Madame Esfandiary, who was also subject to fits of pique, especially when she had been at the bottle. And Soraya's younger brother, who had moved into the palace with his mother, took flagrant advantage of his relationship with his brother-in-law.

But when Soraya appeared in the evening, hair carefully coiffed, face made up, wearing one of her beautiful "sheaths" from Balmain, and looked at the Shah with her large sad eyes, he forgave her everything.

Perhaps, if Ali Riza had not been killed, the dynastic question could have been postponed. But with no heir in sight, it had to be faced now. And there was another, all too familiar reason: once again, a strong man was challenging the Shah's rule: As military governor of Tehran, Teymur Bakhtiar was steadily enlarging the scope of his power. He kept files on everybody, he had a network of agents operating throughout the country. Shades of Razmara began to haunt the Shah, made particularly vulnerable by the lack of an heir.

Every time Soraya left for foreign parts, it was rumored that she was being treated for sterility. Eventually a top religious leader broached the subject to the Shah, who answered with asperity: "I love my wife. Do you love yours?"

"Of course, Your Majesty."

"Would you permit other people to discuss her problems with you?"

"No, Your Majesty."

"So the problem is laid to rest. We won't speak of it again."

But he would have to speak of it with Soraya. The definitive conversation took place toward the end of November, 1954. In a few days, the royal couple was to take off on an official visit to the United States. Mohammed Riza and Soraya were discussing arrangements when he suddenly turned to her and said:

"When we get to New York, I plan to spend three or four days at the hospital for a checkup. Why don't you have one at the same time?"

"Why should I?" she asked. "My health is excellent now."

"I know," the Shah said, looking away, "but you know perfectly well what I mean."

Soraya nodded. Of course she knew.

As soon as they arrived in New York, the royal couple was admitted to Columbia Presbyterian Medical Center's most elegant wing. For three days, the Shah and Soraya were examined and tested. The final verdict was that both were in the best of health.

Then Soraya asked her doctor anxiously: "About the matter I discussed with you . . . What is your diagnosis?"

"We have found nothing that should prevent your Majesty from having a child. You must simply be patient."

"Is there no treatment that might speed things up?"

"No, that would be useless. It's just a matter of time."

When they returned to Tehran, their families and friends pressed them to learn what had happened. Annoyed, the Shah curtly told them what the American doctors had reported. They would have to be satisfied with that for the time being, and the subject was not broached again. But the newspapers would not let it alone. They put forward various theses: While waiting, wouldn't the Shah have to name a crown prince? And if so, who? Ali Riza's son wouldn't do: he was illegitimate. Shanaz? No, it had to be a male. What if Shanaz had a son by Ardeshir Zahedi, whom she had recently married? Out of the question: it would be a Zahedi, not a Pahlevi.

As the months passed, it became evident to everyone— including Soraya—that she was not going to have a child. There were increasing pressures on the Shah. Not only Bakhtiar was nurturing ambitions, but Zahedi, the prime minister, also appeared to have ideas. In addition, it was being rumored that he had amassed a large fortune since the coup d'état, and that several of his ministers had accepted bribes from foreign companies wanting to do business with the government. This in itself did not bother the Shah—after all, it was common practice in Iran—but the plotting did.

Zahedi was placed under close surveillance, his conniving confirmed, and through the mediation of Assadollah Alam, his resignation was demanded. Exposed, the prime minister had no choice. But as is always the case in Iran, the whole affair was conducted with the most exquisite politeness. Zahedi called on the Shah while he and Soraya were at tea and, pleading ill health, requested to be relieved of his duties. The Shah offered him the post of Iranian representative to the European section of the United Nations in Geneva. "It's not a demanding position," he told him," and the city is most attractive. I'm sure you will cultivate a taste for Geneva and in fact will never want to leave it." Zahedi thanked him and took the next plane.

Hossein Ala was named in his place, and two years later, he was replaced in turn by Manutcher Eghbal, a one-time medical student in Paris. On his return to Iran, he had practiced in various hospitals in Tehran, taught in the medical school, and entered politics in 1943. A tall handsome man of great charm and cultivation, he filled virtually every ministerial post before he was named prime minister. (For all that his political career was somewhat checkered; he is now president of the National Iranian Oil Company and remains one of the regime's "éminences grises.")

As the months and years passed, Soraya's "problem" began to have a disastrous effect on their marriage. There were scenes and tears, and the periods of reconciliation became shorter and shorter. Then, in July, 1957, things came to a head.

Eghbal went to the Shah and spoke to him in plain language: "If Your Majesty wishes me to undertake the reforms you have asked for, your own position must be unassailable. Either the Empress produces an heir, or the dynasty's future must be assured in some other way."

That evening, the Shah had a conversation with Soraya. Together they tried to think of a solution. Soraya, who naturally continued to hope against hope, suggested a temporary solution—good for, say, five or ten years. "Why not lift the ban against the Qajars? Then one of your stepbrothers could be named crown prince."

"It's a good idea, but it would require a change in the Constitution, and only the Council of Sages can do that." (This was a kind of council to the crown, made up of the country's top dignitaries.)

"Then summon the Council and put the question to them."

"What if they refuse?"

Soraya hesitated for a moment. "Then we'll have to separate."

The Council met in January, 1958. There was an immediate division of opinion. The priests were in favor of modifying the Constitution, but Hossein Ala united those "against." Eghbal could have shifted the balance, but he chose to remain neutral. When the verdict was finally announced, it was against changing the Constitution.

So, another solution was proposed. It had been on everybody's mind for a long time but no one had dared mention it. A certain Dr. Abdul said it: "Mohammedan law states that to provide an heir, the king has the right to take a second wife. The Empress must accept this solution."

How to convince Soraya?

The Shah didn't dare speak of it to his wife, so he sent three emissaries in his stead. When they had finished, she said indignantly: "How dare you come here and make me such a proposition! You should know me well enough to realize I could never accept it. I prefer to leave."

The dénouement took place on an evening like any other, when the two, who had drawn much closer as the storm clouds gathered, went to a nightclub for an evening of dancing. They chose the Colbey at the Hotel Darban in the heights above Tehran. The evening began with "the game of Cardinal Pap," in which two people sink their teeth into opposite sides of an apple, each trying to eat his half first. Then they burst balloons with lighted cigarettes. After that came the dancing, and the Shah—for whatever reason, to tease or to annoy his wife—invited a ravishing European blond to dance. He danced with her several times, and it seemed to Soraya that her husband was holding the European closer and closer. She held her peace for an hour, then suddenly rose and left.

When the king took note of her departure, he left, looking very upset. Soraya, long since returned to the palace, refused to see him. She spent the night going through her belongings, burned hundreds of letters, woke up her servants and packed her bags. When morning came, she went to see her husband. She was convinced he had already decided to take another wife.

"I'm through. I'm leaving. Please order me a plane."

A little before noon, a car left the palace grounds and drove off in the direction of the airport. The Shah was at the wheel, Soraya at his side, both of them arguing heatedly. Two days later, Soraya was at the Palace Hotel in Saint-Moritz. Not long after, four generals arrived to attempt a reconciliation. As her response, Soraya gave them a list of things she had left behind in Tehran and wished sent to her.

The Shah telephoned her on March 5. Their talk was cool and distant, the conversation of two people who know it's all over. Nine days later, the official divorce was proclaimed. A little later, Soraya received a letter from her ex-husband, stating that he was deeply sorry for what had happened, but that he had been forced to bow to reasons of state. He gave her an allowance—much smaller than was generally believed—but she was hardly in want, for the Shah had been transferring funds to her over the years, funds which his investment counselors had managed very well.

By way of compensation, he named her "Imperial Princess" so that the ex-queen of Iran would not have to resume her maiden name. This title placed her on the same footing with the Shah's sisters and gave her the right to a diplomatic passport. In addition, in Europe, she took precedence over most members of the aristocracy.

Meanwhile, her picture was removed from every city, town and village in Iran, and the text of the divorce was put in its place—a document full of poetry and regret, composed by the king himself.

Chapter 19

No sooner had the Shah resolved the Soraya problem "with much pain and sorrow," than a shower of dollars began to rain down on Iran. Thanks to oil, of course, for after the resumption of production, the country's revenues rose to $936 million in the space of seven years. Also, thanks to loans. The Shah was able to borrow $245 million, most of it from private banks and the remainder from the International Monetary Fund and the International Bank for Reconstruction and Development (today, the World Bank). Not to mention the $45 million from the U.S., at $5 million a month.

With these funds, the Shah launched his Second Five Year Plan, approved by the *majlis* on March 23, 1956. The Plan, which encompassed agriculture, communications, industry and social services, was estimated at one billion two hundred million dollars—the exact sum garnered from Iran's oil revenues plus the total amount of its loans.

On the diplomatic front, the king became a signatory to the Baghdad Pact, on the heels of Turkey, Iraq, Britain, and Pakistan, thus creating a bridge between NATO, to which Turkey belonged, and SEATO which included Pakistan. This was of great importance to the Shah, for it placed his country on a sound international basis and improved his credit with Western financial sources.

Unfortunately, like many a third-world country short on disinterested civil servants, Iran was rife with corruption. Under-the-counter deals, hush money and bribes were a fact of daily life, and foreign advisers were constantly perplexed by the extent of the corruption they encountered. For example, the director of Tehran's electrical installations invited the Shah to the inauguration of a power station that had cost two million dollars. When the Shah turned on the switch, the current flowed into a nearby reservoir, electrocuting two swans. Another example: a former chief of army intelligence was put in charge of a government organization called K.O.K. with a budget of $1.5 million, whose function was to make confidential reports on the Shah's popularity. He turned out to be the sole member of the organization, and his reports were pure guesswork.

The flow of American dollars produced a boom, but not everybody profited. While Tehran changed overnight, the desert and the villages remained untouched. Mehrabad became a luxurious airport, the floors and walls of its entrance hall faced with Italian marble. In the city proper, new neighborhoods shot up out of the desert and climbed the slopes of the Elburz. Everywhere, there were new movie palaces, department stores and buildings. The bazaar was bisected by wide avenues in grids, with electricity and neon lights. The population soared to 1,200,000. But the city had no sewage system. It still doesn't.

For the business community, Iran became a veritable El Dorado. One Iranian businessman admitted to profits of 300 percent a year. In two years, a former shopkeeper managed to build himself a fourteen-story palace. In Shemiran, the chic section north of the city, sumptuous villas with swimming pools, select clubs and night spots blossomed overnight, and the city streets filled with an astonishing array of luxurious cars.

Mollie Panter-Downes, on a visit to Tehran for *The New Yorker* magazine—gave eloquent testimony to the changes in the capital. While she was there, television made its first appearance with four and a half hours of programming a day. Only twelve hundred sets had been sold, but it was a beginning. And she noted further that if Western bread had failed to catch on, Coca-Cola was a wild success.

But in the lower city, far from Shemiran, the poverty remained unchanged, as did the condition of workers and peasants throughout the country. In the burgeoning oil industry, workers earned an average of $9 a month, while the cost of living crept up and the shortage of housing raised rents to dizzying heights. Taxes accounted for a mere 10 percent of the state's revenue, the remaining 90 percent coming from oil royalties and indirect taxes, the latter leveled against everybody to be sure, but affecting mainly the poor. And fiscal fraud was taking on the proportions of an institution.

In the countryside, there was the same inequality: sharecroppers had rights to only one-fifth of their harvest, out of which they had to pay not only taxes but the interest on their debt. Sixty percent of all peasants owned no land at all; 23 percent owned less than a hectare (approximately 2½ acres). Fifty-six percent of the cultivated land belonged to a handful of large landowners, some of whom owned as many as a hundred villages.

During the summer of 1959, a strike in the Tehran brickworks degenerated into a huge work stoppage affecting over thirty thousand workers. Riots broke out and the police retaliated with gunfire. The owner of one of the factories, judged to be a little too severe, was arrested, along with the strike leader. In the arbitration that followed, the salary of the workers was raised to forty-five cents per *hezar*, a load of 1000 bricks, which the factory sold for the equivalent of $6.

Iran's poverty was thus a constant source of unrest. Although the much weakened Tudeh was no longer a political factor, there were still a number of underground cells, especially in the universities. They received their instructions from Baghdad, Warsaw and East Berlin, and despite the intervention of the police and border controls, the party's organ, *Sobh Omid* (The Morning of Hope) — printed "somewhere in Europe" — reached Iran in large numbers. And, for all the Shah's efforts, he could do nothing about the radio broadcasts beamed at Iran from Moscow, Baku, Yerevan in Soviet Armenia, and East Berlin, which daily proclaimed the sins of the Iranian government. The most dangerous of these was *Sedaye Milli Iran* (The National Voice of Iran) which was assumed to be subsidized by the Russians and specialized in social agitation. Every evening, it broadcast what the price of basic necessities in Iran's principal cities had been that morning, emphasizing each rise in price.

The exodus from the country to the cities created an angry "lumpen proletariat." And, thanks to inflation, Tehran was becoming — next to Caracas — the world's most expensive city. Bank robberies and other holdups were on the rise, the black market flourished, while increasingly, the rich sent their assets abroad. Every day, the Shah received new reports on rackets involving Iran's "one thousand families," corruption among its civil servants, and the shameless depredations on American aid and the state's resources.

While the country was skidding toward catastrophe, the Shah acted as if he had decided that corruption was endemic to Iran, hence incurable. To forget his country's woes and to console himself for the collapse of his marriage, he embarked on a series of amorous adventures which the world press followed with relish.

Soon a new name began cropping up — that of Marie-Gabrielle of Savoy, daughter of ex-King Umberto of Italy. The two had met at the home of mutual friends in Geneva in December, 1958. Marie-Gabrielle was living in a small chateau in Geneva with her mother Marie-José and her brother Victor-Emmanuel, crown prince of Italy. Umberto had taken up residence in Cascais in Portugal.

Marie-Gabrielle was eighteen, tall and pretty with blue eyes. She was studying to be an interpreter. She loved sports, especially swimming, riding, skiing, and she shared her brother's passion for cars. At the beginning of 1959, her father received a letter from the Shah asking for his daughter's hand in marriage. This was a source of considerable embarrassment to the former king, as it involved a question of religion, which he explained in his reply to the Shah.

Undeterred, the Shah immediately set off for Rome and an audience with Pope John XXIII, to request that His Eminence grant Marie-Gabrielle a dispensation. He was refused: articles 1060, 1061, and 1070 of the canon law expressly forbid all marriages between nonbaptized persons and those baptized into the Catholic Church. Now, there was no way that the Shah, a Muslim ruler, could renounce his religion and be converted to Catholicism. Nor could he consider raising his children in any but the Muslim faith. What to do?

The Iranian press came to the rescue, proclaiming that, by virtue of her genealogy, Marie-Gabrielle had every right to become queen of a Muslim country. One newspaper came out with a somewhat garbled history, to wit: "Princess Marie-Gabrielle has Arab blood in her veins. Her family tree indi-

cates that her distant ancestor, Maria-Isabella, wife of Alfonso
VI, King of Castile, was none other than Princess Zelida,
daughter of Mohammed II, King of Seville under the Arab
occupation in 1080. Zelida changed her name when she became a Christian. From this union issued, in the fifth generation, Maria, Queen of Spain, wife of Alfonso the Wise. His
second wife, Beatriz [actually she was his illegitimate daughter, but this may have frightened the Iranian press], married
Alfonso III of Portugal, of which the Emperor Charles V was
a ninth generation descendant. Marie-Gabrielle was descended
from Charles V's son, both through her father, Umberto II of
Italy, and her mother, Marie-José of Belgium."

No one doubted that, given the limited freedom of the
press, this article was dictated by the court.

But Marie-Gabrielle was not impressed. When the Shah returned to Geneva to renew his suit, she announced to the
press: "You may say, and keep repeating, that this marriage
will never take place. I shall not change my mind. I will never
marry a man I am not in love with. I don't love the Shah of
Iran; I will not marry him." To which her mother added:
"Besides, he's too old for her."

On May 3, Mohammed Riza was back in Geneva. A little
after 11:00 AM the following day, he drove with Ardeshir
Zahedi and three aides to 31 Chemin de Velours in suburban
Florissant to inspect a handsome villa which was for sale. (It
was later learned that they were looking for a suitable residence for the Iranian representative to the United Nations'
European headquarters in Geneva.) Then he spent twenty
minutes at a jeweler's on the Place Molard. When the owner
was questioned later by reporters, he refused to reveal for
whom the jewels were bought, and when he was asked directly if they were for Marie-Gabrielle, he answered with a

mysterious smile: "It's not for me to answer such a question."

The Shah subsequently spent fifteen minutes at a bank, then drove, still with Zahedi, to l'Or du Rhone, a restaurant on the rue du Strand. Toward the end of lunch, Zahedi asked the owner of the restaurant to call a certain number. He took the call in a private booth. The Shah was meanwhile smoking one cigarette after another, his eyes darting back and forth toward the telephone booth. Zahedi finally returned and leaned to whisper something in the Shah's ear. The king paled, rose abruptly and was driven at full speed back to his house. Intrigued, reporters called the chateau of Merlinge. No answer. They rang at the gate. No answer.

The next morning, a gloomy looking Shah took off in his private plane from the airport at Cointrin.

A week later, Reuter's in Tehran reported: "Well-informed sources have divulged that the Shah has abandoned all ideas of marrying Princess Marie-Gabrielle of Savoy, and that he plans to choose an Iranian wife to carry on the dynasty." (Marie-Gabrielle later married the celebrated French promoter, Robert de Balkany, in a Catholic church, even though he was divorced and the father of two. The Pope had agreed to annul his previous marriage.)

In a matter of months, the Shah was on the trail of another would-be Empress. This time, he was on firmer ground. He had met the girl eighteen months earlier, before his abortive courtship of Marie-Gabrielle.

During the course of a private visit to Paris in May, 1958, he had asked to meet the outstanding Iranian students in the French capital. The ambassador gathered together a dozen young people, among them one Farah Diba. Face to face with their king, the young students blushed and were silent, giving halting answers when the Shah addressed them. All except Farah Diba. First asking permission to speak, she said: "Your Majesty, I hope you will forgive me for taking this liberty, but I must protest the law just passed, reducing the scholarship grants for students in foreign countries. I know that our country is going through a critical period, but how can you expect Iran to have the trained people and civil servants it so desperately needs if poor but deserving students cannot go to Europe and America to learn what our own universities are not yet able to teach?"

The other students were aghast at the impudence of this girl who not only dared address the king, but criticized the government!

The Shah smiled. Farah's boldness was a refreshing change from the eternal obsequiousness that surrounded him. He explained all the problems involved, promised to try to resolve the question, then shifted to general conversation.

One evening, back in Tehran, Ardeshir Zahedi was dining with the Shah at Saadabad. He mentioned an astonishing young woman he had seen that day who spoke straight out, complaining in no uncertain terms of the fate of students going abroad. The Shah asked her name.

"Farah Diba."

"Why, that's amazing," Mohammed Riza replied. And he told young Zahedi the story of their meeting in Paris.

A little while later, Zahedi had occasion to see Farah again — something to do with her dossier — and his wife, Shanaz, the Shah's daughter, happened to be in his study when the girl arrived. Having heard her discussed one night at the palace, Shanaz watched her with curiosity. She liked her and invited her to her house. The two girls were soon great friends. Shanaz spoke of Farah to her father.

A few days before Farah's departure for France, Shanaz invited her to tea. The Shah was there when she arrived. Before the afternoon was over, he announced to Farah that he had chosen her to be his wife. Only if she agreed, of course.

He had already made a thorough investigation of the girl, supervised by court doctors, one of whom went so far as to make a trip to Paris to inquire about her from the French medical fraternity. He wanted to know if Farah had any physical defect, any congenital disease, if there were anything that might prevent her having a child.

The investigation in Tehran spread to her family and their own doctors. She passed with flying colors, until one doctor came up with the discovery that a great-great aunt had been sterile. Consternation. Then it was discovered that the aunt's husband had had a serious accident before their marriage and was incapable of impregnating his wife.

Farah's father, Sohaab Diba, had attended Saint-Cyr, married Farideh Ghotbi in 1937 and entered the diplomatic corps. Farah was born in Rumania. Her father died of tuberculosis in 1948. With her secondary education finished in 1957, a wealthy uncle in Tehran—his family owned the Park Hotel—suggested she apply for a scholarship to study in Europe, and if the money were not sufficient, he would make up the difference. That is how Farah happened to be at an architectural school on Boulevard Raspail in September, 1957. By early October of the following year, the French and American wire services were announcing that the next queen of Iran would be named on the Shah's birthday.

Details about Farah began to flood the press: that she was twenty-one, had black eyes, was five feet nine, had a 23 inch waist, 35¼ inch bust, etc. etc.

The Shah's birthday was celebrated with flags flying, parades, fireworks, processions of wildly honking cars which stirred up clouds of dust. (Tehran had been without rain for a year.) In the middle of the state dinner given by the Shah to members of the government, a telegram was brought to him which he read with visible emotion. Farah wished him a happy birthday. But there was no official announcement. Word went around that it was being postponed until mid-November.

On November 10, Farah appeared at the Paris Opera for a performance of *Carmen* wearing a white mink cape—a present from the Shah. A few days later, her trousseau was ready. Her furs alone were said to be worth forty thousand dollars. She spent her last day in Paris having her hair done by Carita and eating bouillabaisse. On Saturday, she arrived in Tehran, to be greated by the Shah's entire family and a crowd of thousands—but no Shah. His car had been blocked by the excited mob and he couldn't reach her in time. On the twenty-third, an official communiqué announced: "The Minister of the Imperial Court takes great pleasure in informing the public of the betrothal of his Imperial Majesty Mohammed Riza Pahlevi to Miss Farah Diba."

That afternoon at five, the engagement was celebrated in the presence of the Pahlevi and Diba families and high officials of the court. The three-time fiancé, dressed in the resplendent uniform of Commander of the Armed Forces, went into the library to fetch from his desk a small box lying between a bust of Napoleon and a photograph of his father taken at twenty in the uniform of a Cossack officer. Out of it he took a huge diamond ring and put it in his pocket.

His mother and the rest of the family were waiting on the landing before descending the marble staircase. Tadj-Ol-Moluk took her son's arm, and behind them followed the minister of the court, Hossein Ala, and Prime Minister Eghbal. At the foot of the stairs, Farah was waiting, rosy cheeked, with her mother, uncles and aunts. The court chamberlain arranged the guests in the main drawing room with its pale blue walls, Louis XVI and Directoire furniture covered with white silk, and large baskets of flowers scattered everywhere.

The Shah sat Farah at his right on a sofa under a large Empire tapestry. The Queen Mother and Shanaz sat on his left. Then, with a broad smile on his face, he took the ring from his pocket and placed it on Farah's finger, while she in turn gave him a gold ring. Then, following the old Persian custom, the king offered her sweetmeats, and gave the platter to Ardeshir Zahedi who offered it to the rest of the guests as champagne corks started popping. A dinner for four hundred and fifty guests followed at the Queen Mother's, where Farah spent her first night as the Shah's betrothed.

The marriage was set for December 21. She spent her last day as a "spinster" walking with the Shah in the country, after which she played volleyball. Her wedding gown arrived via Air France on the eighteenth. With it, she was to wear a crown with a very rare lozenge-shaped pink diamond at its center. An inlaid platinum comb held the crown in place, for the jeweled confection weighed almost five pounds. Her earrings each had a teardrop diamond hanging by a platinum chain from an emerald fastened behind the ear. Around her neck, she was to wear a diamond necklace.

On the twentieth, a brand new Ferrari with an imperial crown on its radiator cap raced through the streets of Tehran with the Shah at the wheel and Farah and Shanaz laughing like a couple of schoolgirls beside him. On the day of the wedding, Tehran was covered with a fresh fall of snow—as it had been for the king's wedding to Soraya. And one of the first telegrams of congratulations received at the palace was from Saint-Moritz: "Best wishes for your happiness," signed "Soraya."

On the dot of four, Farah walked up the circular stairs of the Marble Palace to the landing where the Shah was waiting for her in his black jacket with gilt epaulets and covered with decorations, pale blue trousers, a sword at his side. Standing by the windows of the Hall of Mirrors where the ceremony was to take place, the orchestra of the Guards played a pot-pourri of Persian military marches, snatches of French cancan music, *La Vie Parisienne*, and marches of the Italian Alpine Light Infantry.

The by-now familiar ritual was spelled out: three times, the Imam asked: "Are you prepared to become the wife of His Majesty the Shah?" and Farah answered only after the third question. The priest then recited verses from the Koran. Farah, deeply moved, turned to her husband, held out her ungloved hand and said: "I am your wife."

The Shah placed a ring set in diamonds on her middle finger, while the Queen Mother scattered sugar, pearls and gold dust on the bride's veil to exorcise the demons and ensure a cloudless future.

After the wedding feast at Golestan, the royal couple slipped away through a back door and drove to the Royal Palace where Tadj-Ol-Moluk was waiting to lead them to the nuptial chamber. The honeymoon was to begin two days later, but a new eruption on the Iraq border and the Iraqi General Kassein's renewed claims to land close to Abadan, forced its postponement. By the twenty-fourth, things seemed to have calmed down enough to permit their departure when news came of torrential rains at Rasmar on the Caspian where they had planned to spend ten days. They were finally able to leave on the twenty-eighth, and the crowd assembled to see them off on the imperial train shouted "May God give you a son!"

Ten months later, on the morning of October 31, 1960, Mohammed Riza himself drove his wife to the Mothers' Aid Society Hospital. Just before noon, Dr. Jahanshah Saleh, the queen's gynecologist as well as minister of health, rushed into the corridor where the Shah was chain-smoking and announced: "Your Majesty, it's a son!"

The Shah immediately proclaimed a two-day holiday for the entire country, a tax reduction of 20 percent and amnesty for ninety-eight prisoners. The sky over the city reverberated with a forty-one-gun salute, and when the Shah tried to leave the hospital that afternoon, the crowd blocked his car and had to be dispersed with fire hoses.

But between his wedding day and the birth of his son, the Shah went through one of the most difficult periods of his embattled reign. The day of reckoning was at hand: the state treasury was empty again, with a deficit of $145 million on a $390 million budget. Eghbal's regime had sunk into a quagmire of corruption which the Shah seemed powerless to control. Worse still were the political shenanigans practiced by the men in power. The Shah had promised that the twentieth *majlis* would be freely elected, so an opposition party—the Independents—had put forth a handful of deputies in Tehran and the provinces. Their leader, Ali Amini, the grandson of a Qajar King, minister of commerce under Mossadegh, and a vociferous critic of the Shah, was the darling of the Americans who nicknamed him Mickey Mouse. When the returns were in, the prime minister's party had polled 75 percent of the vote, a figure so absurdly high that he was accused on all sides of having rigged the election. In fact, the very word "election" had become a euphemism for manipulations so blatant that foreign ambassadors were given the lists of the new deputies three weeks before the voting took place. Years later, when Eghbal was asked to comment on these elections, he simply laughed and shook his head with astonishment that anyone should have the effrontery to ask him such a question.

At a press conference held soon after the elections, an intrepid journalist actually reprimanded the Shah — an unheard of act of lèse-majesté: "The government intervened in the elections," he stated. "This is an unconscionable infringement of our liberties!"

This time, the Shah decided to act. Eghbal was invited to tea, and a few hours later, his resignation was announced — for the usual reasons of health. (He had held on to the post longer than any previous prime minister — forty-one months.) And, in line with the Iranian tradition of compassion for fallen ministers, he was appointed ambassador to UNESCO. Next, his brother Ahmad was invited to resign as foreign minister. In due course, Eghbal was officially charged with electoral fraud and of relieving a number of factory owners of the burden of paying $7,300,000 in taxes. But the investigations were suddenly called off: according to law, an ex-minister could not be brought to trial without a special act of Parliament. So, the Shah dissolved Parliament and called for new elections. A month later, Jafar Sherif Emani, a technician, was named prime minister.

Emani found himself in an impossible situation. Strikes and demonstrations were breaking out in all the larger cities. In January, several thousand students demonstrated at Tehran University, calling for Mossadegh's return to power. The police charged them with bayonets. The students barricaded themselves in the university, armed with rocks and clubs. In the battle that followed, three hundred were injured — both students and policemen. Meanwhile, the Americans' friend Amini was calling press conference after press conference to proclaim the need for a thorough house-cleaning. The situation was becoming explosive. The Shah dissolved the new

Parliament and, to avert a catastrophe, named Amini prime minister. The new minister immediately announced on the radio: "The treasury is empty. The nation must face up to the crisis. I can say no more for fear of unleashing a panic."

Chapter 20

THERE WAS ONE MAN who found the situation much to his liking and took advantage of it with increasing brazenness. And he had recourse to a formidable weapon in the SAVAK, the intelligence agency he had created in 1956 with the technical help of the Americans — and some say, the Israelis.

As a domestic police force, the SAVAK — its initials stand for Sazemane Etelaat va Amniate Kechvar, meaning Security and Intelligence Organization of the Iranian State — took precedence over all other police units, and used its powers to the hilt. Little by little, Bakhtiar turned it to his own ends, and every week, the Shah found that the SAVAK had penetrated deeper into his own services. Worse still, he discovered that the Iranian C.I.A. network was on the best of terms with the SAVAK. And that Bakhtiar was much appreciated in the United States. That was very serious indeed. Disturbed by Iranian corruption and angry at the way American dollars were disappearing into the pockets of traffickers and racketeers, the Americans were using the SAVAK to regain at least partial control of the country. There was talk of a secret agreement between the U.S. and Bakhtiar. In fact, it was beginning to look like a replay of the 1953 coup d'état, but this time against the Shah and for the benefit of Bakhtiar.

The Shah's suspicions were not unwarranted. The Americans were seriously considering assigning the C.I.A. to establish a republic in Iran—with the complicity of the SAVAK.

Every day, as he left his office on Kahke Avenue to return to Saadabad, the Shah drove past a new palace of gleaming white marble: the million-dollar residence of General Teymur Bakhtiar. When Bakhtiar was named military governor of Tehran in 1953, he owned only a small house in the lower city. Now, eight years later, in addition to the new palace in the capital, the chief of the SAVAK had another on the Caspian, eleven farms, three estates, five villas scattered around Iran, three in Europe, not to mention sizable deposits in various international banks.

In the interim, Bakhtiar's vast intelligence agency had accumulated compromising files on thousands of people. Torture, summary execution and unexplained disappearances were the lot of all those who, under the aegis of the U.S.S.R., tried to reintroduce Communism into Iran. And some of his methods were fairly exotic. He was said to be particularly fond of making a prisoner watch his wife being ravaged by a chained and muzzled bear.

What concerned the Shah most was that Bakhtiar was openly promoting a military coup d'état to be served up in a gigantic blood bath. To a group of foreign correspondents, he calmly announced that he was ready, if the Shah gave him the word, to replace Amini's government with a military dictatorship, and its program of reforms with out and out repression. Moreover, as a member of a very old family, he considered himself eminently suitable to found a dynasty which, as he told his friends, would be far preferable to the present one established by usurpers without a past. Bakhtiar was particularly dangerous because he had the support of the large landowners as well as many of the religious leaders who found Amini too "democratic" and westernized.

If he was to put Bakhtiar in his place, the Shah had to move boldly. So, on May 9, 1961, he announced that he was launching "a series of extensive and much needed reforms in all areas in order to resolve the growing difficulties the country was facing," and he concluded: "No obstacle will be permitted to stand in the way of the application of these measures." Clearly, the "obstacle" he had in mind was Bakhtiar.

To reassure the country, he gave Amini his full backing. As a centrist, the prime minister appealed to all those who wanted "change with continuity." At the Shah's request, Amini went before the people and spoke bluntly, calling for an end to corruption, and asking them to join him in a crusade to bring about the necessary economic and social reforms. Then he warned the nation to beware of those whose interests might be jeopardized by his program and who would therefore plot against him. "You must be vigilant, like me," he stated. "We must resist anarchy and the enemy's intrigues with all our might. Without the support and cooperation of the people, I will never be able to lead our country to prosperity!"

The day after his investiture, Amini broke all contracts with foreign firms, explaining that Iran had no more money to spend on its development. The speech had the desired effect. The common people were aroused; the rich called him a traitor to his class. How could he do this to them? Wasn't he himself rich? Didn't he number a Shah among his ancestors, and didn't he have so much land around his house in Tehran that he was able to lease parcels to ambassadors and embassies without even noticing it?

Although Bakhtiar pretended not to react, he was secretly preparing a countercoup, and went drumming up armed support among the Bakhtiari near Isfahan. The Shah's agents kept him informed, and at the end of June, he summoned the chief of the SAVAK to his study. By the time Bakhtiar left the Shah, he had been dismissed and General Hassan Pakravan appointed in his place. An old friend of Riza Shah, Pakravan was an intellectual, an artist and excellent pianist. More important, he was also dependable. In the wake of Bakhtiar's ouster, the Shah arrested thirty-three generals, one of them the owner of a block of flats so luxurious it was nicknamed "the where-did-you-find-the-money-to-build-it building." Another was head of fisheries and controlled the very lucrative monopoly of caviar for exportation. Arrested with him was a female relative of the "king" of Iranian caviar, Ehsan Davaloo, a close friend of the Shah, who was accused of bribing civil servants to get her a caviar concession worth $450,000 a year.

The purge extended to public works and the ministries: At the Ministry of Education alone, 643 top officials were eased out, and another 370 sent to the provinces as school teachers. Those most critical of the corruption in education had been the teachers, so Amini made their leader minister of education. Five hundred officials guilty of holding down several posts — and pocketing the salaries — were dismissed, the head of the University of Shiraz receiving twelve different salaries at the same time.

Then Amini sealed off the borders. No more travel, no transfer of funds, no private imports. For months, only those on diplomatic missions, students, and the seriously ill were allowed to leave the country.

His next move was to legalize Mossadegh's National Front,

banned since 1953, which had been speaking out for months against the corruption and favoritism, and the inadequacy of Iran's social laws. This won him its leaders' backing, and a meeting of the Front to consider Amini's program drew eighty thousand people.

Amini also expanded the scope of agrarian reform, begun many years before when the Shah first distributed his lands. The "thousand families" — the aristocrats plus the new rich — with their palatial villas in the heights above Tehran, their swimming pools, American cars, and estates larger than several counties, were incensed. The days under Zahedi and Eghbal, when they could flout the law with impunity, were over.

With these reforms under way, the Shah felt more secure. To speed the agrarian revolution along, he enrolled the aid of a specialist, Hassan Arsanjdani. From a draconian expropriation limiting properties to 525 acres of irrigated land or 1750 acres of dry land, he moved to the mechanization of cultivation and to educational measures designed to benefit the peasants. The Shah himself gave the last forty villages remaining from the 518 left him by his father to two thousand farmers.

Next, there was the urgent financial problem, particularly the appalling imbalance in the country's foreign trade — $500 million in imports to barely $50 million in exports. Almost everything was imported: radios, television sets, record players, domestic appliances, stoves, refrigerators, etc. Japan was the prime exporter, with America and Europe providing most of the cars. In addition, Tehran was in the grip of wild land speculation. On the main streets of the city, a square foot cost more than in Paris or New York. Interest on loans had reached 30 percent. All this in a country where only 4.5

million out of a population of 22 million could afford to buy any manufactured goods other than textiles. In Tehran, a worker seldom earned more than $80 a month, and in Tabriz, Isfahan or Meshed, it dropped to $20. And they were the lucky ones. Most Iranians subsisted on an annual income of $70.

Then, suddenly, at the end of 1961, the specter of Bakhtiar reappeared.

The Shah learned that the SAVAK's ex-chief had made a second trip to Washington and had met with President Kennedy. Although the Kennedy Administration knew he had lost all support and had little hope of ever returning to power, it was afraid that the Shah's future was threatened by the growing discontent of his people. The Americans were behind Amini's "white revolution," but made it clear at the same time that they considered his reforms too slow and Iran's situation too unstable.

On the strength of the American displeasure, Bakhtiar started stirring things up as soon as he returned to Tehran. When Amini publicly criticized India's occupation of Goa, the Portuguese colony on India's west coast, Bakhtiar promptly called a press conference and congratulated President Nehru for his action. The Shah responded by arresting seven generals suspected of being pro-Bakhtiar, and three hundred officers were retired.

But Bakhtiar would not be put down. He made overtures to the National Front, and in January, 1962, when new troubles broke out at the University of Tehran, hundreds of students applauded Bakhtiar and called for Amini's dismissal.

On January 26, the Shah summoned him to the palace. From the windows, Bakhtiar could see the soldiers lined up, ready to shoot at the slightest provocation. A few hours later, without so much as a suitcase, he was on a plane bound for Geneva.

Three months later, the Shah and his queen left on an official visit to the United States in search of another $800 million in aid. There were receptions, and the Shah and Kennedy exchanged compliments on the beauty of their respective wives — on the surface at least, little else. But an official in the State Department who was close to Kennedy had this to say:

"When the Shah came to Washington in 1962, the President spoke to him mostly about the 'white revolution.' He tried to talk him out of buying so many arms and reduced his military aid. He even sent a military mission to Tehran whose principal instructions were to convince the king that he didn't need the arms he was trying to get. But the Shah kept talking about his dangerous neighbors, Iraq, the U.S.S.R., and Nasser who was a great source of worry. Kennedy took the opposite tack, telling him that the important thing was to satisfy the aspirations of his people. Kennedy had a certain sympathy for the Shah. He found him engaging and amusing. But he didn't take him very seriously."

The Shah did not appreciate Kennedy's advice, and to this day, he seems to have retained a certain animosity toward him. Only recently, the Shah said of Kennedy: "Basically, he wasn't very strong. He kept on making mistakes . . ." Regardless of American opinion, the Shah continued to devote a large part of his budget to arms — and still does, to the obvious detriment of Iran's economic development.

Once back in Iran, Mohammed Riza found himself faced with a by-now all too familiar problem: it was increasingly evident that Ali Amini, too, had ambitions. Reports from his informers began piling up on the Shah's desk and his relations with Amini swiftly deteriorated. But this time, he felt free to act. He summoned Amini and demanded his resignation. Amini had hoped to reduce the king to a figurehead, like the British sovereign. But he failed, and so he left.

There are two views on the quarrel between Amini and the Shah: the Americans, including Kennedy himself, felt that the comparative success of Amini's social reforms triggered the Shah's jealousy, causing him to dismiss the prime minister and take over the "white revolution" for himself. But the Shah's supporters claimed that the king had begun the distribution of his lands long before Amini came on the scene, despite the risk he ran of alienating the large landowners who were, after all, his natural constituency. And that his use of Amini, a rich man himself, was a political ruse to get the project under way without frightening the landowners. Besides, they insisted, the "white revolution" made greater headway after Amini's departure than it had before.

To replace Amini, the Shah chose his old friend, Assadollah Alam. A Qajar prince, and millionaire married to one of Iran's richest heiresses, he was brought up in England, wore Bond Street tweeds and had his nails manicured. He was also known for the elegant dinners he gave at his palace in the Elburz foothills, with its vast rose gardens and Olympic-size swimming pool. His anglophilia was such that when the Shah chose him as prime minister, Alam took it with a typically British wryness: "It's folly!" he told a group of journalists. "I'm much too lazy for the job. I was born lazy. I'll have to work all the time. It's quite impossible. Somebody else should be named in my place."

His westernized wit manifested itself on another occasion when some workmen at his ministry complained to him of their low salaries: "You promised to raise our salaries to 100 rials ($1.30) a day and nothing has happened." To which he answered with a deprecating smile: "Don't you know that prime ministers always lie?"

Fifteen months later, Alam was eased out and replaced with Hassan Ali Manur, a forty-year-old technocrat. Whoever was prime minister no longer seemed a matter of great importance to the Shah. With Bakhtiar exiled and Amini out of the way, he thought he was done with power-hungry politicians who threatened his throne. But he had made one mistake. He underestimated Teymur Bakhtiar.

Chapter 21

ON JUNE 5, 1963, the Shah stood at the windows of Saadabad watching thick columns of black smoke rising over the lower city far to the south. The bazaar was in flames.

It had all started the day before during the course of a religious celebration. The Shiites of Islam had been commemorating the death of the *imam* Hussein, Mohammed's grandson, murdered on the orders of Caliph Yazid. Every year, the memory of the usurper's triumph over the legitimate heir provoked emotional displays of grief and anger.

This time, the *ayatollah* Khomeini, leader of the Muslim Shiites, and violently opposed both to the Shah's agrarian reforms and the emancipation of women, had decided to launch a coup d'état of his own. To set the stage, he delivered a series of sermons in all of Tehran's mosques attacking the Pahlevi regime. Rather than mention the Shah by name, however, he referred to him as "today's Yazid."

The atmosphere in the mosques became so charged that, when prayers were over, the faithful fanned out through the streets shouting "Down with Yazid!" and "Death to the Dictator!"

The next morning, Khomeini was arrested in Qom, the holy city where he had his residence. As soon as this became known, the streets of Tehran filled with people demanding the release of their spiritual leader. For three days, Tehran was a battleground. Cars were burned, stores looted, official buildings attacked. It was 1953 all over again.

From ten thousand, the crowd rapidly grew to forty thousand. Brandishing pictures of Khomeini, the mob destroyed everything in its path and stoned any woman not wearing a veil. Throughout Iran, crowds took to the streets, shouting their hostility to the government, with workers, students and intellectuals joining the demonstrators. When the building housing Tehran's radio station appeared to be threatened, the Imperial Guard was finally called out with orders to put down the revolt at all costs. Tanks and armored cars advanced on the protesters as the sound of mortar fire filled the air. Terrified, the crowd dispersed only to regroup elsewhere. But when they saw that the Shah's troops had carried the day, in their frustration and anger, they set fire to everything — telephone booths, stores, cafés. Then they turned on the bazaar, and the pall of smoke darkened the whole city.

Martial law was proclaimed, and merciless repression followed. One daily paper reported several hundred dead: the opposition put the figure anywhere between one thousand and nine thousand.

The Shah was convinced that someone had orchestrated the rebellion. Only a few days earlier, his secret agents in Iraq had informed him that Teymur Bakhtiar had suddenly left Switzerland and was now in Baghdad — one hundred miles from the Iranian border. Moreover, as soon as the rebellion was put down, Bakhtiar apparently left Baghdad.

That was the first Bakhtiar alert.

The second came a year and a half later.

One January day in 1965, Prime Minister Ali Mansur drove up to the Parliament building. The gates were opened, but his car was immobilized by the crowd assembled on the sidewalk. Now, there is an Iranian custom that permits anyone with an official request to write it on a piece of paper and hand it personally to the official concerned. To refuse to accept a written request is not done. So Ali Mansur got out of his car to mingle with the crowd as his bodyguard rushed to surround him. But not in time. There was a sudden burst of gunfire. One of the "petitioners," a twenty-year-old theology student named Mohammed Bokharai, had a revolver hidden under his written request. He fired three times and Mansur, his hand clutching his throat, collapsed on the sidewalk. Bokharai was stopped before he could escape, as were two accomplices who also had revolvers. On their weapons were pasted verses from the Koran and the slogan "Death to the Shah's anti-democratic regime!"

Mohammed Riza was skiing that day. He rushed by helicopter to Ali Mansur's bedside at Pars Hospital. Surgeons removed two bullets from the prime minister's throat and one from his stomach, and most of his intestines had to be removed. Five days later, he fell into a coma. He never regained consciousness. The Shah saw that he was buried in the royal cemetery.

Bokharai went before the firing squad, but only after an interrogation, during the course of which he happened to mention the name Bakhtiar . . .

As his new prime minister, the Shah picked Amir Abbas Hoveyda, finance minister under Mansur, the pro-Western former student of political science in Paris who fancied orchids in his buttonhole. (Remarkably enough, he is still prime minister today.)

The third Bakhtiar alert came three months later.

At 9:30 one morning, the Shah's metallic blue Cadillac drove up to the Marble Palace and came to a stop at the entrance steps. His aide-de-camp and orderly were standing at attention. As usual, the Shah got out on the left side of the car. On guard, not fifty feet from the entrance, was a young man named Riza-Shams Abadi, only four months short of completing his military service. His assignment that day was to kill the Shah. After the Cadillac came to a stop, he left his post and ran toward the car, his submachine gun at the ready. A gardener tried to intercept him and Abadi shot him. But the Shah had already reached the hall and gone into his office. The two guards posted at the top step fled, and Abadi rushed into the building. One bodyguard standing outside ran after Abadi and fired, wounding him in the calf which brought him down. But Abadi managed to twist himself around and shot him dead. Another bodyguard in the hall pulled out his gun and riddled the assassin, but Abadi kept inching toward the door of the Shah's office, spraying the area with his tommy-gun. One bullet killed the bodyguard, another pierced the door of the office, missing the Shah by inches. Abadi finally collapsed at the foot of the sofa on which Riza Shah had sat while signing his act of abdication twenty-four years before. Once again, luck had saved the Shah.

Recalling the incident recently, he said: "I had just entered my study when I heard sounds of shooting. It seemed to come from every direction and I thought it must be a general insurrection. We stood rooted to the spot—I had no weapon of any kind. Then the shooting came closer. I could hear it right outside in the hall where it made a terrifying din. One bullet pierced my study door and glanced by me. When silence finally returned, I opened the door and looked out into the hall. Three bodies lay there, one a soldier and two of my bodyguards."

Unperturbed, the Shah refused to cancel an appointment with a French admiral scheduled for later that morning, and after lunch, he went bowling with his family. "You see how Allah protects me!" he said to his staff. And the next day, he drove down Istanbul Avenue, one of Tehran's busiest streets, alone at the wheel of an open convertible. The crowd greeted him with shouts of joy.

The investigation turned up six extremists, all with British diplomas, all with Communist ties, one of them with Bakhtiar's Geneva address in his pocket. . . .

The attempted assassination was a terrible shock to Farah. It was rumored that she was expecting another child and lost it as a result.

But the attempts on the Shah's life continued. Two years later, in 1967, forty commandos attacked the Shah's car. Fortunately, he wasn't in it. The same year, an Iranian student in Germany tried to run a booby-trapped remote control car into the Shah's during the course of a visit to West Berlin. At his trial before a German tribunal (which let him off with eight months in jail), the student confessed he had received the money to buy the bombs and the remote control mechanism from Bakhtiar.

The Shah decided that he had tolerated Bakhtiar long enough. But, for the time being, he would restrict himself to legal measures. In August, 1967, the military prosecutor in Tehran indicted Bakhtiar on charges of plotting against the Shah. Not long after, SAVAK agents learned that their former chief was commuting between Switzerland, Germany and France, and had renewed contact with a former classmate at Saint-Cyr, one François Porteu de la Morandière, an ex-member of the O.A.S. (the Secret Army Organization, formed by a group of extreme right-wing generals during the Algerian war).

In April, 1968, Bakhtiar left Nice with his aide-de-camp, Major Shapur, for Beirut. Three weeks later, Shapur was arrested at the wheel of a Land Rover filled with weapons. The Lebanese police had been tipped off by a telephone call from the SAVAK in Tehran. A month later, Bakhtiar himself was arrested on charges of trafficking in arms but protested to the judge that he was only delivering arms to "Iraqi friends in Baghdad where he was settling permanently." He was sentenced to three months in jail and immediately went on a hunger strike. Tehran demanded his return. Charles Helou, president of Lebanon, responded by extending Bakhtiar's sentence to nine months—which would give him that much longer to consider his reply to the Shah's demand for extradition. Bakhtiar greeted the news of his extended sentence with a smile: after all, he had gained nine months.

On September 23, the military tribunal in Tehran voted the death penalty, and the Shah renewed his demand for Bakhtiar's extradition. Helou answered that he must first serve out his Lebanese sentence. They would discuss the matter when he left prison in March, 1969.

Talks were initiated weeks before the expiration date and became increasingly fraught. Ambassadors consulted back and forth, Iran placed an embargo on Lebanese imports and forbade all Lebanese tourists to enter Iran. In Lebanon, some were convinced that the SAVAK, whose agents swarmed all over Beirut, had spent 50 million Swiss francs (12.5 million dollars) to buy the Lebanese government's signature on the extradition agreement. Meanwhile, an international campaign on behalf of Bakhtiar was attracting strange bedfellows: Soraya, his old classmates at Saint-Cyr, the Grand Mufti of Iraq, the Maronite Patriarch of Lebanon, Pope Paul VI,

Charles de Gaulle, and Jean-Paul Sartre in his capacity as president of the Committee for Iranian Refugees. (Sartre may have been less concerned with Bakhtiar than with the legal precedent this might set, since it would provide the Shah with a dangerous tool against left-wing Iranians.)

On March 18, Bakhtiar finished serving his sentence and Helou decided that he would refuse extradition "by virtue of our Lebanese tradition of hospitality and out of respect for our present laws." Bakhtiar was permitted to go to the country of his choice, and so he drove off to the airport with a police escort of four jeeps, boarded a plane guarded by an impressive contingent of police, and took off for Zurich, via Rome.

On March 22, Iran broke off diplomatic relations with Lebanon and recalled its ambassador.

For over a year, Bakhtiar seemed to be forgotten, although the Shah had meanwhile come to the conclusion that he must get rid of Bakhtiar permanently.

Then, out of the blue, on August 23, 1970, Agence France Presse cabled the news that Teymur Bakhtiar was dead.

When he had arrived in Switzerland, Bakhtiar hid out in a villa in Geneva surrounded by fifteen armed guards. He received visitors, all of whom appeared to be Iraqis. Iraq had been accusing the Shah of supporting the Kurds' rebellion in the hope of annexing their lands to his. Bakhtiar was judged a powerful ally, and so he was invited to come to Iraq and stir up the guerrillas on the Iraqi border. Then, Bakhtiar started seeing Russians. Had he gone over to the other side in order to involve the U.S.S.R. in bringing down the Shah? The Russians were a potent influence in Iraq and might well be attracted to Bakhtiar's operation.

Two months after his arrival in Geneva, Bakhtiar left for

Baghdad with his wife and two children. The Iraqis put them up in the old Nuri Said palace near the Presidential Palace. Although he lived in extravagant style (he had yet to pay his Lebanese lawyer), he was a strict Muslim, neither drinking nor smoking, and wore the ballooning pants of his tribe, with a Colt .45 tucked into the waistband which he always removed when he prayed to Mecca, exposing his back to whoever was around. He was known to make frequent trips to the Iranian border to smuggle terrorists across, and to station small units of commandos assigned to pull off *coups* on the other side.

The SAVAK did its best to spirit agents into Iraq but they were usually intercepted before they could reach Bakhtiar. Only one, a man who had worked for Bakhtiar ten years earlier, somehow managed to get inside his former chief's house. Bakhtiar recognized him and said: "You have come to kill me. All right then, kill me." And he went to the wall where he had hung a Russian submachine gun, and handed it to the agent. The young man was so unnerved that he left on the run.

Then came August, 1970. An Iran Air plane was flying over the Iraqi-Iranian border when two passengers leapt from their seats and, brandishing revolvers, headed for the pilot's cabin and ordered him to land in Baghdad. They claimed to be supporters of Bakhtiar and caused quite a sensation on their arrival in Baghdad. They immediately asked to be driven to Bakhtiar's house and were received with open arms. To highjack an Iranian plane in order to join forces with him was a high compliment indeed. But what happened after was a quite different story.

As usual, there are two versions. The Iraqis claimed that a few days after their arrival, Bakhtiar invited his new friends to go hunting near the Iranian border, and that one of them accidentally shot him. The more generally accepted view is that the "friend" shot Bakhtiar intentionally, that the two men were SAVAK agents who kidnapped the plane in collusion with the pilot so that they could get to Baghdad without arousing suspicion.

The bullet did not kill Bakhtiar outright. He was brought back to Baghdad where he died of an embolism two days later, and was buried at Nadja, the holy city near Baghdad. The SAVAK agents succeeded in getting back to Iran.

The Iranians only learned eleven days later that the former chief of the SAVAK was dead. And they were never told officially that the murder was a SAVAK operation. But when the Shah was recently asked: "Who assassinated Bakhtiar?" he smiled and answered casually: "We did. The SAVAK did."

Chapter 22

THE LIQUIDATION OF TEYMUR BAKHTIAR was proof of how far Mohammed Riza Pahlevi had risen since 1941 when the Allies thought they could swallow the young king in one gulp. And ironically enough, Bakhtiar was executed by the very organization he himself had created.

What, then, is SAVAK? When a high C.I.A. official was asked what he thought of the agency, he said: "It's a reasonably professional organization, certainly the best of its kind in the Near East. It has some unpleasant features, but it's effective." Under Bakhtiar, the SAVAK was a very powerful organization. Today, its power has increased tenfold.

When General Pakravan took it over in 1961, his first task was to get rid of Bakhtiar's faithful lieutenants and replace them with men loyal to the Shah. But his greatest asset was Bakhtiar's own files, which the latter had not had time to dispose of when he was ousted. Bakhtiar had thought he was accumulating information for his own benefit, but his sworn enemy turned out to be the real beneficiary. In fact, a large part of the Shah's power today can be traced to the formidable store of information he was able to appropriate while it was still warm.

Pakravan lasted only two years. He was too much the intellectual, and in the Shah's opinion, too soft on his enemies.

His replacement, Nematollah Nassiri, was much closer to the mark. With his fat round pock-marked face, his cold yellowish eyes and lips as thin as knives, Nassiri was not an appealing man. One look at him made it obvious that he was exactly the right person to head a merciless outfit like the SAVAK.

Its many offices are scattered around Tehran in nondescript houses and apartments. But its headquarters are a vast complex of buildings on the new road to Shemiran which looks, from the outside, like a distinguished club—except for the antennae bristling from the roof. The number of people employed is a state secret; the Shah pretends not to know the figure, but maintains it is less than two thousand. Prime Minister Hoveyda puts the figure even lower, at around fifteen hundred. Foreign observers, however, place it as high as twenty thousand, which would make it one of the largest secret services in the world. A highly placed official in the C.I.A. who has worked both in Moscow and Tehran recently stated that the SAVAK's sway over Iran is greater than that of either the NKVD or the KGB in the U.S.S.R.

The SAVAK is everywhere. Every high official, every state secretary, even each minister has a SAVAK shadow who monitors everything he does and has the right to inspect his every move. The same holds true for all the large business enterprises in the country, in particular, SNIP—the National Iranian Oil Company. At the University of Tehran, there is said to be a SAVAK agent for every three students. At people's houses, at dinners and receptions, one is never sure if the per-

General Nassiri of SAVAK. *Archives France-Dimanche*

son sitting at one's left or right isn't in some way connected with the SAVAK. This is particularly true of the hotels, especially the Royal Tehran Hilton and the Intercontinental. They are always full, beehives of foreign businessmen, ravishing young women on the make and, of course, agents of the SAVAK. SAVAK operatives are free to come and go as they please, placing microphones and cameras in rooms, searching them at will. It is not at all unusual for a guest returning unexpectedly to his room to find a SAVAK agent going through his bureau drawers.

Wisdom dictates that it be taken in stride. Better he should help them open his suitcases and then offer to buy them a drink at the bar. The agents may well accept, but don't expect an interesting conversation. They have no conversation. Sophistication is not their strong point. In fact, they can also be dolts. One businessman whom certain officials considered a little too enterprising, heard a knock on his door one night. When he opened it, a gorgeous young woman fell into his arms, saying she had a room down the hall, had noticed him in the dining room, was a little bored, etc. Smelling a rat, he led her politely back to her room and returned to his own bed. Five minutes later, his door burst open to the sound of flash bulbs popping. Too bad; he was alone. Their plan had been to take some compromising pictures, but clumsy teamwork botched the job. A lack of professionalism, like almost everything in Iran.

The Hilton even has a sign outside the hotel postoffice that reads—in English: "We accept only non-coded Telexes."

On the subject of torture, no Iranian will ever open his mouth. But a French engineer who recently worked for the Ministry of Transport, told us the following story: There were two Iranian engineers working in the same office with him. Both belonged to the opposition, but were not Communists. One day, neither of them turned up for work. They had both been arrested. Three weeks later, one of the two was released, but so badly disfigured that his own father didn't recognize him. He had been tortured daily. The other engineer was never seen again. This same Frenchman claimed that secretaries of foreign engineers and missions were always SAVAK agents. Also, one had to be very careful at night clubs or parties with guests who, while appearing to be drunk, said disparaging things about the SAVAK. Ninety-nine chances out of a hundred, they were SAVAK agents.

If Iranians will not broach the subject of torture, there is ample documentation from international humanitarian organizations like Amnesty International, the International Association of Democratic Jurists, and the International Federation for the Rights of Man. (The first has headquarters in London, the second in Brussels, the third at the United Nations in New York.)

Maître Thierry Mignon, a French lawyer, gave eloquent testimony on this problem of torture in his report to the International Federation for the Rights of Man which he had represented as an observer at a trial in Tehran in January, 1971. It was an appellate trial involving a group of prisoners called "The Eighteen."

Maître Mignon stated that although he was authorized to attend the trial and meet General Dehzadi, head of the military tribunal, he was not allowed to meet the military assigned as lawyers for the defendants, the minister of justice, the prime minister, the Shah, or to talk to the accused or their families. He added that he was able to attend only two out of the four sessions, the authorities having "forgotten" to tell him the dates of the hearings.

What were the allegations against "The Eighteen"? They were accused of having plotted with Bakhtiar just before his death, and of being Communists. Mignon maintained that he was given no proof of either accusation. He was simply told that the men had confessed. At the trial, the prisoners claimed that their "confessions" had been wrung out of them under torture and they now wished to retract them. Mignon, who was able to talk briefly with them during a recess, reported: "They told me they had been tortured, and several of them showed me scars and worse, especially on the shins and arms."

He then reported on the defense made by Chokrollah Paknejad, one of the group's ringleaders. The young man had said:

"Mister President, if you will permit me, I should like to throw some light on the way in which SAVAK agents behave toward those who hold antigovernment views, so that you may know how Iranian patriots are treated, and so that the value of the interrogations used as evidence here is made perfectly clear. If you will allow me, I will describe some of the tortures inflicted on me.

"After my arrest in January, 1969, I was taken to the SAVAK cellars in Khorramshahr where three interrogators beat me and undressed me for a supposed physical examination. The interrogation lasted from 8:00 PM to midnight, while the beating continued without let-up. The next day, I was transferred to the Abadan city jail where I was locked up in the toilet. I spent one week in that toilet, naked, with a soldier's blanket, and one meal a day.

"On the eighth day, I was transferred to Tehran, to Ewin, the SAVAK prison. As soon as I arrived, my first interrogation began with torture: two men, Atapur and Beiglari, who called each other 'doctor' and 'engineer,' beat me for an hour without stopping. Then they put me behind a desk and tried to make me write down that I was a Communist and a spy. I refused. Two officers came in, stretched me out on the floor and took turns whipping me for three hours with a metal whip. I fainted twice.

"The interrogation lasted until February 1. Then they put me in weighted handcuffs [the prisoner's hands are placed behind his neck with gradually increasing weights hung from the handcuffs.] They then made me climb onto a stool, and each time I had one leg on the stool, they pulled it out from under me. On the third day, my left ear began to bleed. The beatings had ruptured my ear drum and I couldn't hear anything out of that ear."

On another occasion, Paknejad continued, when the SAVAK torturers saw that an engineer named Nikdavudi was about to die on their hands, they had him transferred from Ghezel-Ghalel prison to Ghars to prove that he hadn't died from torture. But when the officials at Ghars saw how serious his condition was, they had him removed to the city hospital where he died. His death was attributed to blows on the neck and a lesion on his spinal marrow. The doctors all agreed that his death was caused by torture inflicted at Ghezel-Ghalel. His crime: that he "read books."

In a report on a trial held in Tehran and published in *Le Monde* in 1972, two prisoners — Nasser Sadegh and Ali Mihandust — described their experiences at the hands of Iranian justice. The article said: "Sadegh told us that while he was in detention, he had been repeatedly struck on the head with the butt of a revolver which caused internal bleeding from which he fainted several times. He also saw two of his companions strapped to a metal table heated until it was white hot. The victim exhibited the burns on his chest and back during the hearing. Sadegh had seen another friend die under torture."

The same issue of *Le Monde* printed a letter from Riza Rizai, an escaped prisoner, which read: "With the birth of urban guerrilla warfare in Iran, torture has been intensified. Most of it takes place during the first twenty-four hours after the guerrilla's arrest. First he is whipped with electric cables, then he is beaten by specialists in karate and judo. After that, his hands, feet and nose broken, he falls into a coma. Then the SAVAK agents come to get his confession, which includes a statement that he was not tortured and that his condition is good."

Riza Rizai then listed some of the tortures he had witnessed: "One engineer was made to sit in a kind of electric chair for four hours. He passed out when the burns reached his spinal column. The smell was so bad that no one would come near our cell. He did not die, but he had to have three operations and now has to use his hands to walk.

"Medhi Savalani, who belonged to the Siahkal group, is no longer able to walk at all. Both his legs were shattered. Current practices involve the use of electric clubs. They leave no trace but paralyze the body. Injections with drugs like cardiazol and tearing nails out are also common. And again, they train powerful spotlights on prisoners, use ultrasonic waves, and beat them over the head. I also saw a man who couldn't urinate because he had weights hung from his penis.

"The prisons are so dark and humid that even the guards refuse to work in them. The cells are four by six feet, and six feet high, with a twelve by fifteen inch window. There is no electric light. One cell is already too small for one person; we were three in ours."

As a political police force assigned to supervise Iranians, the SAVAK doesn't confine its operations to Iran. It also watches over all Iranians abroad, particularly students attending universities in Europe and America.

The *Sunday Times* of London — which can hardly be accused of harboring Communist tendencies — published a report of an incident that took place in London in 1974. According to the story, in the late afternoon of Tuesday, May 2, as people were going home from work, a fifty-year-old man dressed in black stood waiting outside a "pub" called the King's Arms. Under his arm he held an Iranian magazine, *Khandaniha*, and he kept looking at his watch as he nervously flicked the ashes off his cigarette. The magazine was his identification badge. For Abdol Ali Jahanbin, officially the first secretary of the Iranian Consulate in London, was in fact a member of the SAVAK, and he had an appointment with a new contact — a young woman who might make it possible for them to infiltrate the Federation of Iranian Students. The London-based group opposed the Shah's regime and annoyed him greatly.

At 5:35, the story continued, a tall dark girl in a plaid coat appeared carrying a shopping bag. She immediately took in the magazine under the diplomat's arm and, without a word, went in the "pub" and sat down. The man followed her in and joined her, saying: "May I sit down next to you?" When she said yes, they started talking Persian.

He told her his name was Ali and that he knew everything about her, her friends, her life in London, and earlier in Tehran, adding that, as she must be aware, once they had established contact with someone who interested them, it meant that person had been observed for many months. "And you do interest us, my dear. You interest us very much," he concluded.

Iranian by birth, Eli Powey had become a British subject eighteen months earlier when she married a well-known member of the executive committee of the National Union of British Students. Now, this organization had very close relations with the Federation of Iranian Students, and Terry Powey —

Eli's husband—was particularly sympathetic to opponents of the Tehran regime, and invited them often to meetings at his house.

Then, the story went on, Ali explained what he expected of Mrs. Powey, which was nothing more nor less than to spy on her own husband and betray their guests' confidences by reporting to him everything she learned about the activities of Iranian students, specifying places, dates, how long their meetings lasted, etc. Eli Powey asked what would happen to her if she refused the SAVAK's proposition. Ali replied "nothing," and added: "If you refuse to work for us, I only ask that you forget our entire conversation." But Mrs. Powey was persistent. She wanted to know what the risks were to her family in Iran. "We can exclude nothing, of course," Ali replied. "You, I, they, who knows? We are all running risks all the time."

Mrs. Powey had very real reasons for being concerned. In December, the manager of the Iranian Oil Company for which she worked in London had told her she was to go to Tehran. Two days after her arrival, she received a telephone call summoning her to a nondescript house on Sharivar Street for reasons having no apparent connection with her job. It turned out to be an interrogation about her, her family, her political opinions. And the man questioning her made no attempt to hide the fact that he represented the SAVAK, that he knew where her parents, uncles and cousins lived, that she had spent her last vacation with them on the Caspian coast.

That is why, although she had no intention whatever of spying on her husband, she agreed to meet Ali on this particular Tuesday in London.

When their conversation was finished, Mrs. Powey asked for time to think it over. Ali left, without so much as shaking her hand, got into a blue Mercedes with diplomatic license plates (YMI 260 H), and headed back to a meeting—official, this time—at his consulate at 50 Kensington Court.

What Ali didn't know is that Mrs. Powey's shopping bag contained a tape recorder which had taken down their entire conversation, and that he had been photographed while waiting for her outside the "pub," when he left her, as well as when he arrived back at his consulate. Once the article appeared in the *Sunday Times*, Abdol Ali Jahanbin no longer answered his telephone. So far as anyone knew, the SAVAK agent had disappeared for good.

In its surveillance of Iranian students abroad, the SAVAK plants informers among the students. There are two kinds of students: those from wealthy families who pay their own way, and the poor who have obtained scholarships. The Iranian government gives these scholarships on the one condition that when the student returns home, he goes to work for the government. In numerous cases, this otherwise normal obligation includes working for the SAVAK. When the Shah's political police contacts these students, it takes great strength of character to refuse. Many of the "reasonable" ones have already begun spying on their fellow students while abroad, particularly on those who have chosen exile and publicly criticized the Shah's regime. The Shah has reason to be concerned, for many of the students attack him with virulence, to the point where, in January, 1976, they were staging hunger strikes on behalf of political prisoners in Iran in such far-flung places as Cologne, Rome, Milan, Strasbourg, in Holland and Sweden, and, in the United States, in Houston and New York City. In addition, Iranian students shower their comrades with subversive publications printed variously in Washington, Berkeley, New York, West Berlin and Paris. Some of this propaganda even makes it to Iran.

On a recent visit to Paris, the Shah was interviewed on television and was asked specifically about torture in Iran. The Shah answered that there was none, and that the articles saying there was were lies written by people who had never been there. But the interviewer was persistent and reminded the Shah that there was an association called Amnesty International whose integrity and diligence were recognized throughout the world and which had corroborated the allegations made against the SAVAK.

To this, the Shah replied: "Amnesty International? What is it? I never heard of it."

On another occasion, the Shah said: "I am not bloodthirsty. I am working for my country and the coming generations. I can't waste my time on a few young idiots. I don't believe the tortures attributed to the SAVAK are as common as people say, but I can't run everything. Besides, we have ways of using psychological pressure that are much more efficient than torture." He also stated: "My people have every kind of freedom, except the freedom to betray."

But it must be kept in mind that what may seem shocking to Western sensibilities is viewed differently in the Orient. The SAVAK's methods are like those of political police forces in all autocratic regimes—west or east, north or south. The Shah is really not unaware or ill-informed about what the SAVAK is up to. He simply considers it indispensable to his survival and that of his country.

Chapter 23

How does the Shah's autocracy work?

Curiously enough, if one is to believe Iran's Constitution, he has no more power than Queen Elizabeth of England. "Iran is a constitutional monarchy. The Constitution, established in 1906, was directly inspired by those of the European democracies . . ." So says the plush official brochure of the Ministry of Information. And, accordingly, the National Assembly has the supreme legislative authority and is the court of last resort. The Constitution also defines the powers of the executive, legislative and judicial branches. In other words, it is the mirror image of Anglo-Saxon governmental structures.

With this difference, however: In Iran, for all practical purposes, the executive, legislative and judicial powers rest in the hands of one man, His Imperial Majesty, the Shahinshah Mohammed Riza Pahlevi Aryamehr. And in the exercise of his power, he leans on three massive pillars, two of them known, the third secret.

The first pillar is the Ministry of the Imperial Court. Officially, it is supposed to concern itself with the Shah's personal life, his domestic arrangements, travels, receptions, etc. What it in fact does is surround him with a group of intimates who devote their lives to the creation and maintenance of his royal image. The minister himself practices such humility, deference, bowings and scrapings that the Western observer is torn between suppressed laughter and utter disbelief. He is assisted by two vice-ministers who oversee tactical maneuvers, in other words, what is "done" and what is "not done."

Then comes the Grand Master of Ceremonies and Chief of Protocol, the most recent incumbent having had the task of studying every detail of Queen Elizabeth of England's coronation in preparation for the Shah's own.

The Grand Master of the Stables looks after not only the stables but all the king's carriages and automobiles, and determines the makeup of processions and what cars will be placed at the disposal of official visitors.

The palace bureaucracy is run by the chief of the Shah's private secretariat who handles all requests and complaints addressed to the Shah. There is a parallel bureaucracy for the queen.

And last but not least, the *imam* Djumeh, the highest Shiite authority in the country, rules on all religious questions.

The second pillar is the government, made up of twenty-two ministers who answer to the prime minister. They are the worker ants who execute the Shah's directives and see that the country functions properly. The Council of Ministers meets in the prime minister's office every Saturday afternoon. The Shah presides rarely, confining himself to meetings of the inner cabinet. But no decision is taken without his approval. The ministers are no more than the executors of his will.

The third pillar is the "invisible government." Like all heads of autocratic regimes, the Shah has little confidence in

Prime Minister Hoveyda and his wife. *Marilyn Silverstone, Magnum*

his official services, not even in the SAVAK. So he has created a "super SAVAK," the "Imperial Inspectorat Organization." Its current chief is the Shah's companion at Le Rosey, Hossein Fardust, and he has the power to investigate anything and everything, the SAVAK included. He is answerable only to the Shah. Furthermore, the head of the I.I.O. is chief as well of "Daftare Vijeh," an organization even more secret than the SAVAK and the I.I.O. Made up of fifteen colonels of un-impeachable honesty and loyalty, this group makes rapid, thorough and often brutal investigations on the Shah's be-half. As the "Incorruptibles" of Iran, it is their task to track down corruption in high places.

The Shah manipulates these three pillars with great skill and undisputed authority. Applying the rule of "divide and conquer," he only sees visitors singly, including the chiefs of the armed services. This encourages all those around him to adhere to an attitude of total submission.

Should you ask any Iranian to describe his government, the answer is almost invariably: "A pyramid, with the Shah on top. Everything flows down from him." The irreverent, of whom there are a few, add: "It's a pyramid of salaams."

Once this amazing machine of government has been taken apart, one obvious question remains: what does the Shah do with his absolute power? How does such an anachronism in the last quarter of the twentieth century conduct himself?

Chapter 24

HIGH ABOVE TEHRAN, a large gray helicopter comes clattering from east of the city, followed by a second helicopter two hundred yards behind. Below, in traffic jams, on sidewalks, people look up for a moment, then go their way. The Shah has just passed overhead, he in the first plane, his secret services in the second. (The Shah's helicopter used to be a snappy blue and white. For security reasons, it is now a dull gray.) And since it is a Friday and a little after noon, everybody knows what he is doing up there. He is coming home from an hour's horseback ride and will soon be having lunch, at Niavaran if it were winter, Saadabad if summer.

Week after week, often day after day, the royal helicopter passes over its three million subjects in the capital, and they look up as if to an all-powerful god flying over them. Contrary to most of today's heads of state who think they must look and act like "everyman," the Shah is a sovereign who is not ashamed to display his power. In fact, he parades it for all to see.

The Shah lives his power, and this is physically palpable the moment the visitor arrives at Mehrabad Airport outside Tehran. On the wall of the great hall where he waits for his baggage, he is greeted by an enormous photograph of the Shah, Farah and Riza Cyrus, with the Shah, looking young and vigorous, welcoming the visitor with one arm outstretched, a broad American-type smile on his face, with, as background, Damavend, Iran's highest mountain. The gesture and the smile are the symbols of contemporary Iran. Yet the capital you are about to enter is a replica of the mythic city in Fritz Lang's famous movie *Metropolis*, where there are two cities, the higher one for the master and his favorites, the lower city for the common people – the workers.

In the south, at an altitude of four thousand feet, are the factories, the workshops, the belching chimneys, the hovels of the lower classes. High above to the north, at fifty-two hundred feet, the large houses, parks and palaces. And between the two, the bazaar, with the business district, offices and shops. Here also, the remnants of the vast parks that once belonged to the foreign embassies, which have been gradually nibbled away by ubiquitous modern buildings of steel and glass.

The Shah has abandoned the city for the Elburz foothills. The old Winter Palace is now the museum of the Pahlevi dynasty, its annex the residence of the prime minister. Golestan is also a museum, a gloomy, glacial building full of Sèvres vases and gifts to the Shah from foreign heads of state.

In contrast to the Shah's welcoming smile at the airport, today's royal palaces are imposing and mysterious fortresses, surrounded by disturbingly high walls with armed sentinels every hundred yards, and guarded gates with sentry boxes which open only after a long and detailed inspection of the visitor's permit. Saadabad, built by Riza the Great, sits within its immense walls in a hundred-and-fifty-acre park planted with huge trees of every variety, most of the park being allowed to grow wild. Scattered about are a dozen palaces for various members of the family, with small houses for the children. The palace itself is a massive, white, square, two-story building with a wide flight of steps leading up to a portico with four columns. Since it hugs a western slope of the Elburz, the air is cooler than at Niavaran three miles to the east.

Niavaran was built about ten years ago, and since the royal couple — Farah in particular — designed it themselves, it gives a better idea of the Shah's way of life. The great gates, the entrance, and the interior court are guarded day and night by soldiers of the Imperial Guard, all chosen from tribes of Azerbaijan and Mazanderan, these producing the handsomest men in the country. And in their long Russian-style overcoats with blue foulards at the neck, short-visored caps and clicking boots, these men really do look superb. With their American submachine guns, bayonets and revolvers, they are also intimidating.

If the visitor has gotten this far, it is because he has survived an infinite number of hurdles. He has been studied, scrutinized, screened and filtered before receiving his permit. When he finally reaches the gates, he then proceeds alone, and on foot. His briefcase has of course been searched, and he will also pass through metal detectors.

The Shah's office is to the right, in the old Qajar palace which looks south over Tehran. The Shah has taken over the vast former reception room, with its mirrored walls and ceilings, and furnished it with comfortable couches, Empire chairs, cases full of antique armor, and ancient lances and swords hanging on the walls. His desk is a large Empire table, with smaller tables on either side, books and folders on the right, his gold telephone embossed with the Pahlevi arms on the left. On a table against the wall is a map of the world lighted from below to indicate the time zones in every part of the world.

As adjuncts to his study, the Shah has an ultramodern cubicle equipped with a dentist's chair and all the latest gadgetry—in odd contrast to the Napoleonic grandeur of the office—and downstairs, a hair-cutting parlor. In the basement immediately under the Shah's room, the startled visitor comes upon a "game" belonging to the crown prince. It is a perfect replica of an oil port, laid out on a table, with tankers, quays, refineries, and an electrical system controlled from a command post which sets in motion every activity of a refinery from filling a tanker right up to its departure toward the high seas. In the days of the Qajars, this space was their summer room. To provide natural air-conditioning, a series of miniature canals had been grooved out of the basement floor to carry the cool waters that flowed down the Elburz Mountains and through the park above the palace.

Dominating the old Qajar palace is the new one built ten years ago from Farah's plans. As a student in Paris, she had conceived the palace of her dreams. Now it stands, fully realized, a large cube with a facade of columns reminiscent of the architecture of the thirties. The interior, however, is very different. The visitor enters into what looks like a deep grotto, much higher and longer than seems possible from the outside. Around it are tiers of balconies with railings sheathed in glass to prevent the royal children from hurtling to the bottom. The only light comes from great glittering chandeliers that pick up the subtle colors of the huge Persian rugs that carpet the floor. On the southern end, the grotto opens into a large reception room overlooking the city, furnished in priceless antiques and deep couches. And everywhere, great bowls of gladioli. In one corner, Farah's piano, and here and there, tables covered with bibelots. On one table, under a

(l. to r.) The Shah, Farah, the Queen Mother, Princess Shams, and Princess Shanaz.

glass dome, is a crown of gold laurel leaves, said to be the crown of Alexander the Great. Against the walls, between the many paintings, glass cases display archeological treasures going back to ancient times, all labeled as if in a museum. Next to the reception room is the dining room with a table seating twenty – the royal couple use one end when alone – the walls hung with paintings of all periods. Beyond this room, a series of smaller sitting rooms, a smoking room, and finally, the capacious red and white projection room. On the north end is the state dining room.

The family's private domain encircles the second floor of the grotto. The Shah and Shabanu's apartments are to the south, the childrens' and their governess's rooms taking up the rest. The royal couple's bathrooms give an idea of the general luxury. The Shah himself ordered the bathtubs from Michel de Lacour's shop *Au Bain de Diane* in Paris. They are identical, with pink marble sides, the interior of crystal tinted a Mediterranean blue lit from below. The faucets are in the form of dolphins in bronze covered with gold leaf, with amethyst eyes for Farah's tub, jade for the Shah's.

The servants' rooms are on the third floor.

When he is not skiing in Switzerland or vacationing on the shores of the Caspian, the Shah keeps to a very strict schedule. He rises at 6:30 AM, which is not extraordinary in Iran where offices open at 7:30 if not before. The work day is confined mainly to the morning, although lunch is seldom before 1:30 or 2:00, allowing for his daily horseback ride. Offices close very early in the afternoon, or don't open at all.

The Shah starts the morning with calisthenics. He is in excellent physical condition except for his eyes which are astigmatic, myopic and far-sighted, all at the same time. He also has stomach problems which have cut down his enjoyment of food. He is at his desk at 8:00, 8:30 at the latest, works until

The royal family, 1971.

A typical evening at the palace. It is customary for the guests to sit on the rug. *Archives France-Dimanche*

1:30, lunches usually with Farah and the crown prince, returns to his office at 3:00, and seldom leaves before 7:30. Actually, this routine is often interrupted by official ceremonies and trips around the country or abroad. The Shah is constantly on the move, and always by air, even in Tehran. Since she became regent, Farah and the Shah are not supposed to fly in the same plane or helicopter, but this rule is more often honored in the breach. Moreover, the Shah usually takes the controls himself.

The couple's evenings are as regulated as graph paper, with family dinners, movies and card games succeeding each other like entertainments on a cruise ship. Nothing could be further from the traditional conception of Oriental courts with their debauchery overlaid with opium fumes. Beyond the immediate family, the Shah's friends are few: a prince, a doctor, a surgeon married to a tall blond whose language becomes a little blue when she's had a drop too many, for which the Shah scolds her gently.

The ritual is unchanging: on Thursday and Sunday, he dines at Princess Ashraf's; on Wednesday and Saturday, at the Queen Mother's; on Monday, at Fatemed's. In contrast to the amiable informality of family dinners, the official evenings are notorious for their stiffness. The Shah and Farah usually dine alone at a table off to one corner while the rest of the guests serve themselves from a buffet and eat standing. Since it is forbidden to turn one's back to the king, guests have to go into contortions to keep facing the Shah as they move around. Also, absolute silence is *de rigueur*, the only sound being the rattle of plates, glasses and cutlery.

The ambassadors are invited in groups of twelve — including wives — three times a year, the Shah and Farah at either end of the table and the guests seated according to the strictest protocol. The atmosphere is glacial. In fact, a French diplomat has observed: "The Shah is the most stiff-necked head of state I have ever known." Yet when the king is not acting in his official capacity, he is simple in manner and very relaxed. Such is the price of absolute power.

The Shah's daily horseback ride is a spectacle one is not likely to forget. Every morning, stable boys take out a dozen horses and the grooms walk them around to keep them calm. The king may not come, of course, but all is in readiness, just in case. Then, a little after eleven, throbbing sounds come out of the northwest and as they grow louder, two gray helicopters appear low in the sky. As they touch down, several horses are brought up at a gallop. Mohammed Riza steps out of the plane, wearing pearl gray riding breeches, a heavy gray turtle neck sweater with wine red leather pads front and back, a Tyrolean hat sporting a feather, and gleaming boots of supple chesnut colored leather.

Striding in his usual slow, deliberate gait, head back, chin thrust forward, he looks very regal indeed. He chooses a horse, and after a few warm-up turns in the paddock, digs in his spurs and heads for one of the bridle paths cut through the young forest.

An hour later, he is back, his face pink from the wind and exertion, and immediately steps into the helicopter which has already started up its engines. In a matter of seconds, the two planes are on their way back to the palace.

What does the Shah read? Does he read at all? "I haven't time," he said recently. When asked his taste in literature, he says he prefers Rabelais and Chateaubriand to all other writers. In music, he likes Chopin and Liszt. His taste in movies is confined to thrillers and cloak-and-dagger films, usually French with Iranian subtitles.

To the question, "Do you have any friends?" he answers: "Alas, no. I can't. If I take a liking to someone, I need only the smallest shred of doubt to make me break it off. I am alone, but I don't feel alone." Then he points to the sky, "because God is up there. I know people sometimes make fun of me because I am religious, but I feel this profoundly. God is my only friend."

And he continued: "There was a sharp break in my life after 1953. I came to realize that I couldn't have the same relationships with my friends. Friendship involves the exchange of confidence between two people, but a king can take no one into his confidence. I have even had to put some distance between myself and my old friend Hossein Fardust whom I trust implicitly. I even observe certain distances with members of my family. I had to tell my mother—who is a very dictatorial woman—that it would be better if she didn't ask me for favors for I might have to refuse her."

Farah lives the life of a dutiful and disciplined sovereign—a far cry from Soraya and her indolent ways. The Shabanu is an intelligent, energetic woman who cannot tolerate inactivity. Much loved by her people, listened to by her husband—it is even said that she is the only person who can influence him—she has proved to be exactly the queen the Shah needed. She plays a very important role, and those in the know say she has no enemies. Even in Tehran's high society, where malice is the coin of the realm, one hears only praise of Farah.

Her life consists of work and obligations. Rising early, she first busies herself with those of the children who live in the palace (Riza Cyrus, it must be remembered, lives in his own house on the palace grounds): Farnaz, born in 1963, Ali Riza, in 1966, and the only girl, Leila, in 1970. She keeps strict office hours before and after lunch, but her chief concern is her country's cultural life. She supports Iranian painters, she established the Arts Festival of Shiraz-Persepolis, and she presides over the International Film Festival and is an active proponent of women's rights. She also has access to a number of political files, for her husband is determined that, should anything happen to him, she will immediately be able to assume her role as regent until the crown prince is of age. To the point that when the Shah is away, it is Farah who presides over the Council of Ministers.

The crown prince's life is both harsh and divorced from reality. Harsh because he is made to work very hard, unreal because he has no contact whatever with the outside world. He studies at a school in the palace with twenty-five children drawn from the families of top officials and his royal relations, and the Shah's orders are that he be treated exactly like the others. He is a diligent student, very conscious of his position, but far from putting on airs, he seems to feel it as a burden.

His great love is his French nurse, Joëlle Guyon, a forty-year-old spinster who has cared for him since his birth, and whose word is law. Living as he does in his own house, his relationship with his parents is affectionate but formal, although he likes to invite them to his house for supper. He does the cooking himself, his specialties being soups and omelets. When the Shah was asked if he considered sending Riza Cyrus to Europe for further education, he said "no," adding: "He would pick up too many bad habits." Has the Shah forgotten the virtues he ascribed to his years at Le Rosey, or have they simply become too dangerous in present-day Iran?

With the exception of Gholam Riza who takes part in official ceremonies, Abdul Riza, and of course Ashraf, the rest of the Pahlevi family doesn't amount to much. They fight the boredom of court life with sports, trips abroad, gossip, and spending money. Mahmud gambles away huge sums and recently bought into a nightclub and bowling alley in Tehran. Ashraf's son, Sharam, infuriated the Shah by making fifty million dollars in two years and was told to put a stop to such conspicuous venality. His half-sister Shams engaged the American architect, William Wesley Peters, ex-husband of Stalin's daughter Svetlana, to build her an eighty-room palace in Chalus, resembling the Guggenheim Museum in New York, with a garden in the center lighted by a translucent dome, and in 1975, she bought for $500,000 an apartment in the Shoreham Hotel in Washington, D.C. Then his daughter Shanaz, after her divorce from Adeshir Zahedi in 1967, became enamored of Khosro Djahanbani, a young man with a degree in economics from the University of Michigan, whose father had been ambassador to Paris. When Shanaz announced her intention of marrying Khosro, the Shah exploded. So she went off to Switzerland and got married. Two years later—by that time she had given birth to a son—she telephoned her father to ask his forgiveness and allow her to come home. She said it was all over between herself and Khosro. The Shah was touched and welcomed her home with open arms. All was well until the Shah learned that Shanaz had spirited Khosro back to Iran and had tucked him away in her villa. There were weeks of fireworks, but in the end, the Shah forgave her.

Next to the Shah and Farah, there is no question that the most important person in the country is Ashraf. Ashraf is a fascinating woman. Widely traveled, she speaks perfect English and French, entertains a great deal, and is a charming hostess full of wit and interesting observations. But woe to anyone she doesn't like! Her volcanic rages are famous—to the point where her brother had to ease her out of domestic affairs. To use up her energies, she first tried gambling, losing vast sums in the process. Then little by little, she became interested in her country's social problems, always with the same energy.

The apotheosis of this royal charade was the Shah's coronation on October 28, 1967, and its sequel, the celebration marking the twenty-five hundredth anniversary of the Persian Empire in Persepolis on October 15, 1971.

At first, buoyed by the birth of a second son, the Shah thought to combine the two affairs. Though the Shah had, of course, assumed the throne in 1941, the Iranian Constitution prohibits a coronation ceremony until a son and heir is born; and in the years following Reza Cyrus's birth, political events had caused a series of postponements. Now he and Farah would have a joint coronation, and at the same time celebrate the Empire's twenty-five hundredth anniversary.

Work on the project started immediately. The film of Queen Elizabeth's coronation in 1953 was sent for, and officials plumbed the archives in search of information about ceremonies during the reigns of Darius and Cyrus. By the end of the year's research, it became all too clear that the cost would be prohibitive. Disappointed but realistic, the royal couple decided to stage the coronation by itself. The twenty-five hundredth anniversary would have to wait. Also, this would give more time for the "white revolution" to show results.

There were reasons beyond the pecuniary for rushing the coronation. Attempts on the Shah's life were becoming more and more frequent, and should he die before his son came of age, the Constitution was categorical: "If, when the king dies, the crown prince has not yet reached the age of twenty, the Parliament has ten days in which to choose a regent." So far, whenever the Shah was away, interim power was vested in a commission made up of the prime minister, a brother of the Shah (usually Gholam Riza), the speaker and president of the *majlis*, and the minister of the court. This had to be changed.

In August, 1967, the Shah had the constitutional chamber vote to modify Articles 38, 41 and 42 of the Constitution so that only he could designate the regent. That regent would be Farah, as soon as she was crowned.

Since the parliamentary vote was never in doubt, plans for the coronation began several months before. If the Shah flinched at the cost of the combined cermonies, he did not exactly hold back on the coronation. Farah's white satin dress

Mohammed Riza Pahlevi at coronation. *Marilyn Silverstone, Magnum*

Farah Diba at coronation. *Marilyn Silverstone, Magnum*

would of course be made by Dior, with a cape of green velvet (Iran's color) to wear after the coronation. The Shah's mantle had been a gift to his father from the people of Meshed and Khnassan at the time of his own coronation. The long white cashmere garment was emblazoned with peacock feathers sewn with gold thread and pearls, the edges, pockets and sleeves encrusted with pearls and gold and silver pailettes. The pearls alone weighed almost five pounds. The closing at the neck was an aigrette of diamonds set around one large emerald and five smaller pear-shaped stones, the diamonds disposed so as to resemble flags, bayonets and rifle barrels. This extraordinary confection weighed 781 carats and had been designed for the notorious Nadir Shah in the eighteenth century. The Shah's uniform — that of Grand Marshal of the Empire — would include a black jacket — covered with decorations, of course — blue trousers with red stripes, and at his waist, a belt of gold mail with a buckle set with a 175-caret emerald surrounded by sixty brilliants and 145 diamonds.

The gold scepter, a gift to Riza the Great from the people of Azerbaijan, was surmounted by a globe with three lions, three suns and a gold crown set with precious stones. His sword had been chiseled in 1889 by a famous goldsmith, the hilt and sheath of gold set with countless emeralds, rubies, sapphires and 12,384 diamonds. The crown was also Riza Shah's. Copied after the Sassanian crowns (the tribe that ruled Persia before the seventh century A.D.), it had 3,380 diamonds, 388 pearls and scattered emeralds and sapphires. Riza Shah's head being unusually large, the crown had to be made smaller for his son. Farah's crown was of gold and platinum, set with a profusion of emeralds, rubies, pearls, diamonds, and brilliants.

The throne was, of course, the famous Peacock Throne. Seven feet high, over three feet deep and three feet wide, it was made of gold-plated wood set with 26,733 precious stones. The imperial carriage was brand new, ordered from one of the last carriage makers still in business—Joseph Klieman of Vienna. Made of ebony encrusted with rare pearls and stamped with the royal arms, it represented twenty-five thousand man-hours of work.

This royal treasure, valued at a mere $20 million (the stones are considered second-rate), is locked up in the basement of the Bank Melli in a great reinforced concrete vault. Nothing can be removed except in the presence of seven high officials, even at the Shah's request.

To decorate Tehran for the event, one million green, red and white flags with the imperial lion rampant were ordered from abroad and hung from every public building, house and shop window. Every house along the path of the procession was refurbished, and giant triumphal arches graced every intersection.

A week before the ceremony, all of Iran seemed to have found its way to the capital. People came on foot, on donkeys, on camel back, wearing red kaftans, black sheepskin hats, brown and white *gandurahs*, robes of every color, billowing white pants and turbans with aigrettes. Forty thousand policemen kept watch over the crowds, and General Nassiri took the precaution of expelling twenty-five thousand people judged to be "undesirable."

At 8:30 on the morning of the coronation, fifteen armed battalions took their places the length of the route, and at 9:40, preceded by a motorcycle escort, the royal procession got underway. "Zendeh bad Shah! Zendeh bad Shabanu!" (Hurrah for the Shah!, Hurrah for the Shabanu) rose from thousands of throats.

Since 10:00 AM, five thousand dignitaries had been waiting in the great Hall of Mirrors in Golestan Palace: ministers, generals, ambassadors, members and friends of the family, and foreign royalty, among them Haile Selassie, Hassan II of Morocco, Hussein of Jordan, Mohammed Zahir, King of Afghanistan, Akihito, crown prince of Japan, Mohammed, crown prince of Saudi Arabia, Isa Bin Salman Al Khalifah, King of Bahrain, Karim Aga Khan, Prince Bertil of Sweden, Ayub Khan, president of Pakistan, Sunay, president of Turkey, Bourguiba of Tunis, Maurice Couve de Murville representing Charles de Gaulle, Sir Rupert Neville, for Queen Elizabeth — and many more. The Queen Mother stood in the middle, surrounded by the various princes and princesses, Madame Farideh Diba, Farah's mother, and the princesses' husbands.

The Shah took his place on the Peacock Throne. The ceremony could now begin.

As the trumpets blared, the imperial flag was hoisted above the throne. Then the *imam* Djumeh came forward, intoning a prayer of thanksgiving, followed by verses from the Koran. He handed the Koran to his sovereign who kissed it, then put on his belt, attached the sword to it, and placed his mantle around his shoulders. A soldier from each of the armed services and four officers marched up carrying the crown, and held it out to the Shah. He placed it on his own head, then picked up the scepter.

Now it was Farah's turn. Attendants carrying her crown and mantle approached. Farah kneeled before her husband as her ladies-in-waiting draped the mantle over her shoulders. The Shah placed the crown on her head. Then, turning to his son and pointing to the assembled guests, he said: "This is His Imperial Highness, the Crown Prince," and he gave his son the same sword his father had given him in 1926.

It was all over by one o'clock. The royal couple returned to the Marble Palace where an enormous celebratory buffet was waiting. To bring them luck, the repast included seven symbolic dishes, each beginning with the letter S: Sib (apples), Sabezi (salad), Samanu (sugar), Sertek (vinegar), Sir (garlic), and Setex (pieces of gold and silver). On the center table stood a red fish in a bowl of water (to bring good luck), smoked fish and chicken (to insure prosperity), a mirror (symbol of light) and, of course, a Koran.

The party was ready to begin.

It was soon time for the Shah to prepare the celebration that would stun the entire world—the twenty-five hundredth anniversary of the Persian Empire.

Why did he choose Persepolis for the site? Because that was the place where, in the center of the Marv Dasht basin at an altitude of 5400 feet, Cyrus the Great had decided to build a palace worthy of his empire's greatness, to which he gave the name Persepolis, meaning "City of the Persians."

Of this palace, whose unparalleled luxury—marble, gold, sculptures, paneling, furniture, rugs and fabrics—had dazzled all who saw it, nothing is left but ruins on a platform of earth sixty feet across and ninety to a hundred and fifty feet deep. During an orgy one December night in 331 B.C., Alexander the Great's troops set fire to everything that would burn. Over the centuries, desert winds and plunderers did the rest, though even today, the beauty and scale of the ruins are breathtaking. The Shah could not have chosen a better stage set for his "triumph."

For a year, there was a constant coming and going between Persepolis, Tehran and Paris, for it was in France that almost everything for the celebration was made. First, a vast encampment of tents covering 160 acres to shelter the guests, made of synthetic fiber and mounted on concrete foundations with wooden frames. Flameproof and capable of resisting sixty-mile-an-hour winds, there were three royal tents and fifty-nine for the guests. The interior decoration was reminiscent of the neoclassic palaces dear to German royalty in the nineteenth century: great hangings of embossed purple velvet with gilt bronze appliqués in the reception room, sideboards painted *trompe l'oeil* in fake pink marble, and round tables on pedestals in the dining room. All the tents were air-conditioned.

For a year, a twice-monthly airlift was reloaded onto convoys of trucks that crossed the desert. The security forces were also active. No unauthorized person was allowed within a radius of seventy-five miles, with three concentric circles of armed troops scrutinizing every guest. Virtually everybody was searched during the preparations. One French electrician was singled out for frisking forty times within twenty-four hours. Even the fancy soaps were subjected to a Geiger counter. To keep "troublesome elements" at bay, several thousand people were arrested as a precautionary measure, and the parents of those who wouldn't give their addresses were taken as hostages. The SAVAK went so far as to supply a portable radio beamed into SAVAK's frequency to every operative assigned to a guest.

Meanwhile, two hundred Iranian soldiers gave up shaving so that, at the last moment, their beards could be trimmed to resemble those of the ancient Persian warriors whose uniforms —copies, of course—they were to wear.

The Shah felt keenly the rebuffs to his invitations: Nixon turned him down, sending Spiro Agnew instead; Queen Elizabeth declined in favor of Prince Philip and Princess Anne; and Georges Pompidou sent Jacques Chaban-Delmas. To make up for these galling absences, however, he could comfort himself with the faithful Haile Selassie (who arrived with a black chihuahua wearing a diamond collar), nine kings, five queens, thirteen princes, eight princesses, sixteen presidents, three prime ministers, two governor-generals, two foreign ministers, nine sheikhs, two sultans—representing all together, sixty-nine countries.

The ceremony began with a visit to the tomb of Cyrus at Pasargadae, fifty miles northeast of Persepolis. Then the guests returned to Persepolis for the banquet. The menu included quail eggs stuffed with caviar (the only Iranian food at the dinner, Farah complained), lobster mousse with Sauce Nantua, flaming lambs with arak, a traditional dish of peacock stuffed with foie gras, platters of cheese, a salad of figs and raspberries, champagne sherbet, and to mark Farah's thirty-third birthday, a seventy pound cake. Maxim's was in charge of the catering, and provided 165 chefs, wine stewards and waiters—not to mention 25,000 bottles of wine.

The Shah's imperial "triumph" cost him—according to the most reasonable estimates—one hundred million dollars. To those who reproached him for the cost, the Shah remarked: "This criticism is ridiculous. The twenty-five hundredth anniversary celebration cost me less than the inauguration of each new president of the United States." And as for the banquet's expense, he said: "What do they think I should feed over fifty heads of state? Bread and radishes?"

In a more thoughtful vein, he added: "You Westerners simply don't understand the philosophy behind my power. The Iranians think of their sovereign as a father. What you call 'my celebration' was to them the celebration of Iran's father. The monarchy is the cement of our unity. In celebrating our twenty-five hundredth anniversary, all I was doing was celebrating the anniversary of my country, of which I am the father. Now, if to you, a father is inevitably a dictator, that is your problem, not mine."

There were two other reasons the Shah did not mention: He wanted to show the Iranian people that Iran had once again become a great nation, triggering a national awareness of a new Iran restored to the great days of Darius. And he wanted to record Iran's entry onto the international stage, impress the emirs of the Persian Gulf and the people of the third world. Besides, Iranians point to the fact that part of the expense helped to finance a permanent infrastructure of roads and hotels. Even the great tents now serve to house conventions.

The Pahlevi family is used to thinking in large numbers. The Shah is indeed one of the world's richest men, but his fortune, or most of it, remains invisible. In addition to the land he still owns, he has large accounts managed by the Union of Swiss Banks, with a portfolio of assets that ranges from real estate to oil refineries. The occasional indiscretions leaked by Swiss banking circles place this part of his fortune at several billion dollars.

Everything that bears on the family's finances is a secret. None of the Pahlevis has an official income; it is one of the ambiguities of the Iranian system. In 1958, the Shah created the Bonyad Pahlevi Foundation into which he has gradually transferred – officially at least – everything he possesses. The first transfer made public was valued at $133 million, and it included the assets of the Persian Gulf Shipping Company, the Bank for Development and Rural Cooperatives, the Royal Publications, the Melli Insurance Company, the Golestan Sugar Refinery, cement works in Fars and Khuzistan, several hotels, restaurants and nightclubs, etc. The gifts continue, but they are no longer made public, although it is known that the O.M.R.A.M., one of Iran's largest commercial banks, was turned over to the foundation. Nor has the foundation ever made a public accounting of its assets.

In theory, it is completely independent of the royal family. But there are those who believe that the Shah continues to control it and is in fact the sole owner. In a country like Iran, and with a monarchy as absolute as the Pahlevis', it is difficult to draw a line defining the limits of their possessions, particularly since the foundation's directors are named by the Shah. In another area, a number of foreign businessmen are convinced that the Shah gets a percentage of every contract signed with a foreign firm. Given the Shah's character, this seems highly unlikely. But in view of the degree of corruption practiced in Iran, even among the Shah's entourage, these suspicions are understandable.

It seems fair to say that amassing a fortune is not the Shah's chief aim in life. What appears to motivate him most, the thing to which he devotes all his energies, has much vaster implications: He wants to become a part of history, to engrave his name for all time not only on the history of his country but on that of the entire world. With his mysticism, he might even hope to fill the spiritual void in the Western countries which, in his view, are floundering in materialism.

Chapter 25

THE "WHITE REVOLUTION" is Iran's answer to its critics, the leit-motiv of the Pahlevi saga.

All foreign correspondents working in Tehran in the fifties remember vividly the extraordinary scene that took place at regular intervals in the Winter Palace. The ritual was always the same, and it transported them centuries back to feudal days in Europe. Little did any of them know then that they were witnessing the birth of the "white revolution."

Starting at dawn, hundreds of peasants in their Sunday best (Friday-best in Iran) waited on the sidewalks, looking expectant and a little frightened in the tight lineup imposed by the police. By ten o'clock, the gates were opened, and they timidly filed in toward the great reception hall which they entered, silent, heads bared, looking wide-eyed at the chandeliers and paintings. Facing them as they entered the room was a huge table on a platform piled high with rolled-up papers tied with ribbons and fastened with sealing wax.

The Shah walked in and everyone prostrated themselves. Smiling, he asked the company to rise and the strange ceremony began. As names were called out, the peasants—some

The Shah distributing royal lands to his genuflecting subjects, 1950. *Michel Descamps, Paris-Match*

singly, some in groups—climbed to the platform and received dozens of rolled-up papers from their sovereign's hand. The Shah was giving away his lands: Henceforth, they—the peasants—would be the owners. Each time, as the peasant received his deed, he would kneel before the king and press a kiss on his shoe. And each time, the Shah would quickly ask him to stand up. However many times he asked them to stop the genuflection, they continued the ritual. To kiss the feet of the person who has just made you a gift of his lands is a sacred duty.

Thus, in a few years, the Shah distributed over a million and a quarter acres—a quarter of Iran's arable land—to over thirty thousand families. This was the project dearest to his heart: to lead Iran out of the Middle Ages and turn it into a modern country. The "white revolution" was the first step. By giving away his lands, he hoped to galvanize his people and revolutionize their habits and attitudes. But it wasn't until 1963, when he had finally won out against the grasping politicians and feudal landowners, that he felt strong enough to move forward.

Since 1963, in the government, in the public services, the two words have been the order of the day. Signs, posters, and billboards on all official buildings spread the word. Before oil became the Shah's obsession, his conversation constantly turned to the "twelve points of the white revolution"—they were six at the beginning and gradually added to. And here lies the paradox: How can an absolute monarch speak of "the liberation of the working masses," "positive socialism," "an end to the exploitation of men by men" and even of "a people's democracy," when in the same breath Communism is put down with violence and left-wing parties are denounced as "reactionary"?

In point of fact, the Shah's program rivals—at least on paper—that of any left-wing party on the globe:

1. The abolition of tenant farming and the redistribution to the peasants of all lands owned by large landowners who do not cultivate them themselves.

2. Nationalization of all forests.

3. The selling of all government industrial enterprises to cooperatives and private individuals.

4. The sharing of profits from these enterprises between workers and employers.

5. A revision of the electoral law to provide for universal suffrage and, in particular, woman's suffrage.

6. The creation of an Army of the Educated, for high school graduates who will do their military service as teachers.

7. The creation of an Army of Health, made up of doctors and dentists, exercising their professions in the countryside, free of charge.

8. Creation of an Army of Development to promote agriculture.

9. The establishment of Equity Tribunals in all the villages.

10. Nationalization of all water resources.

11. A national plan for urban and rural reconstruction.

12. Reorganization of all government units, administrative decentralization, and a total recasting of national education.

What, after ten years, has the "white revolution" accomplished? Its first result seems to have been the unleashing of a great economic boom. Everywhere in Iran, there is frenetic activity. At Kharg, a small island facing Abadan, the Iranians have built the largest petroleum port ever conceived for the exportation of oil. From all over southern Iran, across mountains and valleys, then plunging under the waters of the Gulf for twenty-five miles, dozens of pipelines converge in giant reservoirs as high as thirty-story buildings and as large as football fields, on a plateau on the summit of Kharg. Other pipelines have their terminal in a steel and concrete port built in deep water three and a half miles away. Super-tankers from all over the world queue up night and day. (It takes only eight hours to fill a 500,000 ton tanker; the rate of intake is 60,000 tons an hour.)

Petro-chemical works have sprung up in Kharg, Abadan, Shampur and Shiraz; lead, copper, iron and coal mines have been dug; Iran has become the largest exporter of sulfur in the Middle East; iron and steel mills, along with other metals, are constantly going up. The Aryamehr complex near Isfahan already produces—besides gas—over a million tons of steel a year.

Meanwhile, transportation has expanded enormously. In ten years, 21,000 miles of roads have been built; seventeen cities now have airports; a telephone network covers most of the country; and fourteen dams irrigate a quarter of a million acres of land, at the same time tripling Iran's electric power.

To replace oil, whose reserves experts believe will be exhausted in twenty years, Iran plans to shift to nuclear power. From the atom, the Shah expects not only all the energy his country needs, but the desalinization of sea water to solve agriculture's key problem of drought.

Until 1975, the cost of this giant effort was absorbed. In 1974, oil profits rose 400 percent approaching $23 billion. With a production of 6 million barrels a day, or over 12 million tons a year, Iran is the world's fourth largest producer of oil. Together with Saudi Arabia, this represents 50 percent of all the oil produced by the thirteen OPEC countries. With 1974 oil revenues at $1.5 billion a month, the Shah was able to give the underdeveloped nations grants worth $2¼ billion. Between 1971 and 1973, Iran averaged a rate of economic growth of 14.3 percent; in 1974, it climbed to 40 percent. Shifting to another area, between 1968 and 1972, savings accounts doubled in volume, as did the amounts deposited. From 1971 to 1973, assets in Iran's twenty-eight principal banks grew by 70 percent, from $508 million to $880 million. With the first surge in oil revenues, these figures increased three- and four-fold. This made Iran the ninth richest country in the world, after the U.S., the U.S.S.R., West Germany, Japan, France, Australia, Saudi Arabia and Great Britain. What a splendid revenge for the quaking monarch Churchill barely acknowledged during the Tehran Conference! Better still, the Shah was now in a position to bail out Europe and America's ailing economies, distributing loans here and there as he pleased.

During 1974, he loaned $3 billion to Italian firms, $1.5 billion to British industries, $1 billion as advance payment to France for five nuclear power stations, and $7 billion to underdeveloped countries in Asia and Africa.

During 1975, to provide for its own needs, Iran shopped around with the sharp eye of a French housewife weighing the desire for bargains with the need to spread her patronage around. Iran's army numbers 280,000 men, modest enough compared with the armies of some other Middle Eastern powers, but the Iranian air force is probably the world's third largest. In the pursuit of an ever more powerful military establishment—dictated, according to the Shah, by its proximity to the Soviet Union and the necessity of maintaining peace in the Persian Gulf—Iran purchased $6 billion worth of armaments over a two year period. This proved a bonanza for U.S. industries, sliding into the worst depression since the 1930's. In fact, such was the scope of its purchases that Congress erupted in alarm, and the General Accounting Office complained that this would cause a serious drain on vital U.S. matériel.

From Grumman, Iran bought thirty F 14 fighters at a cost of $900 million; from T.W.A., twenty-two used 747 jumbo jets for $99 million; offered to rescue ailing Pan Am for a reputed $300 million; signed a contract with Rockwell to build an intelligence base, and with Raytheon for Hawk anti-aircraft missiles. From the U.S. Navy, it purchased three diesel-fueled submarines and six Spruance-class destroyers — with more sophisticated antiaircraft armament than it provided its own navy.

On a visit to Iran in May, Senator Edward Kennedy, echoing his brother's dismay twelve years earlier, criticized the Ford Administration and Western governments in general for their huge arms sales to the Persian Gulf area. After a speech at the University of Tehran, Kennedy met with a group of students. One of them took offense at the Senator's criticism of Iran's military budget. Kennedy replied: "How many people around this table can tell me what your government is spending on arms?" No one had any idea; one student guessed $5 million. When Kennedy gave them the actual figure, the students were incredulous. (This incident probably did little to dispel the Shah's resentment of the Kennedy family.)

To bolster its own industrial development — much of it not unrelated to its military program and its long-range plan to prepare for eventual oil depletion — Iran forged agreements with all the major industrial nations of the West. The United States always getting the lion's share, Iran signed a trade agreement totalling the incredible sum of $15 billion, to be spread over a five-year span. This, according to Secretary of State Kissinger, was the largest ever signed between two nations, larger even than the Marshall Plan. It included the purchase of 8 nuclear power stations, the construction of 10,000 apartments and other units, 5 hospitals, an electronics industry, a port for agricultural produce, the purchase of fertilizer and pesticides, farm machinery, processed foods and the construction of superhighways. A flap developed in the U.S. over the disposal of the spent uranium fuel from the nuclear power stations since it could be converted into a nuclear arms capability. Iran protested that, as a signatory to the Non-Proliferation Treaty, the problem did not exist. There were sporadic student protests, Massachusetts Institute of Technology objecting to the training of 54 Iranian students in nuclear engineering, and 250 Columbia students and others demanding an end to the university's program with the Iranian government. Harvard's $400,000 project to develop post-graduate facilities on the Caspian coast also ruffled academic waters. On the other hand, Iran's endowment of a chair of petroleum engineering at the University of Southern California, and a $1 million endowment to George Washington University went unchallenged.

In its contracts with individual firms in the United States, Iran spread its net far and wide: Owens-Corning was engaged to make fiberglass and resins for Iran's own Behshahr Company; David Lilienthal, former head of the T.V.A., was hired for the unenviable job of reforming Iran's civil service and other administrations; a subsidiary of General Telephone and Electronics received a large order for communications equipment (including the modernization of Tehran's telephone system). General Motors was hired to build the world's largest truck manufacturing plant, Fluor of Los Angeles, in collaboration with Thyssen in Germany, to build a $750 million refinery in Isfahan, International Systems and Controls of Houston to construct a $250 million wood products complex in northern Iran, and as a cultural investment, Iranians bought $500,000 worth of paintings at a Sotheby Parke-Bernet auction.

In the wake of this buying binge, a reporter asked the Shah during his visit to the United States in May if, to help New York City out of its fiscal crisis, he might be interested in buying the city. The Shah smiled (a rare occurrence with the press) and said: "Owning New York would be a very appealing proposition."

To spread the wealth to Europe and capture an increment of goodwill there, Iran bought from Britain 800 Chieftain tanks, a fleet of Hovercraft, tankers from British Petroleum, a $32 million foundry for manufacturing engines from British Leyland, and help in building a huge naval facility at Chahbahar near the Pakistani border, thus extending its naval reach into the Arabian Sea.

In France, Iran invested $1 billion in the creation of Eurodif (Spain, Italy and Belgium were also included) to build a $2.3 billion plant to produce enriched uranium from which Iran would take out 10 percent of production. It deposited $1 billion with Creusot-Loire for the purchase of two out of an eventual five nuclear power stations, and signed a $2.4 billion trade agreement with the French government for turbojet trains, two Concordes, the joint exploration of uranium deposits, and a subway system for Tehran — fast becoming the most traffic-congested city in the world.

Having bought a 25 percent interest in the Krupp works in Germany the year before, the Shah tried to buy a 15 percent interest in Daimler-Benz, makers of Mercedes cars and trucks, but was outbid by Kuwait. But he was successful in signing an agreement for a 25 percent interest in Deutsche Babcock, manufacturers of power generating equipment, and ordered two nuclear power stations, thus bringing his total in this category to fifteen. The two governments also agreed on a $620 million joint venture pact.

Turning to his dangerous neighbor to the north, Iran signed a $3 billion trade agreement with the Soviet Union, including a large paper complex to be built in Russia with Iranian credit, asked the Soviet to expand its steel plant in Isfahan, build four silos to store 300,000 tons of grain, and construct a heavy machinery plant in Arak.

As a leading member in OPEC, with a natural stake in the peace of the Middle East, the Shah embarked on a series of moves to calm the fractious Arabs on his western flank, and the impoverished countries to the east. His rapidly growing navy patrols the oil routes of the Persian Gulf, and has in the past enabled the Shah to help his friends restore order—as when, in 1973 and again in 1975, Iranian troops embarked for Oman to fight alongside the Sultan's forces in suppressing a leftist rebellion. Few doubt that his ambitions include nuclear weapons. Among the Middle Eastern countries, Libya has quietly annexed an area in northern Chad, known to be rich in uranium; Egypt, Syria and Iraq openly seek nuclear capability; experts are convinced that Israel possesses several nuclear bombs. As mentioned earlier, Iran has acquired, or is acquiring, fifteen nuclear power plants for civilian purposes, five of them from France, with a billion-dollar loan as advance payment. But as of this date (October, 1975) all Iranian deals with France are under a moratorium imposed by the Shah, because of France's supposed refusal to sell him the materials and technology required for conversion to military purposes. By the same token, India's recent accession to the Nuclear Club prompted the Shah to offer France a special low price and easy credit for oil.

The Shah started the year 1975 by carrying the olive branch to Jordan and Egypt where he was given a warm reception despite Iran's large oil exports to Israel. As a peace offering, he promised Cairo a gift of 1000 Mercedes buses, and discussed with President Sadat the possibility of constructing a pipeline parallel to the Red Sea which would also have the advantage of giving Iran a readier access to the Mediterranean. To promote friendly relations in the Persian Gulf, he tried to placate the ornery Saudis and neighboring emirates with offers of loans, and the embattled Israelis with a gift of the oil Israel would lose if it returned the Sinai oil fields to Egypt. (Iran is Israel's principal supplier of oil.)

After decades of trouble with Soviet-oriented Iraq and Iran's flagrant support of the rebellious Kurds in northeastern Iraq, the Shah was able to announce in Algiers in March that the two countries had resolved their differences—with the quid-pro-quo that Iran would oust all foreigners from the Gulf if Iraq ejected the Soviet—"a de facto nonalliance within the Western alliance" in the Shah's words. (The mysterious Mid East.) With the almost simultaneous assassination of Saudi Arabia's King Feisal, Iran and Iraq could now join forces to counter the Saudis' pressure for a lower oil price. Almost in the same breath, the Shah announced the end of parliamentary democracy in Iran which sent a frisson through the West. For the sake of "efficiency," there would henceforth be only one party—with the unambiguous name of National Resurgence Party. Now turning his attention eastward, the Shah also extended the hand of friendship to Afghanistan, Pakistan, Nepal, Bangladesh (India has already been mentioned), with offers of loans at the ready.

In view of the West's nervousness about OPEC and its intentions, it was inevitable that the Shah should make a trip to the United States. His visit in May was not without its bumpy moments. While the energy-conscious Ford Administration turned on the charm (some called it "fawning"), Secretary of the Treasury Simon did an end run by referring to the Shah as a "nut." Reporters on a "Meet the Press" television program asked unfriendly questions about the number of political prisoners in Iran ("Communist propaganda," declared the Shah). President Ford, castigated for engaging Ann-Margret to entertain the royal couple at the White House with a night club act in questionable taste, answered that he thought "the Shah would go for a sexy show." And, always ready with a sensational scoop to suit the occasion, the columnist Jack Anderson quoted a C.I.A. psychological study of the Shah that described him as "a brilliant but dangerous megalomaniac who is likely to pursue his own aims in disregard of U.S. interests." A minor item of passing interest, it was disclosed that the handful of visitors to ex-President Nixon's St. Helena on the Pacific included Iran's ambassador to the U.S., Ardeshir Zahedi.

As if to compensate for her country's conspicuous consumption, Empress Farah was accorded space on the *New York Times* Op-Ed page to condemn the modern world's drift toward materialism and its baleful effect on culture and the environment. "More than ever," she wrote, "'gross national happiness' should stand beside 'gross national product.'" Also, a curious coincidence, at the same time that the royal couple was being feted in the capital of the Western World, the Shah's sister Ashraf—his favorite envoy to Communist countries—was guest of honor at a dinner given by the Chinese deputy foreign minister, Ho Ying, in Peking, followed by a five-day visit to North Korea at the invitation of President Kim Il Sing. Princess Ashraf was also chairman of the United Nations preparatory committee for the International Women's Year Conference held in Mexico City in June, and one of its leading luminaries. Not to be outdone by her brother's largess, she offered $500,000 to help defray the costs of the conference, $500,000 for an Economic and Social Commission for Asia and the Pacific, and $1 million for an international institute for research on the status of the world's women. Enthusiasm for this last plan sagged when it was learned that the institute would be based in Tehran. Early in January, 1976, the Op-Ed page of the *New York*

Times printed Ashraf's dispirited valedictory to the International Women's Year: "What will be the fate of the Decade for Women in the face of schisms in the ranks of women and the apathy of most governments?" she concluded ruefully.

The grandiose gestures abroad had their counterparts at home. Having made giant strides in modernizing Iran's industrial plant, the Shah turned his attention to buttressing his country's self-image. Grandeur and culture were the order of the day. In late January, the Shah announced plans for Shahestan Pahlevi (Shah Pahlevi Town), a "new town" covering 2.5 square miles to be built on empty land owned by the army adjoining the capital at a cost of between $3 and $5 billion. With the firm of Llewelyn-Davies International of London in charge, assisted by Jaquelin T. Robertson, a New York architect, the complex would include a vast square—larger than Red Square in Moscow—to be called White Revolution Square, with housing for 50,000, commercial developments, an opera house, and a university. Aware that urban planning had shifted from the monumental to a more human scale, the planners promised a compromise that would satisfy both proponents. Acknowledging the ugliness and congestion of Tehran, the planners made no bones of the fact that tourism was one of the new town's *raisons d'être*.

In the cultural domain, the towering ruins of Persepolis were used as a backdrop for a Festival of the Arts that surprised many by the catholicity of its fare. All the arts—dance, drama, music, film—were given an airing to thunderous applause by groups representing every political persuasion. Three Greek tragedies were given by the Off-Broadway La Mama Repertory Company, Poland's foremost modern composer, Krysztof Penderecki led the Polish National Radio Orchestra in his own music, Alwin Nikolai's Dance Group performed, as did ritual dancers from Uganda—to name a few.

In view of the Pahlevi munificence on five continents, it came as a considerable surprise when the Shah announced — and in Washington, no less — that due to a loss of 30 to 35 percent of its purchasing power caused by world inflation, Iran would have to consider an increase in the price of oil. At the same time, he tried to calm Western nerves by promising that Iran would temper the "greedier" OPEC countries' demand for a 30 percent rise — all this to be determined at OPEC's September meeting in Vienna. Secretary Simon responded with a declaration that the U.S. would decontrol the price of "old" oil and place a tariff on imported oil. This created a furor in Congress, whose Democratic majority damned the proposal as nipping the precarious economic recovery in the bud.

Resorting to the principle of the escalator clause, the Shah then proposed an oil price linked to that of twenty or thirty commercial and industrial products imported by OPEC countries from the West. In midsummer, the deal to buy Pan Am fell through, Iran giving as its reasons "Pan Am's internal affairs" and that it had "other priorities for its development projects." A week later, the Shah announced a $4 billion deficit caused by a 17.9 percent drop in oil profits, and started looking abroad for loans. By the end of the year, OPEC and oil experts generally estimated that Iran's oil export revenues for 1975 were expected to be $19.5 billion, a drop of 11 percent over 1974, with a budget and balance of payments deficit in the area of $1 billion. The glaring inconsistency between the Shah's gloomy May forecast and the actual figures reported six months later lead one to wonder if he wasn't softening up the West for a rise in the price of oil, and at the same time, warning the eager recipients of his largess that he might have to restrain his generous impulses. To dramatize Iran's plight, he launched a vigorous program to combat the

20 percent inflation at home: 7,500 merchants and shop-keepers were arrested for profiteering, another 10,000 were fined. Within a period of days, prices tumbled 15 percent. As India was demonstrating at the same time, autocratic methods sometimes work where democracies fear to tread.

In the tug of war between oil producing and oil consuming countries, each side blamed the other for the disastrous impact of skyrocketing oil prices on the underdeveloped countries. By including other natural resources in the oil solution, and proposing a loan fund from assessments on OPEC oil production, the Shah assumed the role of Third World champion, the West having forfeited the position with its mixture of crocodile tears and indifference. The role suited the Shah admirably. Not only did he carry more weight in Western circles than any other OPEC leader (the U.S., especially, quaked over every mile of border separating Iran from Soviet Russia), but his country also commanded a strategic position between the victimized countries of Africa and Asia in general and the Arab people in particular, which provided him with an effective bastion against any further loose talk about "strangulation." But Iran's advocacy at the Vienna OPEC meeting of a 28 percent increase in oil prices was gunned down by the more moderate oil producers. With Saudi Arabia in the lead and Venezuela as mediator, the rise was held to 10 percent for a nine-month period—a figure the West could live with, albeit reluctantly.

For all his country's new-found wealth and power, the Shah is well aware that there are blatant discrepancies at home which new towns and arts festivals are unlikely to erase. The rich grow richer, the poor remain poor and multiply.

For a handful of enterprising businessmen, the "white revolution" has been a pot of gold. For instance, Habib Sabet, once a truck driver, is now king of Pepsi-Cola, Volkswagen, Squibb, tires, rubber products, refrigerators, machine tools, Revlon, and he just spent half a million dollars in London on furniture for his new house, copied after the Petit Trianon at Versailles at a cost of fifteen million dollars. His empire encompasses forty-one companies employing ten thousand workers.

In thirty years, Mohamud Ladjevardi turned a small family business into the largest enterprise in Iran. Today he owns forty-eight banks and produces most of Iran's sheet metal, soap, and textiles. He has said that his gross profits in 1974 totalled $280 million, and will double that in three years.

Gholam Khayami, who once washed cars, today has the Mercedes concession and manufactures buses and cars under license. Kachi Iravani, a former shoe-shine boy, owns dozens of buildings. Even the old rich, including the Qajars, have greatly increased their fortunes. Yet the upper middle class is far from being the only one to enjoy the boom: A whole new middle class has come into being, which could be called the "Volkswagen class." In just a few years, a large number of white collar workers, shopkeepers and people on modest salaries have achieved a level of comfort they would not have believed possible a few years before. They buy apartments, the latest electrical appliances, television sets, record players, cars, etc., etc., made all the easier by the almost unlimited availability of credit. Speculation in real estate is the current craze of this new class. Every Friday, on the Muslims' day off, people dreaming of a "second home" line up in front of shacks in the outer suburbs to study maps of subdivisions.

So much for the new rich. But in the country as a whole, more than half the population still lives below subsistence level. The countryside is little changed from ancient times:

poverty and disease, disease and poverty. There is no way of earning a living, and health care is almost nonexistent. By offering an annual salary of $2,000 the government hoped to encourage young doctors to practice in the provinces, yet two-thirds of the country's doctors refuse to leave the larger cities. There are only 9,500 doctors for the entire country, or one to every 3,300 people. There are more Iranian doctors in New York than in any Iranian city with the exception of Tehran.

Education is of a piece with medicine. Seventy percent of Iranians are illiterate, and only 18,000 students graduated from Iran's universities in 1974, the same number as Syria, a much poorer country with a fourth of Iran's population. Meanwhile, 30,000 students study abroad, many refusing to return for political reasons. At first glance, this "brain drain" would seem paradoxical. Why allow the country's best students to go abroad and become seduced by Western ideas, thus either remaining abroad or coming home as potential trouble-makers? It is generally believed that the Shah sees this as a risk he is forced to take. The training is not yet available in Iran, and those who do return make up for those who don't—or almost. And there is always the SAVAK to keep the militants in check.

As for Iran's becoming one of the world's richest countries within twenty-five years, all economic experts agree that the Shah suffers from a "reality problem." He confuses desire with reality. Iran is plagued with bottlenecks: its workers lack essential skills, its autocratic system places men in positions of responsibility for reasons of loyalty and submissiveness rather than qualifications, its bureaucracy is corrupt and inefficient, and its educational system is woefully inadequate.

Discussing recently his difficulties with education, the Shah said: "Our greatest problem is not money—we have that to

Modern Tehran. *Pars News Agency*

burn—but the human infrastructure. We are tragically short of teachers. I am just now studying an educational system operated by satellites where courses are beamed at the school and teachers learn at the same time as the students." Why, then, given the ambitious scope of the project, is Education the only ministry without a marble palace, without guards, and virtually without central heating?

Even the otherwise pragmatic Prime Minister Hoveyda talks about teaching the most remote villages through television, apparently forgetting that few of them have electricity . . .

In his desire to develop his country, the Shah, like all autocratic rulers, is faced with the problem of squaring the circle: the more he improves education, the more he lifts his country out of its poverty, the more he encourages his people to assume political responsibility, the greater the risks to his own power. He has always distrusted intellectuals, yet he needs them to help develop the country. When a professor expresses an independent thought, he is dismissed or even arrested, which obviously paralyzes freedom of expression. As the country gropes toward intellectual maturity, the Shah's ambivalence is bound to cause him trouble. As Iran becomes liberated, his star as king and "father" of his people may gradually fade. Some day, it may even eliminate the second of the three words by which Iranian children learn to read and write —Koda, Shah, Mihane (God, Shah, Country).

Many an underdeveloped country has undergone this process as the price of evolution. Will the Shah of Iran be able to keep absolute power over his people while the "white revolution" pushes them inevitably toward political awareness?